The Equilibrium of Natural Streams

The cover drawing is a stylised portrayal of a full, four-layered *alluvium profile*. The *competence* of the stream which created it would have been, to the same scale, approximately equal to the length of side of the small squares.

THE EQUILIBRIUM OF

NATURAL STREAMS

A new theoretical approach providing a key to

the understanding of longer-term fluvial processes

Elizabeth A. West

ISBN   0   86094 006 3 paper
        0   86094 007 1 cloth

published by Geo Abstracts Ltd.,
           University of East Anglia,
           Norwich NR4 7TJ,
           U.K.

Printed in Great Britain by Headley Brothers Ltd 109 Kingsway London WC2B 6PX and Ashford Kent

CONTENTS

.Contents

Page

Contents

Page

PREFACE

This work is the product of a long endeavour to understand
better the relationship of natural streams to their alluvial deposits. It was begun in the late 1940s, when I was
first closely involved with prospecting for diamonds in West
Africa and able to study alluvial deposits from the insides
of pits dug expressly to sample them. These ideal conditions for observation were at my everyday disposal for over
ten years and they yielded me the germs of certain new
ideas about the transport and deposition of gravel in
streams.

Later, in London and on excursions to look at streams
in England and France, I developed the ideas in two spells
of full-time absorption with the subject. The first of
these, in the mid-sixties, produced the rough outline of
what I believe to be an essentially new general theory of
stream equilibrium; the second, just concluded, has permitted close re-examination of the theory and an improved
statement of it.

Although over this long period observation and reasoning have not been closely synchronised, this has scarcely
mattered, for the work is primarily a study of relationships that do not depend on exact quantitative data for
demonstration of their validity. In fact, many of the
quantities considered, although explicitly defined, are
effectively unmeasurable, either because they are so by
their nature or because they relate to extremely slow
processes.

I have long realised that my approach to the subject
has been out of step with present-day practice. This work
is deliberately one of deduction and synthesis, in which
all kinds of natural streams are modelled conceptually
upon a theoretical framework whose few components, recognised by simple reasoning, are simple fundamental quantities. Although my ideas are derived from observation of
nature, the theory can only be presented deductively.
Actual streams, instead of initiating enquiry, are examined
primarily to see if they will match the deduced models,
and, apart from a few brief examples mentioned earlier on,
they do not occupy the reader's attention until the latter
part of the work, when they are closely investigated.

As discussed in the Introduction, an important feature
of the theory is the restriction of the variable quantities
introduced to the few that demonstrably 'control' the
equilibrium of streams and the exclusion of those that
merely 'modify' it. I believe that this apparent laxness
in fact offers the only means possible of reaching a real
and comprehensive *understanding* of the longer-term processes. The obstacle to achieving the same end through
analysis of empirical quantitative data relating to actual
natural streams is that these data uncompromisingly record

the effects of many variables, which in combination mask
the separate basic relationships that alone can clearly
reflect cause and effect. Although empirical observations
broadly illuminate the problems by demonstrating the
resultant trends, inherently they can do no more than this,
for even where the correlations suggest simple relationships, rarely can they be shown not to be the accidentally
simple models of the products of complex, multi-variable
interactions. Sternberg's Law, considered in this work,
is one example of this. Moreover, the correlations make
no claim to universality, because alone they say nothing
about the variability of the equations' coefficients and
exponents. As J. Hoover Mackin (1963) remarked in a
closely-related discussion, 'the equations are statements
of problems, not conclusions'. On the other hand, laboratory experiments can certainly isolate particular relationships and, I believe, very usefully complement the
deductive approach. Nonetheless their scope is limited,
and the separate solutions they demonstrate can surely only
be linked in a general deductive theory. It seems that
ultimately understanding depends on theory. I think so,
if only because, in all the accounts I have studied of
important empirical work on natural streams, I cannot
recall reading any decisive explanation of *how* the trends
demonstrated were actually realised. Any speculation on
this has always been left unresolved.

So far as I know, I have taken the deductive road
alone. I believe that the only other writer to have asked
the same questions that I have done is the same J. Hoover
Mackin already mentioned, initially in his *Concept of the
graded river* (1948), and it was this paper which set me on
the course I have followed. Thus, and most certainly not
through choice, I have worked in isolation. Briefly, in
1966, I discussed my ideas with Dr. Luna B. Leopold of the
U.S. Geological Survey, who, whilst confirming my mis-
givings about my position, very kindly gave me constructive
advice on how to go on. I was particularly pleased to be
received by him, because his published observations on
streams, and those of his colleagues, had provided me with
so much clear evidence of the effects of the processes I
had been studying. In the same way more recently, I have
been very grateful for the writings of Professor S.A.
Schumm.

I am bound to say that I have full confidence in the
broad statement of the theory, whilst recognising that
there must be many faults in detail. The theory has provided real solutions to every one of the host of problems
to which I have long sought solutions elsewhere in vain.
For example, thanks to the theory I now know how a graded
stream came to achieve its balance, why so many gravel
streams possess bimodal particle size distributions, why
some streams are braided whilst others possess single
channels, what controls the width-depth ratio of these
single channels, why stream drainage densities vary, where
and why gravel-bed streams suddenly change along their
course into sand-bed streams with an equally sudden change
in slope, and how portions of pay-streaks of heavy minerals
can be phenomenally rich. To these questions and many

Preface

others I provide positive and, I hope, clear answers in the
text. Needless to say, I am excited by the theory, which
I can only regard as an instrument of research which, if
fully comprehended, should be welcome generally. The
reservation of full comprehension is necessary because inevitably, for such a subject, the argument, although never
difficult, is certainly quite long and involved, and a
partial understanding is only likely to confuse and be
counter-productive.

Over the years I have had cause to be very grateful
for direct help from various quarters. I have already
mentioned my obligation to Dr. Leopold. Lately, my chief
adviser has been Professor K.M. Clayton of the University
of East Anglia, whose encouragement and counsel are very
greatly appreciated.

For particular reasons vital to the completion of my
work, I am most indebted to Mr. E.C. Wharton-Tigar of
Selection Trust Ltd., the Natural Environment Research
Council, and the memory of the late Mrs. Sheila Hammond.
I also acknowledge very kind help from Mrs. Margaret
Davies, Mrs. and the late Mr. H.F. Brown, Monsieur Bernard
Tagini and the Bureau de Recherches Géologiques et Minières
of France (for the loan of internal reports), Mrs. Christine
McCulloch and Mr. R.L. Wraight. Finally, I thank my friend
Miss Betty Jones for very generous assistance in preparing
the final manuscript.

E.A.W.

March 1977

LIST OF FIGURES

List of figures

LIST OF TABLES

LIST OF PLATES

INTRODUCTION

One source of the pleasure we find in natural streams is
their variety. We feel there can be no end to the cata-
logue of their differences, particularly when our minds
turn to faraway places under extreme climates. However,
for the geomorphologist there is an added satisfaction in
the recognition, often quite unexpected, of distinctive
common properties in streams of otherwise strikingly
different appearance. Thus, despite the diversity, it is
evident that there are controls common to all streams and
a single broad pattern of behaviour.
    The diversity reflects the great number of influences
affecting the form of the finished object. But the common
properties suggest that few of the influences are
controlling and that most are merely *modifying*. So we
might suppose that if the few controlling influences could
be identified and understood, possibly we might build
conceptually the 'structure' of any kind of natural stream
and then invest it with the visible properties that could
make it physically recognisable and familiar, as largely
provided by the many modifying influences. Then, since
the stream might be a self-regulating machine, we might
possibly also foresee how it would evolve if left to
itself, without change in outside influences, for any
length of time. Such anticipation of nature, if observation should show it to be substantially and consistently
correct, would affirm the reality of our understanding.
    This is the approach of the present study, which is a
work of *synthesis* based on simple *reasoning*, but checked
(especially towards the end, in Parts III and IV) against
observation. Much of this observation is as recorded in
the large literature of geomorphology; but much also is
the product of my own close involvement with streams,
especially at one time from the privileged vantage of the
diamond prospector, able to study at close quarters the
very anatomy of 'living' stream deposits from the inside
of countless pits dug to the base of the valley fill.
Whilst such experience provided me with many of the ideas
about to be described, I hope it has also provided a safe-
guard against the misconceptions that can too easily upset
the theoretical approach.
    A comprehensive theory covering this complex subject
demands as a fundamental condition the restriction of the
number of recognised influences to an absolute minimum.
Failure to meet this condition must inevitably reduce the
authority of any conclusions drawn, by rendering it impossible to impose the essential condition for useful
scientific demonstration, that only one influence should
be allowed to vary at a time. A laboratory experiment may
be designed to respect this condition, but a natural
stream, the complex product of the many influences just
mentioned, is by definition not to be so constrained. The

Introduction

problem is of course well recognised and it has been suggested that many situations in fluvial geomorphology can only be analysed by methods of 'statistical mechanics', operating on field measurements whose values have to be regarded as randomly distributed (e.g. see Scheidegger and Langbein, 1966). This approach is necessarily the last resort of enquiries seeking reasonably precise mathematical relationships. Its admitted weakness is that no real understanding of the processes emerges.

However, there is a way out on the conceptual plane. The present work seeks understanding at all costs and is prepared to sacrifice mathematical exactitude to obtain it, without however sacrificing validity. The merely modifying influences, once recognised as such, are simply going to be ignored, when appropriate, in order to make way for the process of reasoning, thereby inevitably introducing distortions into what would otherwise be simple mathematical relationships and hence usually denying the possibility of the formulation of actual equations. But for the present purpose this is no shortcoming. In the interest of understanding alone, it is enough to know the *kind* of relationship, the detail being superfluous.

It will, however, still be convenient to express relationships in mathematical terminology and the following very simple convention will be used. The expression $y = \phi(x, w, 1/z)$ will signify not merely that y is a function of x, w and z but also that as x or w increases, so y increases, and as z increases, so y decreases; and that the opposites are true. Unfortunately there is no choice but to introduce a special notation because the nearest established convention, normally written $y = f(x, w, z)$, does not convey the more restricted meaning needed. It should also be noted that a term such as $\phi(x)$ will not necessarily signify the same function of x throughout the work and must always be considered in its immediate context.

The simplicity of this almost qualitative approach will now be apparent. The argument will usually take the form of a declaration to the effect that as (say) x increases, so y increases until a critical value of x is exceeded, at which point a significant change in the behaviour of the stream is observed, for reasons which are discussed. This work will have much to do with the crossing of such function 'thresholds', which themselves will often be well defined (that is to say, the x, w and z values), although the values, y, of the actual functions will rarely be closely quantified.

Frequently the argument will rest on the assessment of the relative values of quantities which may differ by many *orders of magnitude*. For example, when x is of a certain value, y may be so very small that it can be ignored. But as x slowly increases, so may y increase by a *proportionally enormous* amount until, at a threshold value of x, y suddenly assumes a significant value. This very simple mathematical statement may yet say all that need be said about an important natural process, which could not be better understood by consideration of specified values of y or a sophisticated equation.

An example of this, closely examined in Chapter 16, is the probable explanation of why, upon ancient shield areas in the tropics, even quite modestly rounded quartz pebbles are apparently completely absent of diameters smaller than 5 mm (according to my own specific observations, mainly in West Africa), although well-rounded quartz pebbles (showing Wadell roundings of 0.8 and more) of diameter 7 mm and over are frequently abundant. The reason seems to lie in consideration of the relative orders of magnitude of the mean travel velocities of pebbles of different sizes in rivers flowing on erosion surfaces during the Tertiary period. Pebbles of size 5 mm and smaller travelled so fast that they could never achieve high rounding before the process stopped upon their arrival at the sea or other permanent destination; pebbles of size 7 mm and over could travel slowly enough, and for long enough (perhaps for a very long time indeed) and finally frequently enough (although most of the movement would have been to and fro, in situ, as will be discussed) for them to be both stranded in considerable quantities on the old land surface today *and* highly rounded, as shown in Plate 9. The 'threshold value' for retention is thus about 6 mm. Although this explanation (whether valid or not, as can only be judged later) has a strictly mathematical basis, it may be argued thus, apparently qualitatively, simply because the orders of magnitude of certain of the values involved - namely travel velocity, duration of time and frequency of movement - each varies with particle size across the critical range, 6 mm ± 1 mm, by such enormous amounts proportionally that we have no need to consider their absolute values.

This example also shows that we have to go back quite far in geological time to study the ultimate outcome of some fluvial processes. Often today's streams cannot give the answers, because of interruptions caused by crustal and climatic disturbances during the recent Quaternary past. Nearly all modern streams have been subjected quite recently to more or less active rejuvenation, which has involved increased erosion within the drainage basins and the supply of abundant fresh alluvium into the stream channels. Thus stream processes as observed today are generally in an early and therefore still short-lived stage of development, particularly evident where gravels are being transported. Nonetheless sometimes even these processes may seem to be so extremely slow that they deny the very idea of change and suggest that we are witnessing a timeless 'steady state', and certainly, unless circumvented by the effects of quite different processes (such as the chemical alteration and softening of the hard-rock components of gravel and bedrock), such conditions may persist virtually unchanged for a very long time. Yet they can always be shown to be the result of earlier, more rapid processes (see Chapter 8 for a common explanation) and in the context of geological time only very rarely will any high degree of permanence be demonstrable. Undoubtedly in the long term most streams exhibit a continuous, slow change in their properties, if only in reflection of the inevitable depletion of the stocks available for transport.

Introduction

From these observations we may surmise that whereas at one end of the wide temporal scale there are certain very long term processes operating in which all the significant controls affecting them are *variable*, at the other end, as for instance in the brief time needed to establish a particular sense of 'steady state', there are other, very short term processes operating in which *the same controls* are all effectively *invariable*. We shall examine these situations more closely later, but the incompatibilities just broadly indicated demonstrate plainly enough the magnitude of one aspect of our problem.

Mackin (1948) was the first to emphasise that it is impossible to think far about many stream processes without taking into consideration the time-span involved, and he had in mind, of course, the elusive concept of *grade*. The apparent contradictions and uncertainties that have resulted from use of this term in the past have been reviewed by Dury (1966), who concluded that 'very little now remains of the concept of grade, as usually stated in relation to streams' and indeed we might consider this to be the proper end for a concept which seems never to have been explicitly defined, inasmuch as the variability of the quantities concerned has only been discussed and never specified.

According to Dury, the early proponents of the concept of grade, G.K. Gilbert and W.M. Davis, never actually formulated comprehensive definitions. Nonetheless, we can readily discover the essentials of Davis's understanding, as for example from two brief extracts from his writings (as quoted by Dury):

(i)   Grade, meaning balance, always implies an equality of two quantities ... (it) is an essential balance between corrasion and deposition.

(ii) The maintenance of grade, during the very slow changes in the volume (i.e. discharge) and load that accompany the course of the cycle, involves an appropriate change of slope as well.

The interesting conclusion to be drawn from these remarks considered together is that the concept of grade understood by Davis is in fact *two concepts*. First he recognised the *establishment* of grade as a *shorter term* process in which all the controlling influences except slope were effectively invariable, so that the 'slope for grade' assumed a constant value; second he recognised the *maintenance* of grade as a *longer term* process in which the other controlling influences, discharge and load, could also vary appreciably and therefore cause the 'slope for grade' to do likewise.

Mackin (1948) went half-way to accepting this duality, because whilst he asserted (page 475) that the shorter-term state of grade - which to him was the only real grade - could be recognised only by the criteria of 'no change in altitude or declivity', yet also he recognised the longer-term condition of 'shifting equilibrium' (page 477), in which 'downcutting or upbuilding' continued whilst the stream remained 'approximately at grade'. The paradox he could not accept was that if the stream were at grade in the shorter term and if the conditions then

existing, with the exception that the load was now appreciably changing, were maintained in the longer term, then
the stream must also have been at grade *throughout* the
longer term; for this would have implied that a graded
stream was degrading. Which of course it was, but the one-
concept theory could not embrace such a contradiction.
Mackin left the problem unresolved by saying that 'the
distinction between the graded and the slowly degrading
stream must, and should properly, depend on the nature of
the problem and the point of view of the investigator'.

Here lies the key to the problem, which is to accept
that there are indeed two perfectly distinct 'points of
view', temporally considered, and to identify and define
the two time-spans which they respectively represent.
Then grade can be defined in terms of the state of balance
at once *established* in the specified shorter-span and
maintained, by continuous shorter-span adjustment, throughout the specified longer span. The concept of grade can
thus be rehabilitated.

The first step is to identify the few 'controlling'
influences discussed earlier and examine their effective
variabilities within each of the sequence of increasing
time-spans which they can now identify. Thus each time-
span can be explicitly defined in terms that are independent of absolute measures of time. For example, in the
shorter time-span corresponding with Davis's establishment
of grade, discharge and load are effectively invariable
and slope is variable; but in the longer time-span corresponding with his maintenance of grade, load is also now
variable. We shall see later that these three quantities –
discharge, load and slope (valley slope) – are normally
the only ones that need be taken into account, and on this
basis we can now provisionally accept that we have here
explicit definitions of the two and only distinct time-
spans relevant to the understanding of grade.

In the course of our general enquiry we shall in fact
need *three* time-spans, representing the relatively short,
medium and long terms, which we shall refer to later as
the first, second and third orders of fluvial time. The
two spans discussed above in connection with grade are the
second and third orders. The first order, the shortest
time-span, is the one mentioned earlier, in which 'steady
state' establishes whilst the three quantities (discharge,
load and valley slope) are *all* effectively invariable.
The various conclusions are summarised in the table below.

Time-span	'Controlling' influences			Process
	Discharge	Load	Slope	
Short term (first order)	Invariable	Invariable	Invariable	Steady state establishes
Medium term (second order)	Invariable	Invariable	*Variable*	Grade establishes
Long term (third order)	Invariable	*Variable*	*Variable*	Grade is maintained

Introduction

It may be recognised that this tripartite division of time at least superficially resembles a similar division proposed by Schumm and Lichty (1965). Actually there are fundamental differences, if only because the eleven variables there recognised describe what are, in part, historically conceived periods of time, which necessarily remain imperfectly defined. Also, significantly, no critical relevance is accorded in their system to the variability of the valley slope. Of course the purpose of the classification is not the same as ours, being never intended to provide the basis of an essentially mathematical exploration of the relationships of cause and effect, as is our particular aim.

To this end we shall now select a set of simple conceptual quantities, few in number and each explicitly defined, and be ready to watch how they interact within the model of a natural environment also explicitly defined, in space by the course of a stream carefully specified in terms of the three spatial dimensions, and in time by the three relative orders of magnitude of this quantity, as just discussed. This preparation is essential. Without it we can scarcely stir from base without losing our way. With it we can safely go far, providing we frequently check with reality, and we shall find ourselves able to tackle freely most of the more important qualitative problems of fluvial geomorphology.

However, the reader is warned that the necessary understanding of the basic relationships described in the next few chapters is unlikely to be obtained through a hasty reading. Almost certainly he will find the deductive approach unfamiliar, and possibly even improper, in view of the emphasis geomorphological research normally places on inductive reasoning based on the evidence of field measurements. But I must again emphasise that many of the premises of this study are of a kind that cannot be demonstrated by any kind of measurement, and that they are essential to insight into the major problems investigated in the latter part of the work.

Because it has been necessary to explore a wide range of subjects in order to demonstrate the unity of the theory, this has been a very difficult work to write. In this respect I cannot do better than quote a later paper of Mackin (1963) who, finding himself in the same kind of predicament when explaining his sound views on methods of geological investigation, asked for his readers' indulgence on the ground that he was 'steering a difficult course between non-essential complexity and over-simplification'. Lacking the persuasion of his fine style, I can only appeal to my readers to struggle with the preparatory explanations in the first part of the work, in anticipation of what I venture will be an exhilarating progress of discovery afterwards. The theory, once it is fully understood, really does provide solutions.

Part I

FLUVIAL TIME

Chapter 1

THE STREAM IN TIME

1.1 Recognition of the controlling quantities

Because the approach to this study is deductive, we will
try not to take anything for granted, except respect for
the physical laws.
  On reaching the ground, some rain collects in valleys
to form streams, if the slope is steep enough, bearing
with it *alluvium*, which is stream sediment of any particle
size. As it flows, a stream spreads a layer of alluvium
across the valley bottom, through which it passes in one
or more channels, constantly shifting from side to side
within a zone which we shall refer to as the *floodplain-
belt*. In the case of a meandering stream, this belt is
identical with the *meander-belt* as normally defined, but
we are prevented from using this explicit common term because of our need for a word that is relevant regardless
of whether the stream is meandering or braided. There
seems to be no choice in this context but to use the term
'floodplain' in a special, restricted sense. However,
where the stream is known to be meandering, we shall refer
to its meander-belt.
  The stream's properties vary with the influences we
shall be considering, which are likely to be irregularly
disposed *along* the stream, as governed by the independent
controls of the neighbourhood geology and topography. As
a first step in simplifying the specification of the stream
under consideration, we shall restrict our interest in its
properties to those obtaining at a single vertical trans-
verse cross-section of the floodplain-belt, henceforward to
be referred to more briefly as the *floodplain-belt cross-
section*.
  Our primary requirement is a set of single values of
each of all the significant properties of the stream at
the floodplain-belt cross-section, referable to a simply-
defined time-span. To decide the appropriate time-span,
we will consider each of the only two conceivable, readily
defined periods that are unrelated to arbitrary time
scales. First there is *instantaneous time*, for which the
stream's properties certainly possess single values. But
in no sense are they together representative of the
stream. For instance, the channel is not the shape it is
because of the effect of any one instantaneous value of
the discharge. Clearly the shape of the channel and other
properties relate to influences maintained over a longer

period. Instantaneous time does not meet our need.

The second duration of time worthy of consideration is the well-known statistical concept introduced by Mackin (1948) as 'a period of years' and defined by him as the period that 'excludes both seasonal and short-term fluc-tuations and the exceedingly slow changes that accompany the progress of the erosion cycle'. Despite the title, this period is obviously not tied to any absolute time-scale. This would seem to be the time-span we are looking for, although we shall soon need to have it more tightly defined. However it is invaluable now in showing how over such a period of time the temporal pattern of the dis-charge of a natural stream is a *single entity* which con-ceptually, like any element of the climate over a similar period, we can regard as a single quantity possessing a constant, or nearly constant, value. The value cannot, of course, be expressed, because no single statistical para-meter can adequately summarise all the significant detail of the pattern of variations of the instantaneous values of the discharge, although there are parameters which will do this approximately. Fortunately our reasoned approach puts us under no obligation to consider measurements and we are perfectly free to enjoy the luxury of using the conceptually *ideal* immeasurable value, which being constant over 'a period of years' fully satisfies our demand for a single value relating to a simply-defined time-span.

This quantity is by no means the only one of this kind at our disposal: it happens, as we could reasonably ex-pect, that the constant discharge as just defined, acting within a similarly constant environment, is able to fashion a channel whose properties considered over 'a period of years' can all be represented by similarly conceived single quantities possessing similar unspecified ideal values, which are also constant over this period. These properties are the components of the stream's hydraulic geometry, such as the channel width and depth and the flow velocity, explicit representative values of which have been defined and correlated by Leopold and his colleagues (see Leopold, Wolman and Miller, 1964). The work of these authors is extremely useful to our enquiry, but happily we do not have to use their inherently imperfect quantities, which are necessarily approximations. Instead we adopt the corresponding conceptual single quantities and their *ideal* values.

It will now be evident that the stream is no longer adequately represented by a fixed channel cross-section, but only as the integration of every state of the channel cross-section as it moves within the plane of the flood-plain-belt cross-section 'over a period of years'. During this time the stream's properties undergo complex rhythmic fluctuations, including not only the seasonal changes governed by the discharge, but also the slower, but still systematic, turnings and twistings of the whole channel pattern in plan within the floodplain and the resulting changes in the channel properties at the cross-section dependent on where at any moment the cross-section happens to intersect the pattern. For example, whilst at one moment the cross-section may intersect a channel 'bend',

later a 'crossing' will certainly take its place and provide significantly different properties. All states are
repeated again and again and thus, over a long enough
'period of years', the varying properties can be properly
represented by the 'ideal' constant values we have been
considering. Of course in particular situations even the
'ideal' values may not be constant, because of rapid
fundamental change in the principal controls of the stream
inside the time required, but we are specifically assuming
that this is not happening here.

We now have to identify the principal controls from
amongst many quantities relevant to this situation. As
already indicated, they can be acceptable only if they are
both few in number and fully representative of all the
'controlling' influences in stream behaviour. The first
of these *controls*, as we shall call them, has already been
introduced, the *discharge* (Q), which is the ideal single
value representing the amount of water passing the floodplain cross-section per unit time 'over the period of
years'. The second control is the *load* (Q_a), which is the
similarly ideal single value of the amount of alluvium
passing the .cross-section per unit time, referable to a
particle size frequency distribution. (It will be shown
later (page 66) that this simple concept of load is not
adequate where there are 'immovable' alluvium components
present at the cross-section which are too large for the
stream ever ('over the period of years') to move. In the
present discussion however we can assume that there happen
to be no such particles, as of course is commonly the
case.) The third control is the *valley slope* (S_v) at the
cross-section, which, unlike the other two, has a measur-
able value.

The roles played by these controls can be deduced from
elementary physical principles. The discharge is obviously
the primary control of stream behaviour, governing both
the channel size and, considered in relation to the valley
slope, the force of the stream as judged by its ability to
scour its bed. The load is the stream's burden, significantly so when in the form of bedload. Its effect, whether
in motion or stationary, is to inhibit the ability of the
stream to scour its bed. Too little load, either in amount
or particle size, permits the stream to continue to erode
vertically, which is to degrade; too much causes the
stream to continue to deposit vertically, which is to
aggrade. Thus we infer that increase in either discharge
or valley slope favours degradation; and increase in load
discourages it. These are the fundamental relationships
and we accept them as axiomatic.

The three controls appear to be the sole significant
arbiters of the stream's behaviour at the floodplain-belt
cross-section 'over the period of years'. Two assumptions
qualify this statement. One is that the valley floor is
composed of readily erodible material, and the other is
that the stream is not constrained laterally by steep
valley sides - in other words it is not flowing in the
notch of a gorge. These uncommon situations apart, it
will surely be accepted that the three controls - discharge, load and valley slope - virtually alone represent

at the floodplain cross-section all the known natural
influences on the stream's behaviour, whether they derive
from the topography, geology, climate, hydrology or vegetation, and that they alone significantly govern, directly
or indirectly, the values of all quantities belonging to
the stream's hydraulic geometry. The only other independent controls conceivable are such as the water and air
temperature at the cross-section and biological activity
affecting the cohesion of the channel banks, but these
(and perhaps some others) may unquestionably be ignored in
the general argument as having only modifying influence.

1.2   The three orders of fluvial time

We will now consider the variability of the three controls,
discharge, *load* and *valley slope*, with the passage of
fluvial time conceived as durations of *three distinct
orders of magnitude*. The principal conclusions we shall
draw are summarised in Table 1.
    In the *short term*, regarded as the *first order* of
magnitude, we can imagine that enough time elapses for
establishment of the nearly constant values of the hydraulic geometry of the stream channel at the floodplain-belt
cross-section. We will suppose that there is a single,
meandering channel gradually shifting across a wide, well-
established meander belt. Clearly the stream has attained
the equilibrium of a *steady state*, certainly an imperfect
equilibrium because departures from the mean state are
usually only too obvious, but nonetheless presenting a
constant mean state. The characteristics of the equilibrium will have established, as we shall see, over a comparatively short 'period of years', during which time it
is evident that the three controls have all displayed
effectively *invariable* values.
    Now we will examine a considerably longer duration of
time, a *medium term*, regarded as the *second order* of magnitude. During this longer 'period of years', the channel
has repeatedly swung (the word 'shift' is no longer
appropriate) back and forth across the meander-belt and
each time, on its return to one or other side of the
valley, is seen to have appreciably lowered its floodplain
surface below the previous level, tending to produce
'unpaired terraces'. Clearly the stream has been regularly
degrading, whilst at the same time maintaining the first
order equilibrium of steady state. Now we can accept that
only two of the controls, discharge and load, have remained
invariable, and that the valley slope has become liable to
change, although in fact it may not have done so, depending
on how the levels happen to have changed along the valley.
The critical change observed is thus not that of the
valley slope but of the *elevation* of the stream at the
cross-section. It will be shown later that this elevation
is most usefully designated as that of the *floor-plane*,
which is the plane defined by the points of deepest scour
beneath the channel (see Figure 1). Within the first
order period the *floor-plane elevation* remains invariable,
but in the longer second order period it is liable to

Table 1. The orders of fluvial time.

Order of fluvial time	Criteria			Special properties		Equilibrium states		
	Discharge (Q)	Load (Qa)	Floor-plane elevation	Rate of degradation	Valley slope (Sv) and Competence (Dc)	Titles	Criteria	Valley slope value
1 (short term)	Invariable	Invariable	Invariable	Constant	Invariable	First order equilibrium or Steady state	Regular first order characteristics	Invariable
2 (medium term)	Invariable	Invariable	Variable	Variable	Variable	Second order equilibrium or Grade	Rate of degradation = 0	Constant slope for grade
3 (long term)	Invariable	Variable	Variable	Variable	Variable	Third order equilibrium (unattainable)	Load (Qa) = 0	Zero

11

change, rising in *aggradation*, falling in *degradation*, and remaining stationary when the stream has established *grade*, which is the state of equilibrium peculiar to the second order.

Lastly, we consider the long term, regarded as the *third order* of magnitude. This is beyond the range of the 'period of years'. Now the shape and character of the landscape will have changed appreciably under the effects of sustained weathering and erosion, and in sympathy with this the load will have diminished in amount and probably also in particle size. After this time only one of the controls at the meander-belt cross-section can have remained anywhere near its previous value, the discharge, very likely unchanged in effective amount provided the climate has not drastically altered. As the load decreases, the graded stream scours more deeply into its bed and slowly depresses the floor-plane elevation, a process imperceptible in second order time, but evident and inevitable in third order time. We can now accept without hesitation that the graded stream is degrading, in fact displaying a very common condition, which we shall frequently refer to as *third order degradation at grade*.

To each order belongs its particular state of equilibrium, as shown in Table 1, although that of the third order, whilst recognisable as a concept, is never attainable. In principle it is the asymptotic approach of the value of the load to zero and of the floor-plane elevation to permanent base-level. Sometimes this process is interrupted by the effects of earth-movement, but otherwise is eventually halted by the progressive inability of the weakening stream to scour its bed effectively (at a critical stage we shall later recognise).

An important property of the three orders of time is that they *coexist*, for they are simply three different ways of looking at time. They are merely examples of the familiar concept of a short term happening compared with a long term happening, but extended to embrace three terms altogether. Emphatically the concept has nothing to do with absolute measures of time. Although some of the processes later to be examined may require the passage of very long periods of time, nevertheless the whole gamut of the events just considered, in all three orders, might be observed in a laboratory in an afternoon. Short-lived examples in nature also will be examined, especially such as relate to the passage upstream of nickpoints past our floodplain cross-sections.

In this chapter attention has been concentrated on time relationships, without much reference to process. This is the subject of the next chapter.

Chapter 2

BASIC STREAM PROCESSES

The basic stream processes are regarded as those that take place as interactions between the dominant controls (discharge, load and valley slope), within one or more of the three orders of fluvial time. Although by definition all three controls are invariable in first order time, we shall see how, in feedback processes, a single property of first order equilibrium acting as a 'seed of change' may, first in the medium term (second order time), provoke change in one of the controls, the valley slope, and then, simultaneously but recognisable only in the long term (third order time), regulate the rate of change of another of the controls, the load. This extremely important single property is the velocity of vertical movement of the floor-plane at the cross-section, which we shall refer to later as the 'rate of degradation'. How the interrelated processes act in the promotion of stream evolution will now be examined.

2.1   The floor-plane

To study the processes, we return to our cross-section of a single-channelled stream flowing in a wide meander-belt through valley-fill resting upon a readily erodible bedrock. Here we look specially at a short stretch of this stream in first order time, centred upon the meander-belt cross-section, and note that there are certain *points* along it where, for whatever reason, the level of the stream bed at certain *instants* of time is lower than anywhere else within the stretch at any other instant, meaning of course within first order time. Such a point - it is really a very small area - represents the spearhead of the stream's penetration in depth, however caused, and we call it a *scour front*. Here alone the stream cuts down through its bed of alluvium to reach a level that otherwise is never subjected to scour in first order time. As previously indicated, we call the plane approximately defined by these scour fronts the *floor-plane*, as shown in Figure 1.

As the stream shifts its course laterally, the scour fronts migrate, creating in plan a random pattern, because all parts of the floor-plane within the meander-belt are equally likely to be visited. Since each scour front at any time of activity affects only a small area of the floor-plane, a long time elapses before every part of it is reached in this process and in the early stages the result is the generation of an undulating surface separating scoured ground above from unscoured ground below. We call this surface the *floor*, a term which may also refer to the material composing the ground lying beneath it,

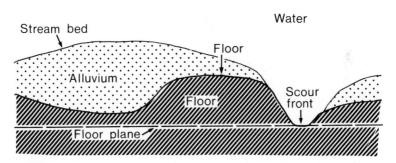

Figure 1. Cross-section along a stream channel to
    illustrate features introduced in Chapter 2.
    Note that the floor may be both the surface of the
    unscoured material and the material itself.

which often of course is bedrock (see Figure 1).

In first order time the *floor-plane elevation* is
invariable, as has already been recognised. But in second
order time the floor-plane may move vertically, the sense
of the movement indicating whether the stream is aggrading,
degrading, or remaining stationary at grade. If, in the
course of second order time, grade is maintained, the
undulating floor is gradually flattened out against the
stationary floor-plane, eventually all but coinciding with
it. Perfect coincidence is impossible because the floor-
plane is only a statistical concept and necessarily even
the flattest, most mature floor is pitted here and there
by holes gouged by exceptionally deep scour fronts developed at times of rare, very high flood. I should mention here that I have actually observed these properties
of floors in various parts of West Africa in alluvial
mining operations, where wide flat areas of very soft bedrock were being exposed in the course of the careful,
selective removal by hand of diamond-bearing basal alluvial
gravels (as in Plate 1).

On the other hand, if the stream continues to degrade,
the floor-plane is continuously being pushed down in
advance of the floor, its position being defined by a vanguard of isolated scour fronts probing down, like down-
stretched fingers, fashioning a convoluted floor, which
also I have seen (especially as remarkably displayed at
Wenchi on the Birim River in Ghana).

Alternatively the stream may be aggrading, with the
floor-plane retreating upwards behind the rising stream.
In this circumstance the floor-plane cannot be identified,
although it remains a valid concept. The floor however
no longer has meaning.

The evidence I have cited is actually superfluous,
because the reality of these processes can be acknowledged
without reference to the kind of physical actions involved,

beyond recognition of the fact that stream channels do
move laterally and that instantaneous values of the discharge do vary. In the present argument the scour front
is simply a reasoned concept, although later we shall
investigate it as a physical phenomenon.

2.2.   First order processes

The first order processes will at this stage be only
touched on. It is enough to know that they produce first
order equilibrium, which can now be more fully defined as
the steady state revealed by constant mean values not only
of the properties of the hydraulic geometry but also of
those relating to the alluvium deposited across the whole
floodplain-belt between the levels of the floodplain surface and the floor.
     The three controls (discharge, load and valley slope)
are invariable. The mechanics of the physical processes
producing the equilibrium are of course exceedingly complicated, in which respect, it may now be worth noting,
they differ strikingly from the simple processes involved
in the pursuit of the non-physical equilibria of the
second and third orders, to be examined later.
     The features displaying the first order equilibrium
will be referred to as *first order characteristics*. In
addition to the well-known elements of the hydraulic geometry already mentioned, they include a few that are less
familiar but are of particular significance to the evolution of the stream and will be introduced into the argument
at appropriate moments. One is important now, the *rate of
degradation*, which is the important single property mentioned earlier as the 'seed of change'. It is defined as
the average velocity of fall of the floor plane. Thus a
positive rate of degradation signifies *degradation*, and a
negative rate of degradation signifies *aggradation*.
     Although a zero rate of degradation normally signifies
grade, there is the common exception to this when a stream
seeking to degrade is prevented by an inerodible floor, a
situation best conceived as imperceptibly slow degradation.
It demonstrates the existence of a fourth, passive control,
the *floor erodibility*. In the present discussion this
control can be ignored, because the floor is being regarded
as readily or immediately erodible.
     The rate of degradation is unquestionably a first
order characteristic. Although by definition the floor
cannot fall in first order time, there is no inconsistency
in this because the rate of degradation is merely the
measure of the tendency to fall and any actual displacement
takes place in second order time. (The relationships are
that of the integral to the derivative, such that if the
fall is h, the rate of fall with respect to time t - which
is the rate of degradation - is dh/dt.)
     Indeed the rate of degradation is the sole link
between the first and second orders. Maintenance of any
positive or negative value of it causes, in the longer
term of second order time, a vertical displacement of the
floor-plane. Differential displacement of the floor-plane

along the valley causes a change in the slope of the floor-plane, and thus of the valley slope, which is one of the first order controls. First order equilibrium has been upset.

Thus the effect of one property of an equilibrium upon external circumstances slowly changes the equilibrium. The two orders of time are clearly distinguishable; in the shorter term an equilibrium is established, in the longer term it is maintained whilst changing. It is a simple example of the effect of feedback.

2.3   Second order processes

A fundamental difference between the first and second orders is that whereas the first is chiefly concerned with the interaction of forces, whose balance creates a physical equilibrium, the second order is involved with *geometry*, which has nothing directly to do with physics.

Our attention is now directed beyond the meander-belt cross-section to a stretch of the along-valley profile including it. In particular we study two geometrical properties of the stream at the cross-section, the *floor-plane elevation* and the *valley slope* (S_V), both now subject to change. The critical change is that of the floor-plane elevation, which now brings about other changes whose quality owes nothing directly to physical considerations, in effect transcending them. We see the shaping of a new spatial arrangement, unique, the final product of a particular geological and geomorphological history. These words relate to a new, entirely different conceptual state.

We have seen that the value of the rate of degradation at the cross-section is determined by the interaction of the first order controls. For different reasons the values of these controls at any time vary along the valley, and consequently so does the rate of degradation. As a result the vertical displacement of the floor-plane over a period of second order time also varies along the valley. The correlation of these displacements is geometrical, not physical, and it is for geometrical reasons that the along-valley profile acquires a new shape and the valley slope at

Plate 1.   The alluvium profile of a moderately-loaded sand stream, typical of the Yengema diamondfield, Sierra Leone. The site of the excavation is the present-day floodplain of the Meya River near Sefadu, about 20 km downstream of the stream's source.
In the background, the *floodplain layer* of silt-clay rests upon a thick *mobile layer* of white pebbly sand. In the foreground, the underlying *lag-cum-immovable layer*, averaging 0.3 m thick, is being removed from the very soft *floor* of decomposed granite. The stream's competence (D_C) is about 60 mm, implying that particles larger than 20 mm in diameter (i.e. $0.3D_C$) are almost entirely confined to the basal lag-cum-immovable layer.

the cross-section a new value.

But now the new valley slope, in its role of first order control, imposes a new first order equilibrium and with it a new rate of degradation, which then maintains the second order geometrical process at a slightly different rate. There is a two-way process between valley slope and rate of degradation, which we call the *slope-degradation interaction*, which is simply an explicit way of describing a fundamental and well-known process of geomorphology. But it may not be so well recognised that this is not a purely physical process, but is part physical and part geometrical, in separate compartments. It is the coming together of the shorter view of 'dynamic' change on the one side and the longer view of spatial change on the other, separate but linked. Below is a diagram of the interaction.

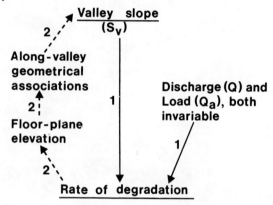

Key

1 ——→ **First order, physical**

2 ---→ **Second order, geometrical**

Second order equilibrium (grade) exists when rate of degradation = 0 (assuming the floor to be readily erodible).

The slope-degradation interaction may be described as follows:
In the short term, valley slope is an invariable quantity and its value, in its control of physical action, governs the rate of degradation. In the long term, rate of degradation by altering geometrical associations, governs the valley slope.

To discover where the interaction leads, we examine all the possible situations and deduce the course of events. These are exercises in geometry. Altogether five significant situations may be recognised, which are listed below according to their stabilities.

	Situation	Rate of degradation	Valley slope
(1)	Grade	Zero	Constant
(2)	Stable degradation	Positive	Declining
(3)	Stable aggradation	Negative	Increasing
(4)	Unstable degradation	Positive	Increasing
(5)	Unstable aggradation	Negative	Declining

   Grade is the state of second order equilibrium, which exists when the valley slope is so adjusted that the floor-plane is stationary.
   The two stable situations evolve towards grade, which is their end state. Stable degradation obtains when a degrading stream's along-valley profile flattens; stable aggradation when an aggrading stream's along-valley profile steepens. In all these second order processes the load is by definition invariable.
   The two unstable situations evolve away from grade to states of increasing instability, which bring into operation abnormal mechanisms. In the case of unstable degradation, the increasing slope eventually initiates processes not directly related to stream action. For example, the very steep stream bed may collapse under its own weight. An extreme case is that the overhanging waterfall, where the main flow of the water is not even in contact with the bed. In the other situation, of unstable aggradation, the declining slope causes blocking of the channel by deposited alluvium and the stream becomes a pond or a lake. The unstable situations do not last long, but provoke some kind of abrupt reaction whose effect is to create a new situation, which may or may not be stable.
   Grade is not the ultimate equilibrium. With the further passage of time, continued erosion in the upstream drainage basin begins to show its effect. As the upstream landscape changes, so does the rate of supply of alluvium to the stream. Until now the load has been deemed invariable, right up to the time of the establishment of grade, which by definition cannot exist without this condition. But now, as we consider yet a longer term, the third order of fluvial time, the load at the meander-belt cross-section changes.

2.4   Third order processes

We have seen that the processes of first order time are physical and of second order time are geometrical, and now we discover that those of the third order are what we might call *supplying*. The reference is to the amount and size of the alluvium reaching the meander-belt cross-section and its influence on stream evolution through variation in the value of the first order control, the

load. The processes have moved into yet another conceptual state. At the same time the field of relevant
action has again expanded, now to embrace the whole of the
upstream drainage basin, all parts of which may contribute to the load at the cross-section.

The third order of time may represent absolute time at
its longest and the argument now requires that certain
conditions should be stated which previously had been
tacitly assumed. If we suppose that our exercise in logic
is really a rather grand natural 'experiment', we expect,
following normal scientific procedure, that the major outside and independent influences have been maintained invariable throughout the experiment. Changes in them are
to be assessed separately, after the inner working of the
system has been understood. Although this stage has not
yet been reached, at least we can identify the influences.

Effectively there are only two *independent influences*.
One is the *climate*, in so far as it is determined from
outside the drainage basin. It controls, directly or indirectly, many variables that govern stream behaviour,
notably the discharge and the rate of disintegration of
the rocks which both furnish the alluvium and constitute
the floor. The other influence is any *external agency*
altering the shape, *attitude and constitution of the land*
- such as crustal tilt, differential uplift and volcanic
action - whose activity disturbs the state of 'stillstand'.
In our 'experiment' both these influences are deemed unchanging, invariable. Consequently the system is self-
governing and the changes involved are of an *evolutionary*
character.

Although the third order processes are obviously complex in operation, they are fairly easily understood. The
cause of change is variation in the load, but the agent of
change is the same first order characteristic, the rate of
degradation, positive or negative. The course of events
is as follows. In second order time, grade is progressively imposed everywhere upstream of the cross-section.
Eventually it establishes not only in the main channel,
but also in the tributaries and every tiny headwater, hillside gully or site of erosion of any kind. Everywhere the
rate of degradation closely approaches or actually attains
the zero value indicative of grade. This means a drastic
easing of erosion and, now in third order time, a tendency
for sharp decrease in the load at the cross-section. However, it is only a tendency, because there is a reaction.

Before considering this reaction, we should note that
variations in the other two controls, the discharge and
the valley slope, can be disregarded. The discharge remains virtually unchanged because we are accepting the
condition of stillstand and constant climate; it will of
course still be subject to some variation, but to a negligible degree in comparison with that of the load. Although
the valley slope will certainly change, it too may be disregarded, because it is now a dependent control. The
slope is now always 'the slope for grade', and its value
adjusts continuously, in the shorter term of second order
time, as demanded by the combined values of the discharge
and the load, through the slope-degradation interaction.

Thus in third order time there is only one significant
variable control, the load.

We have concluded that the universal establishment of
grade in the upstream drainage causes the load to decrease
at our cross-section. The reaction to this is caused by
the resultant change in the first order equilibrium there.
The stream can now scour its bed more easily and the rate
of degradation acquires a positive value, whose effect is
felt only in third order time. The third order degradation
causes change in the upstream geometry. The same process is happening all along the stream and the actual
slopes assumed depend on the particular geometrical associations. But the net result is continued erosion, the
boosting of the load at the cross-section and decrease in
the rate of degradation. Thus there is action and reaction
between the load and the rate of degradation, which we call
the *load-degradation interaction*, similar in concept to
the slope-degradation interaction of second-order time.
It is, of course, a more devious interaction than that one,
because the processes are going on in all three orders of
time, involving both interactions. There are wheels within wheels.

The diagram of the load-degradation interaction is
shown below.

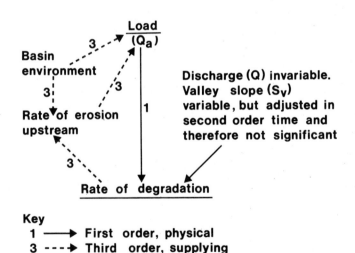

The dual role of the basin environment indicated in
the diagram will be examined later (page 23). It governs
both the potential availability of alluvium of different
sizes and its actual supply to the stream in the process
of erosion, two very different notions. The basin environment is of course the ultimate control of the stream's
evolution and as such is discussed in the next section.

The diagram shows only the relationships, without
distinguishing the sense of the changes. For the interaction does not necessarily induce a positive rate of

degradation. Again we can list all the possible situations
in order of stability.

	Situation	Stability	Load (Q_a)	Rate of degradation
(1)	Ultimate third order equilibrium	Unattainable	Zero	Zero
(2)	Third order degradation	Stable	Decreasing	Positive
(3)	'Third order grade'	Unstable	Constant	Zero
(4)	Third order aggradation	Unstable	Increasing	Negative
(5)	Very unstable situations		Increasing	Positive
(6)			Decreasing	Negative

Before considering the situations severally, we should
note that they belong exclusively to third order time, and
that for any of them the stream may or may not be in second
order equilibrium (or grade).

In third order time there is no readily attainable
state of equilibrium equivalent to that of grade in second
order time. Although the particular load-degradation
interaction just described produces a certain balance
between supply of alluvium and the rate of degradation,
this is not a true equilibrium because the load is still
independently subject to variation and it will only be coincidence if it remains constant for any length of time.
This special case is indicated by situation (3) in the
table, with its mock title of 'third order grade', for in
fact this is an unstable condition. Unlike the valley
slope in the slope-degradation interaction of second order
time, the load cannot remain constant indefinitely in
third order time but must decrease as the upstream slopes
decline and the whole interaction gradually slows down.
Thus the normal tendency is third order degradation. It
is this stable condition, representing the running down of
the system, which heralds the ultimate third order equilibrium of zero load, zero rate of degradation and zero
slope. But this state is for ever out of reach because,
long before it can establish, the stream loses the physical
power of continued erosion and is no longer able to degrade.

The three other third order situations are all unstable, two of them very much so. The most stable of
them (no. 4) is the counterpart of third order degradation,
just mentioned, which is third order aggradation, occurring
when erosion upstream into an abundance of potential bedload is so rapid that the stream at the cross-section

aggrades, a common situation following recent rejuvenation
of a basin. Naturally this reaction cannot continue indefinitely and eventually the situation reverses to third
order degradation, almost certainly not pausing (for there
is no reason for it) at the neutral position of 'third
order grade'.

Of the two very unstable situations, one is common
(no. 5). Immediately after the passing of a sharp nickpoint on its way upstream, the channel slope (and the new
rudimentary valley slope) are suddenly steepened, resulting
in active degradation. As the nickpoint continues its
journey, a greater length of channel is being eroded upstream of the floodplain-belt cross-section and the load
increases, but probably not enough to stop the degradation
at the cross-section. This is the situation in question.
Very soon the second order degradation ceases as grade re-
establishes and is maintained, probably first through a
brief episode of third order aggradation, certainly followed by continued third order degradation as the effects
of the disturbance die out. This is a good example of a
sequence of processes involved in all three orders of time
unfolding within a short duration of absolute time. There
will of course be considerable interference between the
respective processes of the three orders, but the actual
mechanisms of change are unaffected. Nickpoints are considered in greater detail on pages 127-138.

We have now considered all the possible situations open
to a stream at the floodplain-belt cross-section, as specified by self-regulatory changes in the two eventually
variable controls, valley slope in second order time, load
in third order time. All the changes have been induced or
regulated by the sole agent of stream evolution, the rate
of degradation. The system as a whole is illustrated in
Figure 2.

2.5   Stream evolution

We have seen that although many different processes can
take place, few are so directed that they can be maintained
for any great length of time in a system that is generally
running down. In fact we can recognise a definite trend
as represented by only three *normal processes*, (i) degradation (seen in the first, second and third orders of time),
(ii) declining slope (seen in the second and third orders),
and (iii) decreasing load (seen in the third order only).
The characteristic expression of this combination is the
stable situation of *third order degradation at grade*.

Although the immediate single control of this situation
is the load, it is definitely not an independent control
because of its regulation by the rate of degradation,
through the load-degradation interaction. We may therefore
ask what are the ultimate controls of the evolution of the
stream. The answer must lie in the properties of the
basin environment in its fullest expression, relating to
both the potential availability of alluvium of different
sizes within it and the geometrical concept of the attitude of the landscape. It is important to distinguish

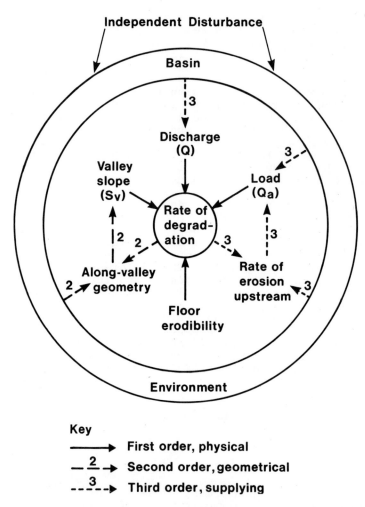

Figure 2.   The processes of stream evolution at a trans-
    verse cross-section of the floodplain-belt.

between these two very unlike aspects of the basin environment, each relating to a different set of dimensions and
each crucial to the understanding of a situation.

    The *potential availability of the alluvium* is governed
by the composition and erodibility of all the ground
possibly liable to erosion and by the resistance to wear
and breakage of the components of different sizes during
transport.   But this factor alone is irrelevant without
knowledge of whether the prospective alluvium is also
actually *accessible*, as determined by the *attitude of the
landscape*, especially as manifested in its 'general slope'.

    It may be helpful here to consider an example.   The
steep incline of the Great Plains of Nebraska and the
enormous amount of potential sand alluvium buried beneath

them have together controlled the evolution of the Platte
River, until the recent disturbance by human agency. The
steep landscape of an early alluvial plain was responsible
for the original steep consequent stream. Because it was
steep, it had a tendency to degrade rapidly. But this
caused the release of abundant sand bedload, whose counter-
tendency would have been to cause the stream to aggrade.
So in the establishment of grade throughout the basin, the
load-degradation interaction ensured that the balance was
maintained by high values of both valley slope and load.
It was a balance of extremes, governed however by a process
of gentle but persistent third order degradation at grade,
gentle because a very little degradation maintained a great
quantity of bedload. The product was the steep, heavily-
loaded, braided Platte River, renowned for this extreme
condition. It is an example of a steep landscape continuing to maintain a steep graded stream through the
medium of a heavy, but inexhaustable, bedload. Most
streams are amenable to a similar kind of analysis, as
will be apparent.

The *normal* pattern of stream evolution can now be
recognised, as shown in the diagram below.

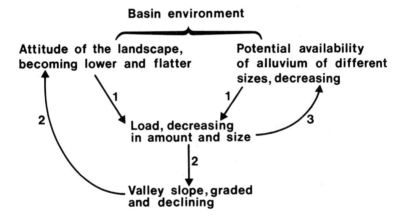

2.6   Independent disturbance

The analysis would not be complete without mention of the
effect on the system of any *independent disturbance*, whose
incidence we have until now been able to ignore under the
condition of stillstand and constant climate.

Whatever may be the nature of the disturbance, it
affects the system only as change to the basin environment,
as illustrated in Figure 2. In its turn the effect of
this can only be change in the adjustment of the 'machine',
whose mode of operation is of course not altered by what
has happened. Frequent or long-continuing disturbance may
well obscure the very existence of long-term effects and
usually the concept of prolonged stream evolution appears
merely academic. But there is evidence of end effects if

Fluvial time

we look in the right places (especially upon the ancient
shields of the tropics, as already mentioned on page 3),
some of which will be presented later (in Chapter 16).

Part II

TOWARDS THE SYNTHESIS OF A STREAM

Chapter 3

THE ALLUVIUM PROFILE

3.1   The stream's competence

The discussion so far has been preliminary to the main
argument. The basic quantities have been first introduced
and then observed in processes of interaction that may
continue to operate for any length of time beyond the short
interval needed for the establishment of a first order
steady state. A three-in-one structure of fluvial time
has been described, able to provide the foundation needed
for any extended argument involving changes in values with
time. We are now equipped for a deductive exploration of
stream evolution.
        The first step is the recognition of a very useful
first order characteristic, the stream's *competence*, defined as the largest size of particle of alluvium transportable by the stream at the valley cross-section in first
order time. Size is the intermediate diameter, referable
to a particular material only when its density differs
significantly from that of quartz. Likewise we shall ignore variation in the shape of the particle, regarding
this factor and that of density variation as examples of
the 'modifying influences' mentioned earlier, which do not
have to be considered in the main argument.
        This simple definition of competence respects the
originals. Mackin (1948) wrote that 'competence (was)
defined by Gilbert as a measure of the ability of the
stream to transport debris in terms of particle size'.
Leopold, Wolman and Miller (1964) equated competence with
τ_c, 'the critical stress necessary for grain movement',
emphasising that the linear measure of competence is in
fact an index of force.
        The simplicity of the concept and the remarkable con-
venience of being able to express force in units of the
size of particles of alluvium suggests its use as a bridge
between hydraulics and geology, which are generally such
mutually incompatible branches of science. The *competence*,
as now specified, is an *index of the 'stream force'* in
first order time. If we now look for the reaction to the
force, we may identify the stream's *load**, referable to a
particle size distribution, as the complementary *index of
the opposing 'alluvium resistance'* in first order time,
whose value governs, as we have already seen, the ability
of the stream to degrade.
        The idea is a very practical one, for we can gauge

*or, more strictly, the *loading,* see page 45

27

both these indices by visual inspection of deposits of alluvium remote from the streams that laid them. Moreover, as will be seen, we can build on the basic relationship and deduce the principal characteristics of a stream from this information alone. Indeed already we can recognise that, equipped with two such convenient, concordant measures, possibly we have simple means of tackling conceptually many of the major problems of fluvial geomorphology.

However, it is essential that the record of the deposits should be examined fully. It is not enough to inspect the more easily accessible upper part of the streambed alluvium, without relating it to the possibly very different ground beneath, all the way down to the floor, which is no less an integral part of the alluvium able to provide 'resistance' to the stream's 'force'. The whole record in depth, from floodplain level to floor, is all relevant.

To see what this implies we will now examine a real situation in West Africa, which I had opportunity to study closely.

3.2   Measurement of the competence of a small West African stream

The Nafayi is a meandering stream 5 kilometres long flowing through the town of Yengema in the Kono District of eastern Sierra Leone. The climate there is humid tropical, the rainfall averaging 270 mm per annum, four-fifths of which falls within 6 months of the year. Vegetation is savannah woodland.

The stream drains an area of lightly-dissected, fairly deeply weathered plateau, eroded to a stage which Thomas (1974, page 236) would classify as 'partially stripped etchplain', implying that very little laterite and only a limited amount of hard rock are to be seen. The solid geology is Precambrian gneissic granite, which weathers preferentially along zones of weakness to a non-plastic kaolinitic clay, 'immediately erodible' in that it almost literally possesses those physical properties which Mackin (1948) recognised as characteristic of cream-cheese. It is 'soft bedrock' of this consistency which almost everywhere floors the Nafayi valley. The commonest material of gravel size in the stream's alluvium is vein-quartz, in particles of size rarely larger than 100 mm in diameter and deriving mainly from sources within the basin. There is also a lesser amount of granite and allied rocks in varying states of decomposition. The sand carried by the stream is principally quartz, together with a considerable amount of granite debris, especially evident in the 2-4 mm size range (usually regarded as just beyond the range of sand, although, as will be explained, we shall consider it as such).

The Nafayi alluvial deposit was sampled for diamonds by hand-excavated pits, each covering a horizontal area of about 3 m^2. The work was carried out in 1947, when no records of specific geomorphological interest were

maintained, and for this reason no detailed plan of the
meander pattern is available. Nonetheless several of the
sampling measurements and descriptions are pertinent to
our enquiry and are perhaps of special interest as being
of a kind not normally available.

Our immediate concern is a middle stretch of the Nafayi
about a kilometre long, where the valley sloped at 4 m per
km and the stream flowed at or near to grade within a
meander-belt of width about 60 metres. The constitution
of the ground in depth was revealed by five channel-side
pits evenly distributed along the course, which showed the
following consistent sequence of layers, whose thicknesses
differed little from the mean values indicated.

(1) Buff-yellow to grey silty *clay*,
sandy at base   1.2 m

(2) Grey pebbly *sand*   0.9 m

(3) *Gravel* of vein-quartz, with
some granite, in sand   0.3 m

(4) Soft weathered granite *bedrock*

The mean granulometry of layers (2) and (3) is indicated
as follows.

Size range	(2) Sand	(3) Gravel
+ 10 mm	3%	23%
6-10 mm	2	11
4- 6 mm	3	9
2- 4 mm	9	17
1- 2 mm	5	5
- 1 mm	78	35
	100%	100%

There was nothing remarkable about this one stretch and
the particulars are typical of streams of this size in the
region. For streams larger than the Nafayi, the thicknesses of the upper two layers are greater, but not, as
shown in Plate 1 (page 16), of the gravel layer, which
rarely differs appreciably from an average of 0.3 metres.

Certain features need to be noted. All the evidence
indicated that the stream was at grade, having been recently degrading. First, the floodplain surface in the
meander-belt was lower than the surface of any other part
of the valley flat, and there was no suggestion of back-

swamp formation; second, deep buried channels were never found beneath streams of this size in the region; third, the bedrock floor was uneven, evident even in a pit, indicative of either continuing degradation or recent establishment of grade (see page 14); finally, the gravel layer was loose and free of clay, unlike the gravel revealed in pits dug outside the meander-belt. From this evidence it may be concluded that *all the alluvium down to the bedrock floor* had recently been involved in the continuing first order processes. This showed that the gravel layer was an integral part of the 'living' alluvium and not a historical relic.

Examination of the gravel layer revealed a highly significant property. A critical particle size could be recognised, equivalent to an intermediate diameter of about 80 mm, distinguishing, on the one hand, particles *larger* than 80 mm which were never found other than resting on the bedrock floor or on particles of the same size or larger, from, on the other hand, particles *smaller* than 80 mm, which could be readily found separated from the floor beneath by particles smaller than them. In other words, in first order time the stream had never been able to transport particles of size larger than 80 mm, although it could and did transport particles smaller than this. This measure of 80 mm is clearly the stream's *competence*, the first order characteristic defined earlier in the chapter. Thus by inspection alone we have obtained a simple but accurate index of the stream force in first order time. Naturally circumstances do not normally allow such inspection of a 'living' meander-belt, but opportunity is often offered in a terrace section, although of course it may not be closely relevant to the modern situation. In any case our present interest in this quantity of competence is conceptual, and we will now use it to pursue the argument.

3.3   Vortical action

We return to the deductive approach, to examine how the deposited alluvium of the Nafayi had come to be arranged in these layers, the number of which we can now recognise as *four*, the composite gravel layer in fact embracing two layers, distinguished from each other by the critical size of 80 mm.

The scour front was introduced in the last chapter as an essentially mathematical concept. It was shown that it had to exist, regardless of how it functioned. We now look at it as a physical phenomenon.

It is well known that a stream scours deepest at the outside of sharp bends when in flood. However caused, the flow is strongest there, in terms not only of along-channel linear forces, but also, as Matthes (1947) described, of intense 'macroturbulence', local and non-linear. The stream bed is deepened at a point by the action of an upsurging vortex - which Matthes called a 'kolk', a word used by Dutch engineers to denote 'bed deepening by vortex action' - capable of lifting particles of alluvium

vertically off the bottom. Matthes claimed that the
velocity of rotation at the pointed end of the vortex may
be many times greater than that of the surrounding flow.
The action of a stream at a scour front is thus also that
of a moving elutriator, passing to and fro across the
deeper spread of alluvium, sorting the particles into two
categories by size, as distinguished by the critical value
of the competence.

The larger particles, if present (which often they are
not), are called the *immovable particles*, because they
cannot leave the floor, on which they form an *immovable
layer*. The smaller or *load particles* are periodically
lifted up by the whirlpool into the zone of linear flow,
which disperses them downstream of the scour front, either
in more or less permanent motion (the suspended load) or
in more or less prompt return to the channel, bed, as
another layer (in fact there are two layers) resting upon
the immovable layer. The process is illustrated in
Figure 3.

It is emphasised that we are here dealing with maximum
instantaneous values of the velocity of flow, which may
differ considerably from the mean values often regarded as
critical to stream equilibrium. Although the mean values
may correlate with the mean rates of transport of the
smaller particles, they are irrelevant to the largest
gravel sizes which perhaps can *only* be shifted at all by
momentary departures from the mean velocity. Kalinske
(1943) has shown that, for turbulent 'linear' flow at the
stream bed, the standard deviation from the mean velocity
is about 25%, which indicates that momentary velocities
are frequently nearly *twice* the mean velocity. One of the
merits of the measure of competence as we define it is
that it perfectly takes into account these highly significant exceptional values.

The scour fronts signify the sites of *maximum* erosion
in depth down to the level of the floor-plane and their
incidence, in space and time, is ever restricted to few
points and short periods of time. On a more modest scale,
the same kind of process is operating with much greater
frequency, in respect to both space and time, elsewhere in
the channel and at more moderate discharges, but of course
without reaching down to the floor-plane. These isolated
excavations, great and small, will be termed *scour holes*.
All stream flow is to be crudely compounded into two kinds,
the *linear* and the *vortical*, and the elutriating effect
produced by the vortical flow is reproduced in some degree
whenever a deposit of alluvium is scoured by moving water,
and the effect is particularly marked in very turbulent
flow over gravel. This means that the larger load particles, such as are usually retained in place during the
process, are often sensibly, and sometimes violently,
disturbed without being liable to downstream transport.
We can visualise the stream bed at any moment as a foundation, fragile indeed but briefly effective, for an array
of *ephemeral potholes*, in which larger particles, of a
certain size range (which we shall investigate later), are
rigorously milled *in situ* in the course of spasmodic and
dilatory progress downstream. Matthes recognised that

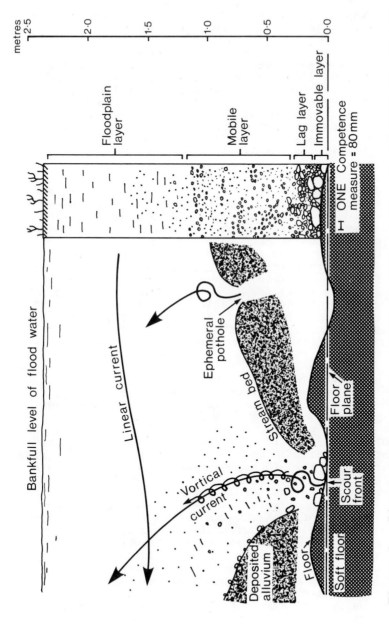

Figure 3. Diagram illustrating aspects of stream action in depth in the channel and the formation of the *alluvium profile*, which is based on the Nafayi data.

kolks can cut permanent potholes in hard rock, so pre-
serving 'casts', as it were, of the probing fingers of
erosion, and we, with our image of ephemeral potholes in
unconsolidated alluvium, are momentarily perceiving almost
identical circumstances that differ significantly only in
the speed with which the foundation yields to the cutting
tools.   This process is very likely an important cause of
the wastage and rounding of slowly travelling gravel in a
stream (as will be discussed again later), but its main
significance in our immediate enquiry is in explanation of
the *sorting* of larger particles of alluvium in depth.

This preoccupation with the alluvium in depth may
appear to produce views that conflict with accepted
opinion.   But this is not really so, for rather the ideas
complement each other.   For instance, Leopold, Wolman and
Miller (1964) emphasise the lengthwise cyclic pattern of
the shape and surface composition of the channel bed,
which in a meandering, gravel-bedded stream shows itself
as a regular alternation of 'pools' and 'riffles'.   But
even as we look for the strongest vortical action in the
pools, we realise that the actual processes we have been
discussing are indeed scarcely ever visible to the investigator concerned with surface features.   As Matthes
remarked, the mechanics of kolk action are 'shrouded in
obscurity'.   The real action in pools can never be seen
because it only happens at times of flood, when the water
is deep and turbid.   Moreover afterwards at low flow, we
find the scene of action discreetly transformed and
camouflaged.   The steep walls of ephemeral potholes have
collapsed and all is blanketed by fine alluvium subse-
quently deposited by weaker currents.   Clues to the recent
violence in depth have been delicately covered up, except
for the important evidence of larger load particles thrown
out of the deepest holes and stranded on the riffles.
Such particles can only move either when impelled by the
strong vortical action or when undermined; and so they
stay immobile upon the riffles whilst finer stuff around
them comes and goes, awaiting the eventual change in the
bed configuration that will allow them to slip from view
back into the depths.   This is a cycle of movement in
depth coexisting with the more familiar cycle of movement
in *length*.

This discussion has been concerned mostly with the
larger load particles whose size is only a little smaller
than the measure of the competence.   The movement of the
much smaller particles is less dependent on encounter with
major vortical disturbance, whose effect may be merely to
deflect them from the generally straight paths already
imposed on them by the weaker but pervading linear component of the stream's flow.

3.4   The competence ratio

From the foregoing discussion we may recognise the existence of two distinct and opposing processes determining,
in first order time, the relative vertical position of all
sizes of particle in alluvial deposition:

(i)   Particles move periodically and gradually *down*, under gravity, when the ground beneath them is cut away by the currents that are too weak to shift them directly.
(ii)   Particles move periodically and abruptly *up* when themselves propelled by the currents strong enough to perform this.
The sense of the *resultant* tendency, which is a first order characteristic, depends on the relative influence of the two processes.   The governing quantities are on the one hand the particle size as denoted by the intermediate diameter D, and on the other hand the competence D_C, representing the force of the stream in first order time. The critical control of the tendency for the particular size is therefore the ratio D/D_C, a dimensionless quantity which we call the *competence ratio*, an extremely useful parameter.

We will immediately put it to use in distinguishing which sizes of particle belong to each of *four distinct layers of alluvium.*

(1) D/D_C *is greater than unity.*   This condition defines the *immovable particles*, for which there is never any upward movement in first order time.   Once an immovable particle reaches the floor, by whatever means, it stays there.

(2) D/D_C *ranges between unity and about 0.3*, a tentative estimate of a critical value whose measurement is discussed later.   This range designates load particles that show a decisive *resultant tendency* to move *down* and indeed most of the time they behave as immovable particles. But occasionally they are thrown up by the strongest vortical currents such as act in the deepest scour holes. Here is a situation best understood through appreciation of the relative orders of magnitude of the frequencies of movement.   Any tendency for movement up of these particles is so extremely rare in comparison with tendency for movement down, that effectively, for the population as a whole, there is no movement up at all and they form a layer on the floor, yielding place only to the true immovable particles.   For, of course, unlike the immovable particles, they do move sometimes and individually they trickle downstream, but imperceptibly, without impairing the identity of the layer.   These are the *lag particles* and they form the *lag layer.*

(3) D/D_C *ranges between about 0.3 and about 0.001*, another tentative estimate discussed later.   These are the load particles which show a complementary decisive *resultant tendency* to move *up*, but are yet too large to be maintained in suspension, and they quickly come to rest again upon the channel bed.   These are the *mobile particles* and they form a *mobile layer* resting upon the lag layer.   The boundary between the two is fairly sharp, because there is no graded bedding within either of the layers.   The reason is that the bulk of the mobile and lag particles differ almost qualitatively, again the effect of the disparate orders of magnitude of the frequencies of vertical movement.   Obviously there has to exist somewhere a middle, neutral range of sizes for which the opposing tendencies of movement up and movement down are fairly easily balanced,

but it is very narrow and the few particles belonging to
it are not to be noticed amongst so many others. For
these others, the great majority, the resultant tendencies
are so definite, either decisively up or decisively down,
that there is no inclination for the sizes to become
graduated in depth and consequently neither of the two
layers formed, mobile and lag, displays graded bedding and
the plane of division between them is sharp..

This is not to say, however, that there is no *local*
sorting within the layers, especially within the mobile
layer for which such a wide range of relative sizes exists
($0.001D_c$ to $0.3D_c$). It will also be noted that this layer
always contains a very small quantity of lag particles in
transit, having been cast out of deep scour holes to lodge
temporarily somewhere above the lag layer. Doubtless
smaller lag particles may sometimes be thrown right out of
the holes and onto the surface of the channel bed, but we
may guess that very few indeed would reach so far.

(4) D/D_c *is smaller than about 0.001.* As the competence factor continues to decrease there comes a value
for which movement down of the particles virtually ceases
altogether, because so rarely is the current weak enough
for them to be deposited from suspension. This is not an
absolute condition because still water may often be found
locally in stream channels, especially at low discharge
and more commonly in braided streams, but it is the general
rule. This description defines the *fine particles*. But
although they do not properly belong to the channel deposits, they do make a major contribution to the alluvium
deposited *outside the channel*, either upon the shoulder
of pointbars or as true overbank deposition upon the
floodplain, wherever the full force of the stream is not
applied. In both these situations flow is shallower without being notably steeper, and therefore is slower and
weaker. We call this uppermost deposition the *floodplain
layer*, which often contains, as we shall see, a high proportion of silt. But its boundary with the mobile layer
is rarely distinct, simply because the shoulder of a point-
bar is always gently and evenly rising from the channel
proper right up to the level of the floodplain (as in Plate
2) and there is tendency for the coarser channel alluvium
to be swept up this shoulder by a sideways component of
the bottom-hugging linear current of the stream (see Allen,
1970, pages 132-3). Here of course graded bedding is
apparent. Nonetheless the concept of the separate layers,
broadly considered, is undeniable and indeed typical expressions of each are distinctive.

Before these conclusions are summarised, we should note
that the characteristic particles of each of the three
lower layers (mobile, lag and immovable) are always accompanied by smaller proportions of other populations. The
voids between both immovable and lag particles are necessarily occupied by smaller grains, including very fine
material which has filtered down from above or entered
laterally after the shifting channel has moved away. We
have already noted that some lag particles will be found
within the mobile layer, mainly near the base. Only the
immovable particles rigorously keep their place.

3.5   The alluvium profile

The four layers compose a sequence which we will call the
alluvium profile. To it all forms of stream deposition
may be referred. The concept resembles that of the well-
known soil profile in that all the layers are developed
simultaneously and there is no stratification in the
chronological sense. Also, one or more, or even all, of
the layers may be missing. The complete sequence is shown
below, with estimates of the critical competence ratios
(D/D_c) relating to each layer.

Characteristic Particles

	Layer	Title	D/D_c Range
(1)	Floodplain	Fine	Less than 0.001
(2)	Mobile	Mobile	0.001 - 0.3
(3)	Lag	Lag	0.3 - 1.0
(4)	Immovable	Immovable	Greater than 1.0
	———		
	Floor		

All the relationships have been ascertained by deduction alone, although of course their recognition has
been prompted by observation. As for the dimensionless
critical competence ratios (D/D_c), the determination of
their actual values, which are the products of complex
physical interactions in first order time, can only be
discovered by field measurements, as will be discussed
presently. We shall refer to them as (1) the *critical lag
ratio*, estimated at about 0.3, and (2) the *critical mobile
ratio*, estimated at about 0.001. We shall also need to
refer to the corresponding absolute particle sizes as
(1) the *critical lag size* (D_l), for which $D_l = 0.3D_c$, and
(2) the *critical mobile size* (D_m), for which $D_m = 0.001D_c$.
We have seen that the competence of the Nafayi was
observed to be about 80 mm. By applying to this value the
critical lag ratio of 0.3 we calculate that the critical
lag size (D_l) is about 25 mm, which is consistent with the
sampling record. The implication is that particles of
size between 25 and 80 mm are confined almost entirely to
the lag layer, although some are bound to have strayed

Plate 2.   A point-bar on the Adour River at Mugron, in
     southern France, here a *moderately-loaded gravel
     stream* carrying quartzite gravel of maximum common
     size about 135 mm. The competence is about 500 mm.
     The horse is taking advantage of the shallow water
     over the riffle bar.

into the mobile layer, mainly near its base. If the immovable particles are scanty, the lag layer rests directly
on the floor and we have a *lag-cum-immovable layer*.

Now applying the critical mobile ratio of 0.001, we
have 0.08 mm as the critical mobile size (D_m), the minimum
size of particle to be found abundantly in the mobile
layer, almost identical with the standard lower size limit
of sand (0.062 mm). This is also consistent with the
record.

I did not see the Nafayi deposit being mined, but have
witnessed such operations in many similar streams (e.g. as
in Plate 1, page 16) and can affirm with certainty that all
four layers would have been found evenly spread both across
and along the meander-belt, as the pitting results suggested. Gravel may have been lacking very locally where
exceptional activity in abnormally deep scour fronts had
dispersed it, but generally a remarkable uniformity would
have been observed. Also there would have been no difficulty in identifying within a few centimetres the boundary
between the mobile 'sand' layer and the lag 'gravel' layer,
always an important decision to the operators because only
in the latter would the diamonds be found in quantity. In
fact it was a very palpable boundary, which could be de-
tected accurately from the surface by means of a simple
steel probe, use of which was standard practice in assessing depths prior to excavation.

Possibly the most significant feature of the alluvium
profile of the Nafayi is the very fact that all four layers
were represented. In most streams of the world the two
lower layers are missing, simply because there are no immovable or lag particles in the alluvium. For this there
may be two quite different reasons. One is obviously that
there may be no gravel-sized particles, or only very small
ones. But an equally likely explanation is that the
competence of the stream (D_c) is much greater than the
size of even the largest of perhaps very large gravel
particles. This can only happen where a stream is heavily
loaded with gravel. In such circumstances, as we have
seen, the stream slope is kept steep (through the slope-
degradation interaction) in order to maintain grade, the
steepness having imparted extra force to the stream and
therefore a larger competence. Thus we may have mountain
streams carrying boulders of diameter up to (say) 500 mm
maintaining competences in the order of 3000 mm, and of
course there would be no immovable or lag particles in
such a stream.

At the other extreme we have relatively lightly loaded
streams like the Nafayi. Because of the seasonally restricted rainfall of 270 mm per annum the discharge of the
Nafayi is high for its drainage area. Set against this,
the 'potential availability' of bedload alluvium is low,
because in this area of thoroughly decomposed granite
virtually the only source of gravel is in the sparsely
scattered quartz veins, and the only source of sand is the
small amounts of residual quartz and fine granite debris
weathering directly out of the granite. Finally, as we
consider 'the attitude of the landscape' as the other
factor influencing the amount of the load (page 24), we

recognise that the rate of erosion in this generally level region of low relief can only be modest. Thus high discharge and low load are the controls of the Nafayi, which is accordingly a relatively lightly loaded stream, maintaining a competence for grade of measure actually smaller than the largest particles of alluvium. Now it so happens here that the sand sizes and the gravel sizes make nearly equal contributions to the deposition (by processes examined later), with the result that sand sizes preponderate in the mobile layer in marked contrast to the gravel sizes that preponderate in the combined lag and immovable layer. Clay is the principal constituent of the thick floodplain layer. The total effect is a fully represented alluvium profile illuminated by layers of sharply contrasted granulometry, as shown in Figure 3.

3.6 Estimation of the critical competence ratios

Explanation will now be given of how the values (0.3 and 0.001) of the two critical competence ratios D/D_c were obtained.

The estimate of 0.3 for the *critical lag ratio* (D_1/D_c) derives from my own observations, which, although unavoidably of limited scope, would appear to give an adequate first approximation. My association with alluvial diamond deposits in West Africa ended before I had reached my present understanding of the alluvium profile and consequently I never made express measurements to discover either of the critical ratios. Fortunately rescue has been provided by a collection of properly scaled, close-up colour-transparency photographs of a number of relevant examples, which, supported by recollection of other alluvium profiles observed elsewhere, allow me to submit the figure with some confidence. But in fact there is no call for concern about the accuracy of the figure, in that the *existence* of both critical values has been demonstrated both by theory and observation, and precise estimation of the values is not an important consideration in this work for the reasons explained in the introduction (page 2), although obviously we need to know them approximately.

The photographs mentioned were taken in Sierra Leone and Ghana. Three types of measurement were read from them: (1) the actual competence measure D_c, available where immovable particles were recognised; (2) the minimum sizes of lag particles in the lag layer, giving the critical lag size (D_1), clearly indicated in certain types of alluvium profile discussed later (e.g. see pages 113 and 115); and (3) the maximum sizes of mobile particles commonly found in the mobile layer, this also giving the critical lag size (D_1). In all the situations photographed, whether or not immovable particles were present, approximate values of D_c were known through interpretation of other properties, as will be apparent later, and it was gratifying to find single figures emerge which fitted every situation. It is very difficult at this stage to discuss all the relationships governed by the value of competence, many of which

Towards stream synthesis

will have to wait until other characteristics of first
order equilibrium have been investigated, but it will gradually become apparent how the values estimated are always
consistent with the general pattern of properties. Unfortunately the photos individually are not of quality fit
for useful black-and-white reproduction, but the composite
picture of Figure 3, which relates to the Nafayi data,
demonstrates the more important relationships.

The Sierra Leone photographs are of alluvium profiles
more or less similar to the one of the Nafayi, with competences ranging between 40 and 70 mm, whilst the Ghana
photographs, depicting alluvium profiles of the Birim
River some 150 miles downstream from its source, indicate
competences of about 150 mm at Edubia and about 300 mm at
Wenchi (where the slope is steeper), both sites displaying
a mobile layer consisting principally of gravel. I am only
able to speculate about the value of the critical lag ratio
for competences greater than this, but see no reason why
it should not be the same as for smaller competences, or
nearly so.

The estimate of 0.001 for the *critical mobile ratio*
(D_m/D_c) was obtained in a rather different way. The concept of critical mobile size (D_m), the absolute measure,
is already well recognised, and reports of values of it
have been reviewed by Moss (1963). He refers to Lane's
(1938) assertion that 'many rivers, although transporting
huge quantities of suspended material to the sea, have
beds of clean sand, rich in particles in the 0.1 - 0.3 mm
size range, but containing little smaller material', and
quotes other measurements of the critical size, varying
between 0.06 mm and 0.35 mm. Similar values may be inferred directly from published size frequency distributions
for streambed samples, whence may come many good estimates
of the critical mobile size. But these figures alone
obviously do not give the ratio D_m/D_c, for which we must
also have the complementary values of the competence (D_c).
Fortunately here also we are provided for, because many of
these frequency distributions record the presence of relatively coarse gravel particles. Such particles are of
rare but nonetheless significant occurrence in sand bed
material, and of course are characteristic of gravel bed
material. To take an example of a stream with a *sand bed*,
according to particle-size analyses published by Scott and
Stephens (1966), the Mississippi River at St. Louis yields
gravel particles up to the 16-32 mm size range in a bed-
material notably deficient in sizes smaller than 0.06 mm.
The data are too limited to allow any definite conclusion
to be drawn, but they suggest that the competence here may
be about 75 mm, indicating critical lag and mobile sizes
of about 20 mm (D_l) and 0.07 mm (D_m). Surer estimates for
other streams with sand beds are discussed later (pages 111
and 113). To take an example of a stream with a *gravel
bed* (and a rather extreme case), data provided by
Fahnestock (1963, Table 2) for a site on the Upper White
River on Mount Rainier, Washington State, indicate critical
sizes of about 500 mm (D_l) and 16 mm (D_m), suggesting a
very large competence of over 1500 mm.

These are rough and ready estimates, but they do not

for this reason invalidate the apparently important and universal relationships which they represent. Also there can be no doubt that research specifically directed to measuring the critical sizes would produce very much more reliable assessments of the two ratios. Meanwhile the approximations 0.3 and 0.001 will adequately serve our enquiry.

Chapter 4

THE RELATION OF THE COMPETENCE TO THE LOADING IN A GRADED STREAM

4.1 The loading

Already we have had occasion to describe a stream as being either heavily or lightly loaded. The reference has been clearly not to the actual load of alluvium carried, but to the *relative* load judged in relation to the size of the stream, as measured by the discharge. Obviously quotation of the value of the load alone without reference to the discharge would say nothing very useful and we are bound to take both quantities into consideration, load and discharge. This might seem an awkward requirement in that the load and the discharge are independent of each other, so that any change in the 'relative load' cannot be identified with either of its two components. Fortunately there is no problem. The general argument supposes that at any one floodplain-belt cross-section the discharge is invariable in all three orders of fluvial time and consequently can be ignored as an irrelevant constant in any consideration of changes in the other variable quantities. Thus the 'relative load' at a cross-section is effectively governed, regardless of the order of time considered, only by variation in the load, and at once we can recognise this quantity as a simple and potentially extremely useful first order parameter. Henceforward we shall refer to it as the *loading*, denote it by the symbol Q_R and define it simply as first order load per unit discharge.

It may perhaps be recognised that the loading is the first order equivalent of the 'discharge-weighted' concentration recorded at the U.S. Geological Survey gauging stations, as described by Leopold, Wolman and Miller (1946, pages 186-188), but there is good reason for us not to adopt the same terminology. In the first place we do well to distinguish the loading clearly from the other and very different 'static' concentration discussed by the same authors, whose near counterpart in this present study is the 'alluvium cover', described in the next chapter. Also, and particularly, we need to emphasise the relevance of the loading as essentially an expression of the load alone and all that this control signifies in the context of stream evolution.

We are generally unable to assess the loading in absolute units, if only because there are very few records of measurements available for the *bedload sizes*, which, regarded as the combined mobile and lag sizes, are those that concern us most, and these few belong only to certain kinds of streams. But happily for our kind of approach we shall manage well enough by broadly distinguishing between 'light', 'moderate' and 'heavy' bedload loadings, or, more often than not, by simply considering which of two loadings is the 'lighter' or the 'heavier'. Rarely however can even these judgments be made reliably from direct observation of alluvium under transport, except in the case of heavily-loaded streams in arid or mountain regions where rapid displacement of large quantities of gravel or sand may be visually very evident. Indeed direct assessments can easily be in error because an obviously heavy loading of silt and clay, which alone cannot fundamentally affect the stream's equilibrium (this claim will be substantiated in Chapter 11), may disguise a relatively light loading of the significant bedload sizes. An example of this is the notorious Rio Grande of New Mexico, often extremely heavily charged with silt, which yet, as discussed on page 113, is only 'moderately' loaded with sand.

However it is possible to assess the bedload loading very surely, although of course only broadly, from consideration of a number of channel characteristics which, in a graded stream, it exclusively determines, for we shall see that ultimately the bedload loading, considered in relation to its particle size distribution (and also taking into account the possible presence of immovable particles), is the dominant control of stream equilibrium at a floodplain-belt cross-section. Already we can recognise several such distinguishing attributes, for instance in the valley slope and the competence, the values of both of which increase with increase in the bedload at any one cross-section of a graded stream, and therefore also increase with increase in the bedload *loading* there.

Indeed by means of such relationships we can reliably assess the bedload loading merely by inspection of the alluvium profile. To demonstrate this, let us now compare two imaginary cases, differing only in the values of the bedload loadings, fairly light in the one case, heavy in the other. We assume that there are no immovable or lag particles present in either situation, so that the evidence provided by each is only to be discovered in the mobile layer. Moreover the granulometric constitution of the mobile layer is assumed to be the same for both cases, and the distinguishing clues are thus further only to be seen in the relative disposition of the particles of different sizes to each other. We will assume that they are mostly of gravel size, predominantly about 30 mm in intermediate diameter, with a maximum size, commonly represented, of 90 mm, which is just within the cobble range. From this information, remembering that there are no lag particles and that the critical lag size is equal to about $0.3D_c$, we deduce that in neither case can the competence be less than 300 mm, assuming the streams to be at grade. The evidence we are seeking derives from the differing behaviours of the cobbles in the two original streams.

We first consider the case where the bedload loading is fairly light. Here the competence is relatively small and presumably not much over the limiting 300 mm. We can suppose it to be 400 mm. In comparison with this measure the size of the cobbles (90 mm) is quite large and we infer that

they are moved only very infrequently. We would expect to
see evidence of their inertia. Flung by a rare chance to
the surface of a bar from a deep scour hole, they stay
there as a surface ornament, a thin spread of dispropor-
tionately large particles (the feature is well described
by Leopold, Wolman and Miller, 1964, page 211), which has
become a kind of residual deposit. During the eventual
disruption of the bar, they slump, but keep together in a
ragged bunch, which will later settle as an isolated lens
simulating a lag layer, waiting to be thrown to the surface
again. They do not form a continuous and genuine lag layer
in depth, because they are mobile particles. They are
still small enough to be vulnerable to vertical upward
propulsion sufficiently frequent to keep them almost continuously somewhere within the mobile layer.

In the second case, the bedload loading is heavy and
consequently the competence is much larger. We will suppose it to be 800 mm. Here the cobbles behave in quite a
different way, for they are so frequently mobilised that
they show none of the ponderous quasi-lag characteristics
we have just been considering, but scatter evenly amongst
the smaller mobile particles and behave with the con-
formity we would expect of particles whose degree of
mobility is not markedly exceptional.

As will be discussed more fully later (Chapters 10 and
12), evidence of both these different styles of behaviour
is always displayed clearly in the mobile layer of the
alluvium profile, provided that a wide range of gravel
sizes is represented. Thus we can gauge the values of
both the bedload loading and the competence despite the
absence of any particles of size equal to or larger than
the competence. Plate 6 (page 112)provides a clear demonstration of this. Of course in neither of the cases just
examined is the bedload loading so very light as to be
satisfied by a competence of less than 300 mm, for this
circumstance would be positively revealed by the presence
of a genuine lag layer, which in our examples does not
exist.

No mention has been made here of the fine particles,
such as are carried always in suspension. We shall see
later (more immediately on page 48) that the fine particle
loading, even when very heavy, has only small influence
on the equilibrium of a stream, and will not often have to
be mentioned. For this reason and in the interest of
brevity, we shall henceforward refer to the bedload loading
quite simply as 'the loading', without qualification.

4.2   Correlation of the two indices

In the analysis of fluvial time in Chapters 1 and 2, we
considered only the fundamental controls of stream behaviour, recognised as the discharge, the load and the
valley slope, regardless of whether they would be convenient instruments for extending our enquiry. They are
the bases of theory and we are obliged to respect them as
such, but we shall find other quantities deriving from
them more useful in providing the understanding we seek.

The most important of these have already been defined as
the *competence* (D_C) and the *loading* (Q_R), and they will be
referred to, for reasons given below, as the *two indices*.
We shall now see how they represent the fundamental controls and how they may be correlated. All the quantities
mentioned are first order quantities.

One of the shortcomings of the defined fundamental
controls (discharge, load, valley slope) as research instruments is that they possess little in common with each
other dimensionally and therefore, when together held up
to view as a specification of a particular situation, are
incapable of conveying any immediately useful information.
Indeed only empirical mathematics can link them at all and
then, as is normal, without offering real explanation of
the relationships. Another inconvenience is that two of
them, the discharge and the load, can only be conceived as
numerically expressed absolute quantities of such kind as
cannot be measured easily, even approximately. In fact it
must be almost impossible by any means to measure a bedload of particles of large competence ratio and yet this is
the load which exercises the greatest control of the
stream's equilibrium.

The two indices avoid both these handicaps. Their
values may be compared directly and immediately upon a
size frequency curve, actual or imagined, depicting, if
only very roughly, the particle size frequency distribution
of the loading; and all the information needed for this,
together with adequate assessment in relative terms of
the amount of the loading, may be gauged from quick inspection of an alluvium profile, either in its entirety or
enough of it to know its salient properties. As will be
shown, this information alone can provide a very full
understanding of the behaviour of the stream.

The role of the two quantities is that each serves as
an 'index' of one or other of the two forces into which
first order physical interaction may be resolved. Without
analysing them closely, we may accurately depict the processes involved as confrontation between the 'stream
force', representing the active force of the current seeking to scour down below the floor plane, and the 'alluvium
resistance', representing the passive reaction of the
alluvium which by its mere presence at the seat of action
tends to prevent this scour. As already indicated, the
competence is a true index of the stream force, and the
loading, which is a measure of the amount and size of the
alluvium involved in the confrontation, is a true index of
the alluvium resistance. The result of the confrontation
is indicated by the rate of degradation, positive if the
stream force prevails and there is degradation, negative
if the alluvium resistance prevails and there is aggradation, and zero for the balanced state of grade.

Before accepting the indices, we should check their
relationships to the three controls.

The *competence* may be envisaged as a representative
value of the stream's maximum tractive force at the stream
bed, regarded as a first order characteristic. Tractive
force (τ), the well-known measure of hydraulic shear
(force per unit area), is related to instantaneous values

of the depth (h) and the slope (s) in the formula $\tau = \gamma hs$, where γ is the specific weight of water. Leliavsky (1955, pages 41 and 42) explains the derivation of this formula and states that 'so long as we do not attribute any particular, specifically prescribed, quantitative significance' to the value of τ, the formula is 'axiomatic', and this of course fully satisfies our approach. In first order time, the depth (h) is governed primarily by the discharge, although modified by the load in its influence on the width-depth ratio of the channel (see pages 103-106). Also, the slope (s) is governed primarily by the valley slope, although it too is modified by the load, in its influence on the channel sinuosity, for rather similar reasons (see pages 117-119). But there is no doubt that the dominant influences determining the value of (hs) are the discharge and the valley slope together, and consequently the main argument may disregard the effect of the load as merely modifying. It follows that the competence is effectively governed only by the discharge and the valley slope, increasing as either of these quantities increases, and vice versa.

The *loading* is by definition load per unit discharge, and no more need be said about its relationship to the controls. We should however remember that a full reckoning of alluvium resistance has also to take into account the contribution of the immovable particles, of size larger than the competence, which cannot be expressed by a time function. This contribution, measured as the 'immovable cover' in units of amount per unit *area*, can sometimes be the dominant component of the alluvium resistance, as will be shown later, but at present we will continue to assume that there are no immovable particles involved.

The diagram below summarises the relationships deduced so far, the numbers indicating, as before, the order of fluvial time in which the action operates.

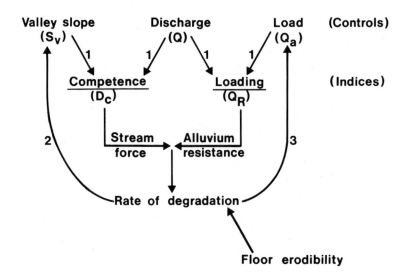

We now take the important step of detaching our study from dependence on the three controls and transferring it to the two indices. We have already noted that the discharge of the stream at the floodplain-belt cross-section may be regarded as invariable in all three orders of fluvial time and therefore may be ignored except as a constant. Thus we can simplify the diagram as follows.

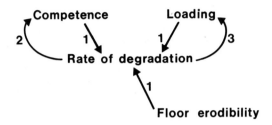

The indices pair off with the only two effectively variable controls, with the competence governed only by the valley slope, and the loading governed only by the load. It follows that we can substitute the slope-degradation interaction by a *competence-degradation interaction*, identical with it in its relationships (see page 18), and the load-degradation interaction similarly by a *loading-degradation interaction* (see page 21).

Remarkably, the further we venture from the foundations of our study, the simpler become the relationships. Indeed the diagram becomes even more concise when we consider streams *at grade*. We have seen that through the working of the slope-degradation interaction the stream establishes in second order time a particular value of the valley slope appropriate for a zero rate of degradation, which we call the 'slope for grade'. We can now understand that there must be a corresponding *competence for grade*, also establishing in second order time, and we have the following very simple relationship between the two indices of a graded stream.

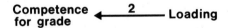

Competence for grade adjusts itself continuously to the loading. Both quantities are expressed in the common units of size of particle of alluvium. Both quantities may be gauged from inspection of the alluvium profile. This is *the heart of the argument*, though we have yet to see how to use it.

Chapter 5

ALLUVIUM COVER

5.1 Alluvium cover recognised

We are now ready to begin the 'synthesis' of a real stream
from its two conceptual elements, stream force and alluvium
resistance, as conveniently represented by their indices,
the competence and the loading. It will be a two-stage
process of construction, in which the link between the
abstraction of the indices and the substance of the
alluvium profile is provided by an intermediate concept,
the alluvium cover.

We will begin at our usual point of reference, the
floodplain-belt cross-section, but now will limit our
attention to the vertical column of mixed alluvium and
water overlying a small *area* of the floor, situated in the
channel.

First we examine the column at an instant of time. In
the upper part of the column is the moving water, with some
moving alluvium. In the lower part is stationary alluvium,
protected from the scouring action of the water by the
presence of those particles of alluvium that are actually
in contact with the water. We may regard the protection
as being due to the 'resistance' of these particles against
the 'force' of the stream. The resistance, however conceived in mechanical terms, is provided by the *cover* of the
alluvium above the small area of unscoured material, a
shield of solid particles, some stationary and some moving.
In fact the particles of the cover exist in three states,
which we will examine in turn: (i) some particles sweep
past in suspension, (ii) some bowl along as bedload, and
(iii) some rest motionless on the stream bed.

The particles in suspension, which we call the fine
particles (page 35), make a negligible contribution to the
resistance. As Nordin and Beverage (1965, page 11) have
expressed it, the rate of transport of suspended material
is governed only by its availability and is not function-
ally related to the flow. There is no question of it being
so abundant (within reason) that the excess is deposited
and consequently it has no direct effect on the ability
of the stream to scour in depth. Admittedly it has certain
indirect effect, whose influence however is only modifying.
An increase in suspended load dampens turbulence and
diminishes the roughness (such as Manning's n), but we
know nothing of the net effect of all this on scour in
depth and can safely assume it to be secondary. Nor does
the amount of suspended material transported significantly
affect the amount of it deposited anywhere in the alluvium
profile, including the floodplain layer, for we shall see
later (pages 99 - 103) that the *only* important control of

the content of suspended material in any stream deposition
is the independent one of the competence alone. Thus we
may generally ignore variation in the supply of suspended
alluvium as having any significant influence, either one
way or the other, on the 'resistance' of the alluvium as a
whole.

However, the *larger particles* in both the other states
may make very significant contributions to the alluvium
resistance and it is to these that we shall now restrict
our attention, ignoring the suspended fine particles.
Moreover, as recognised earlier (page 40), this means that
we can usually ignore all particles smaller than about
0.062 mm (the grade limit distinguishing silt from sand,
as commonly defined), and indeed it will be convenient for
us to terminate particle size frequency curves at or near
this measure.

We infer that the mere *presence* of these *larger
particles* at each instant of time, in a physical involvement we do not have to investigate closely, restrains the
current from scouring the underlying material; for it is
self-evident that particles so large that they form a
carpet of solid material hugging the stream bed, whether
they be stationary or moving, must, if abundant enough,
provide a barrier to erosion.

From this we gather that a measure of the effectiveness
of such a cover is its 'thickness' and that the resistance
of the alluvium may be represented by the amount of this
alluvium instantaneously forming the cover per unit
horizontal area of the channel. The amount is referred
to a particle size distribution. This quantity is the
alluvium cover.

Local, instantaneous values of the alluvium cover are
continuously varying in sympathy with changes in the
corresponding values of the discharge and the position of
the 'area' in relation to the channel pattern. But following our earlier practice (see page 8), we may visualise
a single value ideally representative of this quantity
qualifying as the *first order characteristic*, similarly
titled the *alluvium cover* and denoted by the symbol C.
Also we may visualise its two components, the *load cover*
(C_{load}), representing the load particles, and the *immovable cover* ($C_{immovable}$), representing the immovable
particles. Although for a while we shall continue to
suppose that there are no immovable particles and that the
immovable cover is of zero value, it is apparent that later
we shall have no difficulty in fitting this latter quantity
into the general scheme.

Alluvium cover is evidently an alternative expression
of the first order 'alluvium resistance' at the cross-
section, differing from the loading (Q_R) in that it relates
to unit *area* instead of unit *time*. Also, whilst the
loading is governed only by the load (with discharge
assumed constant) and is thus independent of 'stream
force', alluvium cover is governed by both the loading
and the competence, representing both sides of the 'confrontation', as will be seen. The special significance of
cover is provided by its dimension, *amount per unit area*,
which is the same as that of the wholly stationary alluvium

Towards stream synthesis

in the alluvium profile, which we shall refer to as the *deposition* (Y). As illustrated in Figure 5, cover stands conceptually midway between loading and deposition and is a link promoting understanding of the formation of the alluvium profile, as will also be seen. The stages are summarised below.

(1) Loading (Q_R) — amount transported per unit *time* (per unit discharge)

(2) Load Cover (C_{load}) — amount moving and stationary per unit *area* of floor (within the channel)

(3) Load Deposition (Y_{load}) — amount stationary per unit *area* of floor (in the alluvium profile)

If the load cover represents 'alluvium resistance', there must also exist a notional critical value of the cover, relating to similarly constituted alluvium, which would produce a zero rate of degradation and thus exactly represent the actual 'stream force'. This quantity, which is simply the notional *cover for grade*, denoted C_p, expresses Gilbert's (1914) concept of *capacity*, defined by him as 'the maximum load a stream can carry' without 'deposition' ensuing. For a stream at grade, this cover for grade and the load cover are identical; for an aggrading stream, the load cover exceeds the cover for grade; and for a degrading stream, the load cover is less than the cover for grade.
We shall see shortly how the value of the load cover is governed partly by the loading, which determines the rate of supply of alluvium to the vertical column of mixed water and alluvium described earlier, and partly by the varying *travel velocities* of the different sizes of particle. Although these velocities will require careful definition in respect to direction, we can understand now that they vary across an infinite proportional range, from a maximum value equal to that of the stream flow itself for the fine particles down to zero for the immovable particles. The slower the velocity, the greater the cover for a given rate of supply, until we reach the limiting case of the perpetual cover provided by the zero supply of the immovable particles. If this correlation between cover, supply and velocity should be difficult to visualise, a simple analogy may help. When motor traffic is slowed down for any reason, the vehicles 'cover' the road densely, bumper to bumper; but as soon as the traffic increases speed, the gaps widen between the vehicles, which now 'cover' the road thinly, even though the number of vehicles passing per unit time (the rate of supply) may have been the same throughout. Similarly, a small quantity of coarse gravel creeping reluctantly downstream may cover the stream bed much more densely than a much greater quantity of sand hastening by.

This question of travel velocity is of the first
importance because it influences not only the relation of
loading (Q_R) to load cover (C_{load}) but also, and in much
the same way, the relation of load cover (C_{load}) to load
deposition (Y_{load}). We will now see how the travel velocity is governed exclusively by the competence ratio D/D_c,
in a simple relationship.

5.2   The travel velocity of alluvium

Travel velocity (U), the first order characteristic, is
the mean downstream distance travelled by particles of a
stated size per unit time, and it takes into account both
periods of motion and periods of rest.
    Let U be the travel velocity of particles of size D.
U can be visualised as the product of two quantities, one
of which is the mean downstream velocity of motion, V,
relating only to periods of actual displacement downstream
(but not to undirected movement *in situ* in ephemeral potholes under the impulse of vortical currents), and the
other is the *frequency of motion downstream*, F, regarded
as the proportion of the whole time spent in such motion.
Thus U = VF.
    Both the quantities V and F are functions, in the same
sense, of a parameter representing the disparity between
size of the particle, D, and the competence, D_c, which we
have already recognised as the competence ratio, D/D_c.   As
D/D_c increases, so both V and F decrease.
    Thus we can write, using for the first time the conven-
tion described on page 2,

$$V = \phi(1/(D/D_c)),$$

and

$$F = \phi(1/(D/D_c)).$$

The first quantity V is unimportant because its range of
values, *proportionally* considered, is very narrow in comparison with that of the second quantity F, whose range is
infinite.   The actual movement downstream of a particle is
always fairly rapid, however rare or brief may be this
event in the case of lag particles, and yet it can never
be quicker than the speed of the current, which is always
limited.   Thus, in relation to an infinite range, V is
virtually a constant and we can disregard it.
    But F, the frequency of motion downstream, is by no
means a constant.   Its value is influenced by considerations
of both *position* and *time*, both important.   A grain of sand
on the stream bed is liable to be put in motion almost
wherever it lies in the channel pattern and during flows
that account for much of the time.   On the other hand a
cobble of size nearly as large as the competence will not
budge except in the rare conjunction of circumstances that
puts it within the reach of one of the very few, very
strong vortical currents that the stream can *anywhere* and
ever muster.   And we infer that it will only make a short

hop, probably of only a few metres at the most, before it
begins another long spell of immobility, waiting for re-
establishment of the exceptional spatial and temporal
conditions required for movement. For such particles, the
frequency of motion downstream F, is very small indeed, and
it is easy to understand that the proportional range of
values of F is in fact infinitely wide.

Thus there is no doubt that V can be regarded as a
constant in the equation U = VF, and we may write

$$U = \phi(F) = \phi(1/(D/D_c)),$$

noting that the range of values of U, the travel velocity,
is also proportionally infinitely wide.

This is an important relationship, but before accepting
it we should consider briefly the implication of the inter-
changeability of particles of the same size as they make
their way downstream, referred to by Fisk (1944, page 51)
as 'trading'. Laterally, particles leave the channel on
burial in point-bars, only to be replaced by counterparts
emerging from the opposing concave bank. Longitudinally,
particles disappear downstream only to be replaced by
counterparts coming from upstream. For first order equilibrium there is a balance of give and take in all directions
within the plane of the floodplain-belt, and thus we can
maintain our study of the movement of every size of particle, regardless of its travel velocity, by supposing that
the focal point of our study within the small area in the
channel described on page 48 is continuously moving across
the floodplain-belt cross-section even as the channel itself moves. Consequently we are not tied to any specific
set of particles but are free to consider the whole population of particles involved in the first order process right
across the floodplain-belt, whether or not at any instant
they lie within the channel. Thus we are certainly dealing
with true first order quantities referable to the whole
floodplain-belt cross-section and can recognise, as yet
another first order characteristic, a continuous gradation
of the values of U, of proportionally infinite range,
referable to all the sizes of particle involved and governed
exclusively by the competence ratio D/D_c. By our theoretical approach, an extremely complex situation resolves into
the very simple but wholly adequate formula just stated.

Plate 3. A point-bar on the West Dart River just downstream of Two Bridges, on Dartmoor, here (along a short
stretch) a *moderately-loaded gravel stream* carrying
a granite and vein-quartz gravel of maximum common
size in the mobile layer of 120 mm. The competence is
about 400 mm. Lag and immovable particles were visible
in the pool in the foreground.

Towards stream synthesis

5.3   The cover formulae

We can now relate alluvium cover to the two indices by other simple formulae.
    Suppose the load of alluvium of a limited size-range is Q_a, in units of amount per unit time, and the corresponding travel velocity is U, in units of downstream distance per unit time. Both are the first order quantities referring to the floodplain-belt cross-section, where the width of the stream is W.

Load per unit width = Q_a/W.

Let C_{load} be the load cover, in units of amount per unit area, for the same size-range.

$C_{load} = Q_a/UW$.

If Q and Q_R are the corresponding values of the discharge and the loading,

$Q_R = Q_a/Q$,

by definition, and

$$C_{load} = \frac{Q}{W} \cdot \frac{Q_R}{U}.$$

It has just been shown that

$U = \phi(1/(D/D_c))$,

where D/D_c is the competence ratio for a particle of size D and a competence of size D_c. Whence

$$C_{load} = \frac{Q}{W} \cdot Q_R \cdot \phi(D/D_c).$$

At the one floodplain-belt cross-section, Q/W may be regarded as constant.

    Thus we obtain the *basic cover formula* for a limited size-range D at a floodplain-belt cross-section,

$C_{load} = k \cdot Q_R/U = Q_R \cdot \phi(D/D_c)$,

where k is a constant. The equivalent formula for all sizes of alluvium is

$$C_{load} = k \sum_{D=0}^{D=D_c} Q_R/U = \sum_{D=0}^{D=D_c} Q_R \cdot \phi(D/D_c)$$

The *general cover formula* for an alluvium cover C comprising both load and immovable particles may be written

$$C = k \sum_{D=0}^{D=D_c} Q_R/U + C_{immovable} = \sum_{D=0}^{D=D_c} Q_R \cdot \phi(D/D_c) + C_{immovable}$$

The relationships are shown in the diagram below.

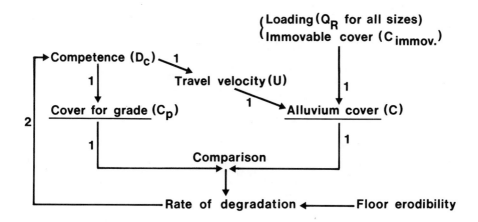

Cover for grade C_p is the notional cover for grade for similarly constituted alluvium and clearly, for a given alluvium, is governed by the competence D_c alone. Whence

$$C_p = \phi (D_c).$$

Chapter 6

THE DEPOSITION CURVE DERIVED FROM THE
LOADING CURVE

6.1   The granulometry of alluvium

The key formula of the last chapter is C_{load} = k.Q_R/U, valid
for a limited size-range D.   The link is U = $\phi(1/(D/D_C))$.

An implication of the formula is that whatever may be
the shape of the complete particle size frequency curve
for the loading (Q_R), the corresponding curve for the cover
(C_{load}) is a *distortion* of it, because of the infinite
proportional range of the values of the travel velocity
(U) between D = O and D = D_C.   It has already been mentioned, though as yet without demonstration, that the
deposition (Y_{load}), relating to the alluvium profile, is
a product of the same influences and its curve represents
an even greater distortion of the loading curve.

Virtually all the alluvium ever seen in nature is a
manifestation of this distorted frequency curve for the
alluvium profile and it is evident that direct measurement
from nature will not help us much in discovering the
characteristic shape (or shapes) of the loading curve.   We
therefore do better to begin our enquiry by investigating
the raw materials of alluvium in the products of disintegration of weathering rock more or less in situ and
thence *deduce* the composition of the supply to the stream.
Afterwards we can distort the frequency curves so obtained
by application of the formula and see if the result matches
the deposited alluvium of familiar observation.

An important property of these raw materials is that
they furnish a mixture of three *kinds* of material, which
are easily distinguished because their sizes happen not to
overlap closely.   These three kinds will be referred to as:
(1) gravel, (2) sand, and (3) silt-clay, all very familiar
terms, but it is emphasised that we are not talking about
size-ranges as such but about kinds of material, qualitatively distinguished.

The *gravel* consists of coarse fragments of rock or
mineral of any composition - be it basalt or hardened mud
or vein-quartz.   The sizes of the fragments are rarely as
governed by the texture of the parent material and so tend
to cover a wide range, and they are evenly distributed
across it, representing the progressive disintegration of
larger sizes into smaller sizes.   There may originally
have been a relatively large modal size, reflecting the
structure of the parent rock, determined perhaps by jointing, as in granite, or by vein thickness, as in vein-
quartz.   But when we consider the *supply* of gravel to
streams these genetic modes are unimportant because the
great mass of the material reaching the channel consists of
fragments of the rock, and the genetic mode normally

endures, if at all, only as a very secondary mode representing what we can broadly regard as 'the largest size
commonly supplied'. This conclusion, however, by no means
corresponds with the impression often gained from observation of the stream beds displaying coarse gravel, the
dominant size of which may be nearly the same as the
genetic, structural model size seen in nearby outcrops.
Nonetheless it is an illusion to suppose that the modal
size of gravel so *deposited* ever even approximates the
modal size of the gravel *supplied*, for it is always much
larger. The reason is evident from the basic cover
formula just quoted, $C_{load} = k.Q_R/U$, where $U = \phi(1/(D/D_c))$.
This shows that the larger sizes travel the more slowly
and therefore 'cover' the stream bed more densely, and in
particular that the *largest* sizes, especially if close to
the size of the competence (D_c), by travelling, *very slowly
indeed*, must provide most of the cover. If the supply of
these largest sizes is also favoured by the existence of
the secondary mode mentioned above, then the preponderance
of these sizes in the deposition is even more marked and
we observe a well-sorted gravel of modal size approximately
equating with the secondary supply mode. And yet the
smaller-sized gravel, the products of fragmentation, will
almost inevitably have provided the more abundant supply,
but by travelling so quickly reveals no visual evidence of
this fact.

This process of disintegration into smaller and smaller
fragments does not continue at an even rate indefinitely,
because eventually a size is reached corresponding with
the upper size limit of another *kind* of material, the
sand, recognised essentially by its abundance within a
narrow range of comparatively small sizes. These properties are exhibited conspicuously by quartz sand, which
is able to perpetuate them by possession of another property, that of durability, resulting from combined
chemical inertness and mechanical toughness. The abundance
of quartz sand is also a reflection of the general common
occurrence of acid plutonic rocks, which are coarsely
and evenly granular in *texture*, and on weathering release
large quantities of quartz grains of size ranging between
0.1 and 0.5 mm.

The importance of quartz sand is yet also linked with
a curious phenomenon, which is the ultimate consequence
of such material existing in a small world, wherein the
land is drained by streams of limited length from source
to sea. As we are coming to recognise, any alluvium
abundant enough to provide at least a moderate loading is,
even if coarse-particled, always assured of at least a
brisk travel velocity (U) by virtue of the actual or
potential control exercised by this loading over the
graded stream's competence, and it follows that sand
in quantity cannot linger in any graded stream on earth.
It may of course be stranded *beside* a stream in a terrace
deposit or *beneath* it in the floor (after aggradation),
but it cannot tarry within the dynamic environment of the
stream as we define it. Moreover because quartz sand is
very durable and also by reason of its invariably low
competence ratio (D/D_c) as presently explained briefly

(on page 59) and more fully later, Kuenen (1959, page 16) could remark that even 2000 kilometres of travel could not cause more than the slight abrasion of a quartz grain. The long term result is that quartz sand, liberally supplied by eroding plutonic rocks, continues to accumulate and disperse across the face of the earth in a process of intermittent short, sharp displacements. Crustal upheavals of terminal deposits of quartz sand cause its reintroduction into streams, which thereupon promptly expel it. We can discount the contributory effects of wind and sea because, even though sometimes they may be exempt from any such irreversible urge and then are able to sustain particle wear to the point of destruction, their fields of effective intervention are nevertheless restricted. So we have ready explanation for both the abundance and the ubiquity of quartz sand and its almost universal major contribution to stream alluvium, where it forms such a distinctive population that the term 'sand', although essentially the designation of a kind of material, has come to be regarded in geomorphology primarily as the designation of a range of particle size.

In this study we shall consider sand neither as a particular material nor as a defined range of size, but as the population of particles possessing the essential qualities considered earlier on, that is to say of abundance within any limited range of comparatively small sizes. The flexibility of this definition is useful, for we can now, for instance, safely designate as sand the abundant coarse granite debris, of modal size 2-4 mm (in deposition), which plays the role of sand in helping to maintain the equilibrium of the Nafayi River (pages 28-29).

The third kind of material composing alluvium is *silt-clay*, which refers to all particles of size smaller than those of the sand population which we have just qualitatively defined. The critical size for this is normally in the region of 0.1 mm, as relating to quartz sand, and it will be both convenient and appropriate for us to regard silt-clay, qualitatively considered, as the exact equivalent of silt-clay, the granulometric size-range, whose maximum size is commonly considered to be 0.062 mm. It happens that this measure is approximately that of the commonly observed smallest size of alluvium to be found in any quantity in the channel bed of a stream, which we have recognised as the critical mobile size (D_m, equal to approximately $0.001D_c$), as already discussed on pages 37 and 49. Hence silt-clay particles almost invariably play the role of fine particles, which are transported only in suspension and are deposited in quantity only outside the channel in the floodplain layer. We conclude that the silt-clay contribution to the alluvium supply is relatively unimportant in this study, and its composition, although obviously differing considerably in kind from that of sand, does not have to be examined. In fact, as already mentioned, we shall always terminate particle size frequency curves at or a little above the silt-to-sand boundary of 0.062 mm. Nonetheless, as we shall see in Chapter 11, the presence of silt-clay does play a significant (though subordinate) role in the establishment of the first order equilibrium of certain kinds of stream.

So we are effectively reduced, in terms of both *kind* and *size*, to the two populations of *gravel* and *sand*, each displaying distinctive properties and, as will be seen, each able to play the principal role in controlling stream equilibrium. Henceforward gravel and sand alone, but separately considered, will be the principal subjects of our argument.

6.2   The loading curve

Loading is the rate of supply of alluvium per unit time to a floodplain-belt cross-section per unit discharge. The best place for a first assessment of the loading curve is a short way downstream of the last point of supply of gravel. Upstream of this point it is difficult to distinguish trends against the confused pattern of the irregular feed of friable gravel debris spread along the channel. But as the travelling alluvium is followed downstream of all the gravel sources, the distinctive properties of the separate gravel and sand populations reveal themselves. The gravel wastes freely, becoming both smaller and less plentiful as much of it disintegrates into sand and silt-clay; whilst the sand, if only because of its low competence ratio (D/D_c) as discussed below, keeps itself intact, both in size and amount.

If we consider any one cross-section of the floodplain-belt and assume that the gravel is of uniform composition, the processes are governed by a simple relationship $I_z = \phi(D/D_c)$, where I_z is the average rate of proportional size reduction with distance of a particle of size D, as defined in the derivative expression $(dD/D)/dz$, where z is distance along the stream. The relationship is considered closely later (page 140 et seq.) and we need now only accept that the competence ratio D/D_c here owes its significance to its control of the ratio of the duration of motion of the particle *in situ* to the corresponding duration of motion *in any direction*, that is to say both in situ and *along* the stream. The concept of motion in situ has already been introduced (page 31) in connection with the sorting effect of vortical action in situ in 'ephemeral potholes'. We can understand from this that whereas a very small particle transported in suspension tends to travel straight down the channel without ever lingering in a pothole on the way, by contrast the movement of a lag particle is almost exclusively restricted to some kind of oscillation in situ, with negligible effective displacement along the stream. The 'wastage' of gravel obviously varies with the duration of motion in *any* direction and thus the amount of 'wastage' per unit distance along the stream, as expressed by the quantity I_z, increases with particle size relative to the competence, as expressed in the competence ratio D/D_c. Hence, other things being equal and at any one cross-section, $I_z = \phi(D/D_c)$.

On the assumption that this relationship is correct, it is simple to deduce what happens to a uniform gravel as

it travels downstream away from its source. The first
conclusion is that the larger gravel particles are decreasing in both size and amount with *distance* along the
stream more quickly than the smaller particles. We then
notice two effects:

(1) Even a short distance downstream of the last point
of supply of the gravel, the loading of the larger sizes
is light compared with the loading of the smaller sizes,
which in any case has been reinforced by the products of
the disintegration of the larger. As already observed,
this is contrary to appearance, because the largest gravel
particles as deposited are so much more abundant in the
stream channel deposition because of the thick cover they
maintain by their slow travel.

(2) Because larger particles waste and disappear as
such more quickly with distance, there soon establishes,
as we move downstream from the last point of supply of the
gravel, a statistically sharply-defined *maximum common
size* (D_{max}). The clear identity of this measure of course
only holds outside the area supplying the gravel. This
conclusion is readily verified by searching on any gravel
point bar for the largest gravel particle, which, subject
to the condition just stated and the absence of lag
particles, always shows a clearly-defined measure.

By contrast with the gravel and for reasons now
apparent, the sand, by virtue of its small competence
ratio D/D_c, wastes very slowly with distance along the
stream, and of course all the more slowly if composed of
durable quartz, and thus the sand loading does not alter
appreciably downstream.

From this analysis we can deduce the general shape of
the loading curve at our point of reference, as shown in
Figure 4a (page 64), which bears little resemblance to the
familiar deposition curves. The coarser gravel is essentially residual material and there cannot be much of it
travelling in comparison with the smaller material, even
near the rocky headwaters, and the contrast must be even
more marked downstream. The characteristic shape is that
of a topographic 'peak and spur', whose gradual change in
profile we will watch as we move further downstream.
Gradually the tip of the gravel spur, representing the most
quickly wasting particles (in respect to distance) creeps
towards the stable sand peak, which eventually towers over
it, as the second characteristic shape (Figure 4b) emerges.
Although there is no critical difference between the two
curves, they nonetheless represent the two characteristic
shapes, distinguished only by the broadly specified
position of the tip of the gravel spur.

Of course the curve alone gives only part of the
information required in a statement of the loading, for it
says nothing of the *amount*. As earlier explained, the
amount rating can be expressed only by the broad distinctions of 'heavy' or 'light' loading, qualified by comparative remarks as required, and it will now be apparent
that we must also know the *separate* amount ratings of
both the gravel and sand loadings. Here we need to note
a simple *convention*, which is that the qualitative
expressions of relative amount link only gravel-to-gravel

measures, or sand-to-sand measures, and *never gravel-to-sand measures*. This is because although the absolute values of the gravel loadings are usually much less than those of the sand loadings, they may not be effectively so because of the much higher competence ratios (D/D_c) and lower travel velocities (U) of the gravel sizes. The full relevance of this will be discussed in the next section, but we can see now that the gravel and sand loadings are virtually unlike quantities and cannot be meaningfully compared quantitatively. Thus we can understand that if, according to the convention, a stream possesses a heavy gravel loading and a light sand loading, in absolute units the sand loading may indeed be the heavier of the two.

6.3   Gravel and sand regimes

We recognise that the loading exercises its influence in two different ways - both through the particle *size* of the alluvium supplied, and through the *amount* of it. This is the key to understanding how either the gravel loading or the sand loading, each acting virtually alone, may control a stream's equilibrium through its controls of the value of the competence for grade. Which of the two loadings dominates depends on the circumstances. Each possesses an advantage over the other in one of the two unlike attributes, like opposing gladiators in the arena. The gravel has the advantage of particle size (D), and the sand of amount supplied (Q_a); one or other of the 'contestants' usually prevails easily, though in certain circumstances they may be evenly matched.
    The situation is expressed in the following equations, which are substitutions of the specific gravel and sand values, as indicated by the suffixes g and s, in the general cover equation obtained in the last chapter (page 54).

$$C = (C_g + C_s) + C_{immov}$$

$$C = k(\frac{Q_{Rg}}{U_g} + \frac{Q_{Rs}}{U_s}) + C_{immov}$$

where

$$U_g = \phi(1/(D_g/D_c))$$

and

$$U_s = \phi(1/(D_s/D_c))$$

D_g is greater than D_s, and therefore U_s is greater than U_g. But Q_{Rs} is greater than Q_{Rg}. The differences are all big. The greater values of Q_R and U pair off in the parameter Q_{Rs}/U_s and the lesser values in the parameter Q_{Rg}/U_g. Thus, despite massive disparities between the values of like quantities, the values of the two cover parameters can be a match for each other.
    Hence, depending on the relative values of the *cover parameters* and not of their component quantities, the load

cover ($C_g + C_s$) is likely to be composed of either dominant gravel or dominant sand. Parity is uncommon because the values of Q_R and U can each vary over wide proportional ranges. The consequence of all this is that either gravel or sand must usually preponderate in the visible alluvium of a stream channel and we should not often see an even mixture of the two populations.

Common observation confirms this, and we may recognise two distinctive *alluvial regimes*, specified as follows.

Alluvial regime	Condition
GRAVEL	Q_{Rg}/U_g much greater than Q_{Rs}/U_s
Transitional	Q_{Rg}/U_g nearly equal to Q_{Rs}/U_s
SAND	Q_{Rg}/U_g much less than Q_{Rs}/U_s

6.4   Estimation of the competence for grade from the loading curve

The competence of a *graded* stream is governed exclusively by the loading, through the mechanism of the competence-degradation interaction. This is the important relationship demonstrated in Chapter 4 and we will now discover how to determine this value of the competence from the loading curve.

The rate of degradation of a stream was shown in the last chapter to be governed by the value of the alluvium cover (C) relative to the notional cover for grade (C_p), which is the cover value appropriate for zero rate of degradation for the particular competence in force. When C is greater than C_p, the stream is aggrading; when C is less than C_p, the stream is degrading; and when C is the same as C_p, the stream is at grade. This last is the condition we are investigating. We have:

$$\text{Alluvium Cover} \quad C = k\left(\frac{Q_{Rg}}{U_g} + \frac{Q_{Rs}}{U_s}\right),$$

as shown on page 61, in which

$$U = \phi(1/(D/D_c)).$$

$$\text{Cover for grade} \quad C_p = \phi(D_c),$$

for identically constituted alluvium.

It will be seen that for a given combined gravel and sand loading, the only variable governing either C or C_p is the competence D_c and we have the following pair of relationships:

$$C = \phi(1/D_c)$$

$$C_p = \phi(D_c)$$

Thus, for example, an increase in D_c increases C_p, but, by speeding up the travel velocity U for both gravel and sand, decreases C.

For the graded stream, $C = C_p$, and the problem is to find the value of D_c which, from the data provided by the loading curve, procures this equality. We know that nature finds the answer by means of the competence-degradation interaction, but our purpose is to discover how to anticipate nature and so achieve a vital objective in our progress towards 'synthesis' of the stream.

On the conceptual plane, where our concern is princi-pally with relative values, the procedure is quite simple. By the method of trial and error, we test in turn the effect of different values of the competence D_c upon data as provided by the loading curve supplemented by statement of the amount of the loading. We have already recognised that this amount normally *cannot* be expressed except qualitatively (light, heavy, etc.) and so in any case we cannot hope for a precise estimate of the competence for grade. On the other hand, because we can know the particle sizes accurately, which also govern the competence for grade, we are nonetheless able to specify a *range* of absolute sizes wherein must lie the value of this com-petence and which in some circumstances may be quite narrow. Thus we are always able to quote an actual value, however approximate, and furthermore will understand *why* it seems to be a reasonable estimate, so fulfilling the main purpose of the exercise.

To illustrate the procedure, we will now estimate the values of the competence for grade appropriate to the two imaginary curves of Figure 4 and a selection of amount ratings relating to them.

We start with the curve of Figure 4a, which is typical of a stream just emerged from a rocky highland area, and suppose the *gravel loading* to be *light*. The tip of the spur is at 500 mm. Applying the trial and error method, let us first assume the competence to be 2000 mm. The relevant equations are $C_g = kQ_{Ag}/U_g$ and $U_g = 1/\phi(D_g/D_c)$. The competence ratio (D/D_c) for the largest gravel part-icles is $500/2000 = 0.25$, which is just below the lag range. Evidently the travel velocity (U_g) for the gravel generally is fairly high for a gravel loading (Q_{Ag}) stated to be light, and we have no doubt from this that the gravel cover (C_g) is thin.

Turning to the sand portion of the curve, whose mode lies at about 0.25 mm, we note the competence ratio (D/D_c) is $0.25/2000 = 0.000125$, which, we can suppose, is re-latively very small, even for sand, and we are sure that its travel velocity (U_S) is very high indeed. It follows, from the equation $C_S = kQ_{AS}/U_S$, that the sand cover (C_S) would be very thin even if the sand loading (Q_{AS}) were heavy. Thus, whatever the sand loading, the sand cover is negligible.

Hence, the whole load cover for the assumed competence of 2000 mm is the sum of a thin gravel cover (C_g) and a negligible sand cover (C_S), which together would provide an inadequate barrier against scour in depth. The stream is degrading. We must try a smaller competence.

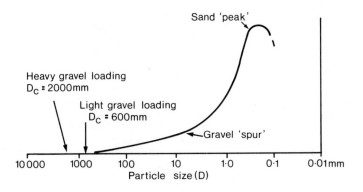

(a) Gravel regime

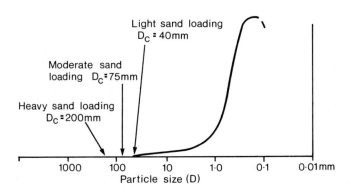

(b) Sand regime

Figure 4.   Examples of the two types of size frequency
curve for the *loading* (Q_R) of alluvium of particle
size greater than 0.01 mm.
D_C is the value of the *competence for grade* corresponding with each of the loadings discussed in
Chapter 6.

For progressively decreasing values of D_C, the competence ratios (D/D_C) increase and the gravel cover parameters (Q_{Ag}/U_g) increase, moreover at an increasing rate
as D_C draws closer to the tip of the gravel spur at 500 mm.
Eventually in a situation determined by the precise value
of Q_{Ag}, the parameter attains a value such that the whole
load cover (C), provided almost entirely by C_g, equates
with the cover for grade (C_p), thus showing that the
competence D_C is the competence for grade. Because the
gravel loading is light, this value of D_C is likely to be

in the region of 600 mm, very close to the tip of the
spur, so providing a substantial, very slow moving cover
of lag particles, able to withstand the scour in depth.
The competence is still too large to permit an appreciable
sand cover, and obviously we are dealing with the gravel
regime.

Next, let us suppose the gravel loading, for the same
curve, to be *heavy*, and we can see that for this condition
the value of 2000 mm for D_C could be appropriate for grade,
or even too small. Despite the high travel velocity of
even the largest gravel particles, the gravel is still
able to provide a substantial cover because there is so
much of it.

This procedure is not so laborious as may at first
appear, for it is easier to act upon than describe, as is
usual with the trial-and-error method. Nor is it so
crude, for it is based on a truly theoretical appreciation
of all the controlling fundamental relationships. Moreover, although the assessments are only approximative,
this is consistent with the nature of the data and more
cannot be asked for. Above all there has been no compromise with the quality of our *understanding*, for we
really do understand why values of 600 mm and 2000 mm are
generally appropriate for the two situations considered;
and already we can see faint images of the real streams
emerging.

We will now examine the other characteristic loading
curve, shown in Figure 4b, which might belong to the same
stream as that of 4a but lower down its course, and considerably further from the gravel sources. Here the
gravel spur is only a vestige of its previous shape, with
its tip withdrawn to a value of only about 50 mm, and
inevitably the gravel loading is light. Now the critical
loading is that of the *sand* (Q_{AS}) and we will begin by
supposing it to be *moderately heavy*. Again we seek the
competence for grade by process of trial and error, and
start by assuming a value of 75 mm. The relevant equation
is now $C_S = kQ_{AS}/U_S$, and we note that the sand travel
velocity (U_S) is governed by the competence ratio D/D_C =
$0.25/75 = 0.0033$. For sand this is relatively large and it
implies a relatively low sand travel velocity. Because
Q_{AS} is moderately heavy, the sand cover (C_S) is thick, in
fact so thick, we may suppose, that alone, even without
the support of a possibly significant gravel cover (C_g),
it provides a more than adequate barrier against scour in
depth, and the stream is aggrading. Evidently the competence for grade is larger than 75 mm.

So we will try the slightly larger value of 100 mm for
the competence. The competence ratio for the sand mode is
now $0.25/100 = 0.0025$, giving a sand travel velocity that
is just so much higher than for the previous trial and a
sand cover that is just so much thinner, appropriate, we
may suppose, for grade, if the contribution of the gravel
cover is disregarded. Nonetheless we must assess this
gravel cover, which may well be appreciable because the
competence is so small. We will suppose that the gravel
loading is light. For a competence of 100 mm the competence ratio of the largest gravel particles is

50/100 = 0.5, which is within the lag range. But for a
light gravel loading, we might conclude that the gravel
cover is insignificant in comparison with the sand cover
and that there is no need to amend the original estimate of
100 mm on its account. Thus we can accept this value of
the competence for grade, and also recognise this as an
example of the sand regime, although probably the sand
cover is rather pebbly.

Other amount ratings for the sand loading may be considered (again see Figure 4b). First, we can suppose it
to be *heavy*, as in an ephemeral stream in a semi-arid
region (see page 109), where we might expect a competence
for grade of about 200 mm. Here all the fine-grained
gravel (all of size less than 50 mm as considered before)
is within the mobile size-range, but travelling so briskly
and providing such thin cover in comparison with that of
the abundant sand that the resulting channel deposition
(as representing simply a further distortion of the loading
curve, as we shall see) is found to be that of an almost
gravel-free sand.

Alternatively we can suppose the sand loading to be
light, as we might expect for a stream flowing wholly
within a plain underlain by soft, mainly argillaceous sediments (see page 114). If the gravel loading were any more
than merely 'light' it would alone control the competence
for grade and impose a gravel regime; but, assuming a *very*
light gravel loading, we could only expect a competence
for grade as small as about 40 mm, as imposed by the sand
loading, and a channel deposition including an appreciable
amount of silt.

These are just a few examples of the many possible
relationships that can exist between the loading and the
quantity dependent on it, the competence for grade. We
have seen that we can always deduce an approximate real
value of this competence to fit the circumstances. No
attempt has been made to describe the whole range of
possibilities systematically, which must wait until a
logical classification of graded streams has been presented.

Meanwhile we will digress to examine the special but
common situation of the stream that shows a substantial
immovable cover.

6.5   Immovable cover

We are now ready to consider the immovable particles,
which we have ignored until now in the interest of keeping
the main argument simple. It has been in order to do so
if only because immovable particles are often lacking
altogether. In many streams however they are the principal
constituents of the alluvium profile, and we cannot go on
turning a blind eye to their existence.

The immovable particles never move in first order time
because they are larger than the competence. They constitute the immovable layer, which lies on the floor, and
obviously this layer has much in common with the floor.
But it differs from it in that the components of the immovable layer are discrete particles periodically subject

to the full force of the stream's scour and in their
reaction to it they make a genuine contribution to the
combined resistance of the alluvium as measured by the
alluvium cover.

We have seen that the load cover relates to the supply
of the load particles through dynamic processes complicated
by the different travel velocities of particles of different sizes. Immovable cover, on the other hand, relates on
the simplest basis possible, that of actual physical
identity, with the 'supply' of the immovable particles,
which, being stationary in first order time, we can only
regard as already an expression of the 'basin environment',
discussed earlier (page 23). The history of their origins
may in fact be complex, but it is of no interest in the
context of first order time, where all we need to know is
that the particles are there. Thus load cover and immovable cover are expressions of the same quantity, a
measure of presence in a certain place, and they are linked
by simple arithmetical addition to make the combined
alluvium cover.

By definition immovable cover is a variable in second
and third order time, because the competence is then a
variable. Increase in the competence implies a subtraction
from the immovable cover of the contribution of certain of
the smallest sizes and consequently the total immovable
cover diminishes in value. Thus $C_{immovable} = \phi(1/D_C)$,
which corresponds in sense with the relationship of the
load cover, C_{load}, to the competence. Thus immovable
cover may be regarded conceptually as merely a supplement
to the loading, despite the difference in dimension,
reacting with variation in the competence to produce change
in the same sense to the value of the combined alluvium
cover. Correctly therefore, the 'index' of alluvium
resistance is not the loading alone, but the combination
of the loading and the immovable cover; and in the same
way the fundamental 'control' expressing the whole supply
of alluvium is not the load alone, but the combination of
load and immovable cover, which we may henceforward refer
to as the *alluvium supply* (Q_a + $C_{immovable}$). Undoubtedly
immovable cover is an awkward quantity, for it is incapable
of being correlated directly with the time-rated supply
quantities until we can consider the state of cover as
relating to all sizes of the alluvium. Thereafter,
happily, there are no problems, as Figure 5 shows diagrammatically.

The physical location of the immovable particles
beneath the load particles is significant in that it
relegates the role of the immovable particles to one of
mere reinforcement, when required, to the first line of
resistance provided by the load particles. Potential immovable particles are called into service only if the load
cover alone cannot equal the notional cover for grade
required by the particular competence in force. If these
potential immovable particles are not needed, then of
course they do not belong to the alluvium at all but to
the floor. We recognise that load cover plus immovable
cover cannot exceed the cover for grade, for if that were
so the stream would be aggrading and part or all of this

Towards stream synthesis

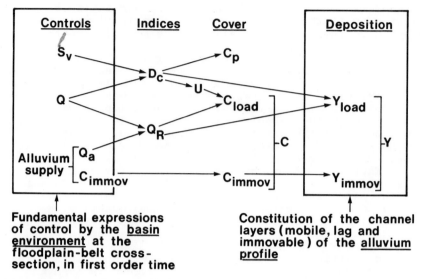

List of first order quantities

Symbol	Title	Definition	Basic formula *
S_v	Valley slope	Slope along floodplain-belt	Independent
Q	Discharge	Amount of water passing per unit time	Independent
Q_a	Load	Amount of alluvium passing per unit time	Independent
D_c	Competence	Size of largest particles transportable	$D_c = \phi(S_v, Q)$
D/D_c	Competence ratio	As for symbol	As defined
Q_R	Loading	Load per unit discharge	$Q_R = Q_a/Q$
U	Travel velocity	Distance travelled per unit time	$U = 1/\phi(D/D_c)$
C	Alluvium cover		$C = C_{load} + C_{immov}$
C_{load}	Load cover	Amount (stationary and moving) per unit area above the floor, in the channel. (For grade, $C = C_p$.)	$C_{load} = k \cdot Q_R/U$ $= Q_R \cdot \phi(D/D_c)$
C_{immov}	Immovable cover		Independent
C_p	Cover for grade		$C_p = \phi(D_c)$
Y	Channel deposition	Amount (stationary only) per unit area, in channel layers of the alluvium profile.	$Y = Y_{load} + Y_{immov}$
Y_{load}	Load deposition		$Y_{load} = Q_R \cdot \phi(D/D_c)$
Y_{immov}	Immovable deposition		$Y_{immov} = C_{immov}$

*Basic formulae apply only to a limited particle size-range D

Figure 5. Diagram illustrating the principal first order relationships.

immovable cover would then belong to the floor; and it
will be evident that the alluvium of an aggrading stream
cannot contain any immovable particles. On the other hand,
if the load cover is less than the notional cover for
grade, then any underlying potential immovable particles
do become involved with the scour, although only so far
down as the scour can penetrate. This will not be far,
because a single continuous layer of immovable particles,
even if only a little larger in size than the competence,
is almost enough alone to provide an effective barrier to
scour. In demonstration of this, Lane and Carlson (1954,
page 459) observed that artificially induced immovable
layers serving as permanent linings for canals conveying
virtually unloaded water flow were no more than two immovable particle diameters thick, as indicated by the completely unaffected constitution of the underlying ground,
in which the spaces between the potential immovable
particles were occupied by fine gravel and sand. Thus
immovable cover is certainly always thin, even when underlain by an inexhaustible supply of potential immovable
particles.

We can now recognise that there are two kinds of
immovable cover, as illustrated in Figure 6, depending on
the 'replaceability' of the immovable particles. One kind
is the *irreplaceable immovable cover*, for which the wasting
of the immovable particles through breakage and wear and
their conversion into lag and smaller particles is not
compensated by adequate, or any, replacement by new immovable particles emerging from the floor, whence alone
they can appear, as the floor gradually falls through
third order degradation. This happens wherever the floor
is of such composition that it disintegrates entirely, or
almost entirely, into particles of size smaller than the
competence, and naturally it is common. Such immovable
particles as do exist are probably all of extraneous
origin, although sometimes, as for sarsens, their place of
origin may have been situated vertically above their
present resting place, whence they have gradually been
let down in the course of a probably long history, always
acting as immovable particles. In any case, once destroyed,
such immovable particles are gone for good, without possibility of replacement. Even though they may be extremely
resistant to wasting, the tendency is invariably for
depletion of the stock, and this is why irreplaceable immovable layers are found mostly in streams of relatively
small competence, of 100 mm and smaller, where alone unflawed, durable immovable particles are likely to exist in
any quantity, usually composed of vein-quartz or other
durable siliceous material.

The other kind is the *replaceable immovable cover*,
whose distinguishing feature is a permanently full complement of immovable particles derived by continuous replacement from the floor. This happens where an easily erodible
floor disintegrates into at least fairly durable particles
of size larger than the competence. Thus an inexhaustible
supply of immovable particles is always waiting. Any
shortage in the alluvium present causes the stream to
degrade, and immediately the shortage is made good. The

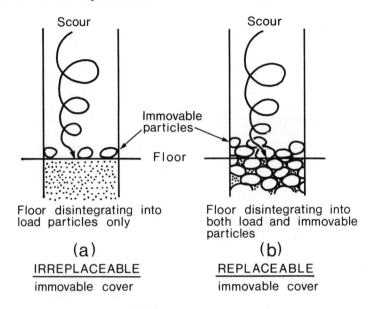

Figure 6. The two kinds of immovable cover, determined
by the 'replaceability' of the immovable particles
from the floor as its level falls.

combined alluvium cover, of both immovable and load
particles, is always equal to the cover for grade and
the stream maintains permanent grade. The situation
commonly develops where streams drain highland areas of
ground weathering into resistant boulders of modal size
larger than the competences of the streams flowing
over them, as shown in Plate 7 (page 133). How this relationship evolves will be discussed later (page 83), and
we need now only note the ambiguous situation in which we
can regard the 'immovable particles' as belonging as
equally well to the floor (supposed to be undergoing
active though slow degradation) as to the alluvium (supposed to be maintaining an arguably questionable state of
grade). The former interpretation is certainly the right
one if the 'immovable particles' are of such varying
size that many of them, although exposed at the surface of
the stream bed, are not wholly released from the bedrock.
On the other hand, where the immovable particles are all
never much larger than the competence, as can happen if
the floor is an old well-sorted alluvial deposit, there
can exist a perfectly distinct, continuous layer of immovable particles every one of which is wholly detached
from the floor, and this layer is certainly playing the
role of alluvium cover.
      There can be no profit in pursuing this dilemma
further and it is enough to be able to assess the actual
effect of these particles, however labelled. Usually this
is not difficult. As indicated, an irreplaceable immovable cover is normally an unimportant, discontinuous

residual deposit that can be ignored in relation to the influence of the load cover. By contrast, a replaceable immovable cover represents the special situation where in effect the stream is in a state of active degradation and there is virtually no load cover at all.

6.6   The deposition curve

The main argument is now nearly complete (see Figure 5) and we are only a step away from the quantity which describes the most solid manifestation of the real stream. This is the *deposition*, which, as a first order characteristic, is defined as the average amount of alluvium of a specified range of particle size deposited by the stream per unit area of the floor across the floodplain-belt.
     This quantity relating to all sizes is conveniently quoted by means of a particle size frequency curve, presented in the same way as for the loading. We shall, however, limit its reference, unless otherwise indicated, to the *channel deposition*, denoted by the symbol Y, comprising the combined depositions of the three lower layers (immovable, lag and mobile) of the alluvium profile as deposited inside the channel. The uppermost layer (floodplain), although formed at the same time as those below it, is deposited outside the channel and is not directly involved in the processes we have been considering. Two components of the channel deposition need to be recognised, as distinguished by particle size, which are the *load deposition* (Y_{load}) and the *immovable deposition* ($Y_{immov.}$).
     Cover and deposition, although of the same dimension, differ significantly in the roles they play. Cover (measuring amount per unit area of both moving and stationary particles at the seat of action in the channel) is useful only as a conceptual gauge by which the stream's competence for grade may be estimated; in this it serves a valuable function, but the quantity is of no interest in itself. Deposition (measuring amount per unit area of exclusively stationary alluvium beside the seat of action) is by contrast an end-product, being the measure of a property that is important for its own sake, describing the very essence of the first order steady state. Both quantities are characteristics of this equilibrium, derivatives of the loading. We have seen (page 56) how the cover curve would be a distortion of the loading curve, as caused by the differential effects of the varying travel velocities of particles of differing sizes, and we shall now discover how the deposition curve takes the same process a little further.
     The linking quantity is the mean *frequency of rest* of particles of alluvium of size D, considered as a proportion of the time spent by particles of this size 'at rest' compared with the whole time. We have already considered the complementary frequency of motion downstream F and can recognise the frequency of rest as of value (1-F). We saw that $F = \phi(1/(D/D_c))$ (page 51) and consequently can accept, without further enquiry (though the same kind of argument would demonstrate the relationship from first principles),

that frequency of rest = $(1-F)$ = $\phi(D/D_c)$.

In the present context the significant difference between cover and deposition is that cover records an amount of particles both in motion and at rest, while deposition records a corresponding amount but only for particles at rest. The proportion of particles at rest compared with those in both states is clearly a function of the frequency of rest and we have

$$Y_{load} = C_{load}\cdot\phi(1-F)$$

$$= C_{load}\cdot\phi(D/D_c)$$

This equation applies to all particle sizes. For immovable particles, frequency of rest, $(1-F)$, = 1, and hence Y_{load} = C_{load}, which we know. For fine particles, which in this process never settle in the channel, frequency of rest = 0 and Y_{load} = 0, which also we know. For the intermediate sizes of the mobile and lag particles, there is a gradation of values of the frequency of rest between these limits, governed by the competence ratio D/D_c.

Thus we reach the second stage of the distortion of the loading curve, accomplished each time by the instrument of the varying competence ratio. The two stages are summarised in the equations:

(1) $C_{load} = k\cdot Q_R/U = Q_R\cdot\phi(D/D_c)$,

which is the basic cover equation,

(2) $Y_{load} = C_{load}\cdot\phi(1-F) = C_{load}\cdot\phi(D/D_c)$.

The complete process is expressed in the single *basic deposition formula*, in which there is no reference to the cover,

$$Y_{load} = Q_R\cdot\phi(D/D_c).$$

It may be noted that because $U = \phi(F)$, as shown on pages 51-52, the two stages are governed respectively by the complementary frequencies of motion (F) and of rest (1-F), but in such a way that the effects are produced in the same sense through the same instrument of the competence ratio D/D_c. The combined process, involving the establish-

Plate 4.   The *lightly-loaded boulder gravel stream* of the West Dart River about 1 km upstream of Two Bridges, on Dartmoor. Lag and immovable boulders dominate the channel. The maximum common size of particles in the narrow strips of mobile deposition is about 180 mm (diameter), suggesting a competence of 600 mm. The width of the channel is about 5 m. Between this point and the road crossing at Two Bridges the stream is characteristically both moderately and even heavily loaded (with braiding) over short stretches along a stepped profile (see page 138).

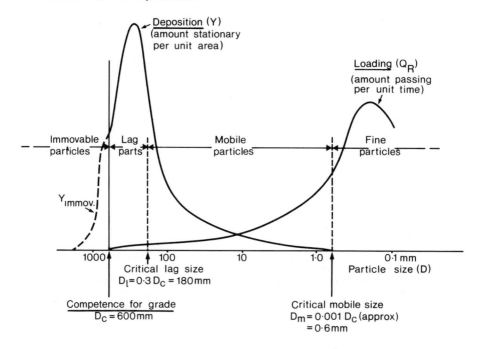

Figure 7. The derivation of the deposition curve (Y)
    from the loading curve (Q_R) in a graded, lightly-
    loaded gravel stream.
    The process is governed by the formula $Y = Q_R \cdot \phi(D/D_C)$.
    N.B. The graphs are only diagrammatic.

ment of grade at the appropriate competence, is complex
and yet is governed throughout by the single, easily
understood control of the competence ratio. We will be
grateful for the simplicity of this relationship as we
pursue our enquiries further in the latter part of this
work.

    We will now look at the actual mechanism of the pro-
cess of the distortion of the loading curve, using as an
example one of the curves already discussed but adapted to
show the presence of immovable particles. The resulting
deposition curve is shown in Figure 7, in shape very
different from the loading curve from which it was derived.
The distortion is the outcome of differential increase in
the relative amount of the larger sizes at the expense of
the smaller sizes according to the demands of the basic
deposition equation $Y_{load} = Q_R \cdot \phi(D/D_C)$. The value of
$\phi(D/D_C)$ increases from right to left on the diagram. At
the extreme right, where D is less than the critical
mobile size D_m, the value of $\phi(D/D_C)$ is zero, and we have
already recognised that $D_m = 0.001D$ approximately. As
D increases beyond (to the left of) D_m, the value of
$\phi(D/D_C)$ increases at an increasing rate until $D = D_C$,
where $U = 0$ and the value of the parameter is infinite,
although of course at the same time the amount of the

loading (Q_R) for the largest sizes, if present, is zero
where $D = D_c$. Where D is greater than D_c we have the zone
of the immovable deposition Y_{immov}, whose value obeys
other controls (as already discussed on pages 66-71). The
process of distortion relates only to the zone of transportable particles of size smaller than the competence D_c
and we see that for this zone it can be likened to the
process of stepping on one side of a balloon and noting
the shift of the unchanging amount of air to the other
side where the pressure is less.

For a light gravel loading, as in the example, the
position on the diagram of the competence for grade D_c is
at or near to the tip of the spur of the gravel loading,
where the corresponding U values are very low, and the
consequence is the prominent gravel mode near there. But
for a heavy gravel loading, as shown in Figure 8a, the
inevitably larger competence for grade is located well to
the left of the tip of the spur, for which the competence
ratios are nowhere near to unity. Thus for none of the
gravel is the value of U very low and the resultant distortion is more evenly spread out. Figure 8 also shows
(c and d) how the sand deposition curves are derived for
streams where the sand regime is in force. Invariably
there is shift to the left of the diagram, resulting in
increase in the modal size of the sand particles. The
process also explains the usual *bimodality* of mixed
gravel and sand depositions, which is not the expression
of any universal bimodality of detrital particles in
nature, but simply the result of differentially applied
mechanical action upon a unimodal supply. Inevitably the
gravel particles in such mixtures are normally of small
size, because large sizes require large competences and
generally preclude any appreciable sand deposition.
Exceptions are discussed in Chapter 12, page 123.

Finally we may note that the 1000:1 ratio of the
competence (D_c) to the critical mobile size (D_m) determines
the maximum width of the Y curve, equal to approximately
10 standard (Udden) size grades or a Krumbein phi range
of 10. The width may of course often be smaller than
this, either where the gravel loading is very heavy and
there are no gravel particles approaching the competence
in size or else where there is only small-particled
gravel in the loading; but the width will never be
appreciably greater than this. Minor exceptions occur,
especially in braided streams, where there may be a little
deposition of silt-clay particles locally at low discharge, but always the amounts are small and the sizes
not much smaller than the D_m value. Examination of published size frequency distributions for the beds of gravel-
bed streams will show how this 10-grade limitation is maintained, if due allowance is made for the presence of immovable particles in stretches where they might be expected. Conversely, where only the surface of the mobile
layer is exposed in the channel and no particles are
eligible to be present larger than the critical lag size
($D_l = 0.3D_c$), the limiting ratio is about 300:1.

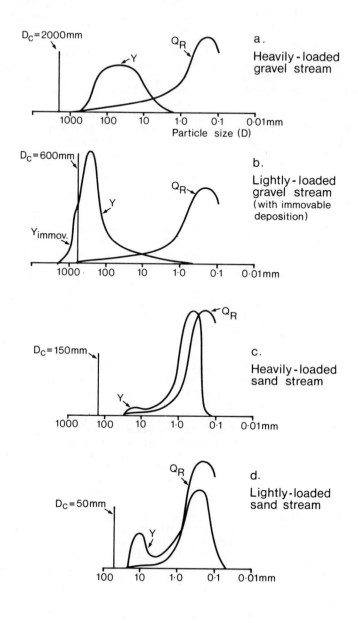

Figure 8.   Examples of characteristic diagrams of graded
             streams.

6.7 A classification of graded streams

Earlier in this chapter we recognised the difference
between the gravel and sand *regimes* of stream equilibrium,
as determined by whether the load cover had been provided
dominantly by gravel or sand. Cover (C) is a conceptual
quantity which cannot be assessed directly from observation, but we now know how it relates simply with the very
palpable reality of the alluvium profile as expressed in
the deposition (Y), in that the particle size frequency
curve of the deposition is merely an exaggeration or
caricature of that of the cover. It happens that the
exaggeration is not marked in the case of those particles
that form the mobile layer conspicuously visible in the
stream bed, because the temporarily stationary component
of the value of the cover is, for such sizes, overwhelm-
ingly the predominant one. For this reason we may safely
rely on the visual evidence of the alluvium profile for
identification of the regime in force. Usually this may
be assessed immediately from a first impression, for the
stream bed usually appears either as a continuous spread
of gravel devoid of sand, or as a continuous spread of
sand devoid of gravel. This impression may be belied by
closer inspection, but there will be no doubt about the
dominant particle size. So we are able to make instant
recognition of the two principal types of stream, clearly
differentiated, henceforward to be referred to simply as
the *gravel stream* and the *sand stream*. The relatively
uncommon transitional type, in which gravel and sand are
evenly represented, will be referred to as the *transitional
stream*.

We now have a theoretical framework for a simple
classification of graded streams, based *first* on the regime
in force (i.e. whether we have a gravel or a sand stream)
and *second* by the amount, qualitatively expressed, of the
ruling loading (i.e. of gravel or of sand) determining
this regime. For a gravel stream, only the gravel loading
can be ruling, and for a sand stream, only the sand loading
can be ruling, and there is no need to repeat the specification ('gravel' or 'sand') for both regime and loading.
As for the amounts, we shall see later that for both gravel
and sand streams the amounts of loading may be conveniently
divided into three ranges, titled 'heavy', 'moderate' and
'light', for each of which simple, visual criteria may be
specified. Thus we have six principal classes of graded
stream: heavily, moderately and lightly loaded gravel
streams, and heavily, moderately and lightly loaded sand
streams. In addition, we require the single class of
transitional streams, undifferentiated, representing the
special case of the transitional regime.

The classification is tabulated overleaf.

The more important properties, including the distinguishing criteria, of the classes of gravel and sand
streams are presented in Tables 2 and 3 (pages 94 and 121).

Towards stream synthesis

Gravel streams	Sand streams	Transitional streams
- heavily loaded	- heavily loaded	
- moderately loaded	- moderately loaded	
- lightly loaded	- lightly loaded	

6.8   The characteristic diagram of a stream

First order equilibrium is the state of a stream not as we
see it during any one of many observations but as we *know*
it as the result of all of them, assuming we have seen it
in all its moods. This knowledge is far more than an
appreciation of an average condition, because it takes
into account every variation from the mean, conceived both
in time, when we experience incidents within first order
time, and in space, when we perceive varying aspects of
the channel pattern as it changes form within the plane of
the floodplain-belt cross-section. We have called the
properties of this integrated recognition the *first order
characteristics*, as expressed by ideal conceptual quantities, in practice unmeasurable, which only thus can claim
to represent the totality of the 'character' of the stream.
It is because these characteristics are ideally representative of the concepts we have in mind that we can use them
confidently as the conceptual mathematical units required
in this study.
    We have now identified and correlated the most import-
ant of these characteristics of first order equilibrium,
which are
    (1)   the *loading* (Q_R)
    (2)   the *deposition* (Y)
    (3)   the *competence* (D_c).
All three quantities may be conveniently displayed in a
single *characteristic diagram*, as shown in Figure 8, (page 76)
for graded examples of both gravel and sand streams.
    The characteristic diagram is a model of the 'structure'
of a stream, upon which we can build its body as recognisable in the endless variety of the dependent first order
characteristics, in fact all that renders a stream perceptible and particular. From the classification of graded
streams just introduced, we know broadly the range of all
the possible variations, which we will now investigate
systematically.

Chapter 7

RECOGNITION OF GRADE

An essential preliminary to study of the properties of
the different classes of graded stream is to check our
ability to recognise the graded state and the two states
of departure from it, second order degradation and second
order aggradation. A special significance of grade is
that it possesses the qualities of an ideal 'standard'
condition, in that its critical properties are explicitly
defined and it is the commonest state met. But to be
useful it must also be recognisable.

Grade, or second order equilibrium, can now be fully
defined in terms of first order quantities as the state of
a stream at any particular floodplain-belt cross-section
in which, whilst the discharge and alluvium supply (load
and immovable cover) are both considered invariable (the
prerequisite of second order time), the valley slope is
so adjusted that the rate of degradation is zero, assuming
a readily erodible floor. Alternatively, grade is the
state in which, in second order time, the floor-plane is
stationary, assuming a readily erodible floor.

However precise the definitions, the situation they
describe is not always easy to identify. First, there is
the obvious difficulty arising when the processes peculiar
to each of the three orders of fluvial time are all operating vigorously at the same time, as happens briefly after
the passage of a nickpoint. The stream may well be at
or near to grade, although the controls of the state are
continuously changing. But at least the turmoil of this
situation may be understood, as already described on
page 23.

Generally we are more interested in situations where
the first order equilibrium or steady state is already
well established, but even here we may be unable to distinguish between continuing second order degradation (for
load considered constant) and perceptible third order degradation at grade (for rapidly decreasing load). But the
problem is academic and normally we need only be aware of
the existence of the two possible processes, which may of
course co-exist.

Undoubted second order *degradation* is evident wherever
a floor of bedrock is frequently visible in the channel.
We can discount the occasional appearance of large boulders
or local ridges of rock which do not extend all the way
across a meander-belt generally floored by soft bedrock,
but recurrent outcrops along the channel, especially if of
weathered rock obviously in situ, are sure indicators of
degradation. They show that the stream force is not being
resisted by alluvium alone, or even by alluvium principally. This criterion may however be hard to recognise

where the floor is old valley-fill of constitution similar
to that of the alluvium, although often such floor may be
identified by difference in colour or by induration.

When the alluvium profile can be inspected (usually
only in a terrace deposit), we can recognise degradation
by the existence of a continuous hard rock floor, especially one whose surface contours obviously relate more to
the physical structure of the rock than to any pattern of
randomly disposed scour fronts. Hard rock may impose, at
least temporarily, an unassailable barrier to stream scour,
with the result that the valley slope may become considerably steeper than is (or was) needed for grade. This means
that the competence in force is (or was) much larger than
the competence for grade required by the loading, and it
creates evidence in the channel deposition. The floor of
such a stream is being incessantly assaulted by the stream
scour, even at low discharges, so that any deposition displays the characteristics of the upper parts of the mobile
layer, revealing a loose, bedded aspect indicative of
involvement with purely linear currents. Certainly there
may be occasional immovable or larger lag particles present, lying on the hard floor, but unlike such particles in
graded streams which occupy a generally undisturbed,
privileged non-bedded zone vulnerable only to the very
strongest local vortical currents, these have been subject
to frequent hunting by the linear currents. Hollows in
the hard rock may sometimes shelter conventional lag
depositions, which however are not representative of the
alluvium profile generally. Often there may be no channel
deposition at all, when the fine-grained floodplain layer
rests directly on the hard rock, signifying that the
channel itself had been simply a stretch of pavement,
perhaps supporting occasional boulders or thinly overlaid
by spreads of sand or gravel dropped as a recent flood
receded. These are all features I have seen regularly in
degrading trunk streams in West Africa, both in floodplain
and in terrace deposits (in pits) and in the actual
channel.

Such cases of degradation are obvious enough, but
subtler evidence must be sought where a stream is cutting
down into a soft floor. We have already noted the significance of an uneven floor (page 14), indicating that it
lags (or has lagged) above a falling floor-plane, although
of course this kind of evidence is scarcely ever accessible
(except in pits) for a stream that is still flowing. However, where the degradation is quite rapid, the surface of
the floodplain (broadly considered) will also be uneven,
and the true meander-belt will be no more than a slightly
entrenched narrow zone enclosing the channel meanders.
Corroborative evidence may be provided by unpaired terraces
at the valley sides.

Aggradation is indicated where the meander-belt is an
'alluvial ridge' overlooking flanking belts of backswamp,
although to establish that the aggradation is continuing
we must also know whether the ridge is still rising. The
classic case of an aggraded stream is the lower Mississippi
(see Fisk, 1944), which is now at grade. An example of a
stream continuing to aggrade in a quite spectacular way

is the meandering Fly River of Papua, described by Blake
and Ollier (1971), debouching from highlands onto a
crustally back-tilted coastal plain which is now almost
dead level. The stream is building itself a prominent
causeway into the plain, whilst overflowing its banks
several times a year.

This last fact highlights another criterion of aggradation. Most streams are at grade and it also happens that
for most streams the recurrence interval of the bankfull
stage is about 1.5 years, implying that overflow of the
banks occurs at all only during two years out of three on
average (Leopold, Wolman and Miller, 1964, page 319).
This would appear to be the fairly constant 'characteristic'
of all streams at or near to grade. But clearly a rapidly
aggrading stream will overflow its banks more frequently
than a graded one, because the level of the whole deposition in and beside the channel is continuously rising,
causing a permanent difference between the level of the
earlier-formed floodplain on the concave side of a channel
bend compared with that of more recent origin on the convex
side. Leopold (1973), discussing changes observed in the
small Watts Branch stream in Maryland over a twenty year
period, states that 'the number of floods exceeding channel
capacity increased dramatically from an average of 2 a year
to 10 a year' and then demonstrates aggradation from actual
level measurements. In Sierra Leone I noticed that streams
in recently intensively cultivated areas overflowed their
floodplains for a long period every year in response to
the filling up of their channels with sediment to levels
above the top of the sand mobile layer, as revealed by
pitting. This is an extreme case and very clearly demonstrates the tendency.

In the alluvium profile aggradation is indicated by the
absence of a recognisable floor, inevitable with a rising
floor plane. Moreover this state precludes the existence
of immovable particles completely and of lag particles if
concentrated in a distinctive single layer. The bottom of
the alluvium profile of an aggrading stream cannot by its
nature ever be identified exactly, although floor material
lying well below the alluvium profile can usually be recognised as such by properties imposed on it by long freedom
from contact with the stream.

Finally we consider direct recognition of *grade* itself.
The obvious evidence of long-established grade is a clearly
defined meander-belt merging without change in level with
a very wide flat floodplain, overlying (though this evidence is usually hidden) a very wide flat floor. There
will also be a smoothly-rounded channel pattern and of
course no sign of the floor visible in the channel itself.
These properties together signify an environment where
third order decrease in the loading has been very slow, and
it is not uncommon.

Newly-established grade is more difficult to recognise,
although satisfaction of the following three criteria will
indicate that the stream is at least very near to grade:
    (i)   no sign of the floor visible in the channel;
    (ii) a channel pattern (for meandering streams) that
    is curvilinear, not rectilinear, so demonstrating freedom

from bedrock control;
(iii) the surface of the channel bed lying at the same
level as some part of the mobile layer as seen in a
bank opposite a point bar, so ruling out active aggradation.
As already emphasised, the criteria of grade are frequently
blurred to some degree by the effects of the normal condition of third order degradation at grade, caused by the
slow decrease of the load, and allowance has to be made
for this. In any case we never need to demonstrate grade
absolutely, but only important departures from it.

Finally it must be emphasised that most streams that
flow over readily erodible floors are at or near to the
state of grade. Normally second order degradation is only
obvious close to nickpoints and even there, as we shall
see, temporary third order increases in the loading may
effectively maintain a continuous approximate state of
grade. Thus, except where the floor, hard or soft, is
conspicuous in the channel at low water, it may be assumed
that effectively the stream is at grade. This conclusion
is very important because it implies that the loading-
competence relationship, which we have recognised as the
'heart' of the theory (pages 47 and 62-66) and is valid
only for graded streams, is *very widely applicable*.
Through this relationship we shall shortly be deducing all
the principal properties of all kinds of graded streams
and, therefore, by implication, effectively of *most
streams*. In any case, even where veritable grade is
demonstrably disproved, we can recognise that minor departures from it merely 'modify' the cardinal relationship
in a way that we can perfectly understand.

Chapter 8

FLOOR ERODIBILITY AND THE MOBILISATION

OF COARSE-PARTICLED ALLUVIUM

Floor erodibility was introduced on page 15 as an independent and passive fourth control of first order equilibrium because of its obvious influence on the rate of degradation. The range of its effect can be great, because whilst a virtually inerodible floor, in the form of massive hard rock, may hold back establishment of grade almost indefinitely, an immediately erodible floor, like that of the Nafayi discussed earlier, provides virtually no resistance to scour whatever.

However, floor erodibility is not necessarily an independent control, because if the floor should be composed of discrete particles of the size of gravel loosely held together, then its erodibility is immediately governed by the *competence* of the stream to which it relates.

Let us suppose that the passage upstream of an important nickpoint has suddenly (for reasons of geometry such as will be examined fully on pages 128-134) imposed a very steep valley slope at a meander-belt cross-section where the floor is bedrock weathered into even-sized boulders of hard rock. Prior to the passage of the nickpoint, the competence will probably have been much smaller than the size of these boulders and the floor will then have been almost inerodible. But subsequent to the passage of the nickpoint, the competence may have become much larger than this size, suddenly rendering the floor *readily erodible*. The immediate result is rapid degradation and the quick transport of the boulders now behaving as load particles of alluvium and playing the principal role in the establishment of equilibrium. The situation has completely changed, in the mobilisation of a whole new population of active particles of alluvium, which previously had not been alluvium at all except possibly as outsize immovable particles.

The process may be very important, permitting the rapid incision of deep gorges through ground which previously had been extremely resistant to erosion. The gorges of Dartmoor in Devonshire are examples, cut through granite dividing into fairly even-sized boulders of the order of one or two metres in diameter. Wherever a stream here is seen to have deeply penetrated the granite mass, we may suppose that it did so when it was once possessed of a very large competence (of the order of 5 metres and more), as focussed in a near-precipitous nickpoint slope (or headcut) moving like a knife upstream. The process is illustrated in Figures 17b and 18 (pages 131 and 134). For very brief periods and at very particular locations the normally unyielding granite would have become as vulnerable as clay, soon however, as the tool passed on, reacquiring its previous ascendency as the value of the competence declined to less than the critical value for mobility as determined by the boulder granulometry. Such waves of erosion would have quickly dissipated; however imposing their effect on the landscape, they were the expressions of brief reaction to comparatively sudden changes in spatial circumstances (as discussed in the next chapter and analysed closely later, on pages 131-132). Certainly nothing of the kind is to be seen in action today on Dartmoor. It is true that the nickpoints remain (as 'arrested nickpoints'), but they are relics of the past event, dividing the steeper stretches downstream, which had been mobilised, from the gentler stretches upstream, which (again for reasons of geometry) had escaped. The old force is now completely spent, following the further and gradual decrease of the competence for grade as a result of third order degradation, now proceeding extremely slowly, as also will be described in the next chapter.

Other and more direct causes of mobilisation may be noted. One is crustal tilt, which increases the valley slope S_V, so increasing the competence. Another is sudden release of more water into the drainage, as from quickly melting ice or snow following change in climate, or by river-capture, which increases the discharge Q, likewise increasing the competence. Both these agencies can be effective, although in general their role is undoubtedly unimportant in comparison with that of major nickpoints.

We shall call the variable property just discussed the *alluvium mobility*, defining it as the facility with which a deposit of actual or potential alluvium may be eroded and transported as governed by the competence ratio (D/D_c) of the particles of its 'dominant' particle size range, on whose separate readiness to become mobilised depends the mobility of the whole. This imprecise definition suits our need adequately in that we shall not need to specify the 'dominant' size range accurately, although we have to know approximately where it lies. For example, in the case of a Dartmoor boulder gravel deposit, considered either as an alluvium deposition or as a floor vulnerable to erosion, we can say that for small competences its mobility is zero and stays so for continued increase in the competence up to a *critical mobility size* (D_b) equal roughly to the modal size of the boulders, beyond which the alluvium mobility increases from low to high with further increasing competence.

This property of alluvium mobility is the last on the list of first order quantities we require to obtain a comprehensive view of the processes of stream evolution, involving all sizes of alluvium in relation to the competence, all variations in floor erodibility, any range of time and an appreciation of fundamental causes. The pattern of interrelationships, seen through the governorship of the simple concept of competence, is summarised in Figure 9, which may be recognised as an amplification of the diagram presented earlier on page 25. We should be able to apply the diagram to any situation, although of course the 'normal tendencies' indicated there (by the notes in brackets) may not always obtain.

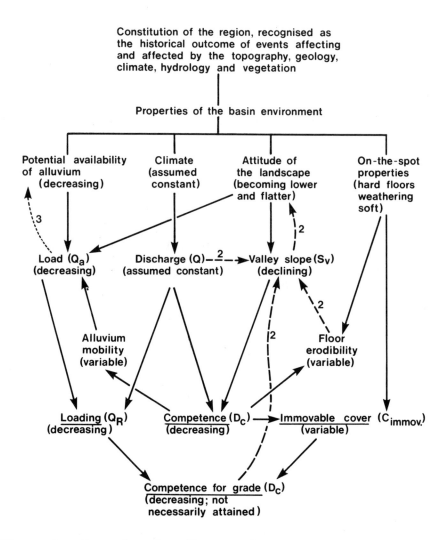

Figure 9. Comprehensive diagram of stream evolution, showing the relationship between the principal first order characteristics (underlined) and the properties of the basin environment. The changes indicated in brackets are the normal tendencies shown in third order time, induced both by decrease in the potential availability of alluvium and by lowering and flattening of the landscape.

In the next chapter we shall apply the diagram to a fundamental situation and use it for initiating the 'synthesis' of the particular stream required by this situation.

Part III
THE STREAM REALISED

Chapter 9

THE SYNTHESIS OF A STREAM FROM KNOWLEDGE OF ITS BASIN ENVIRONMENT

The unavoidably long trail of the basic argument is now concluded. A theoretical demonstration should avoid appeal to natural examples and the aim has been to keep the argument on the plane of simple reasoning. This is not to say that the normal scientific approach has been spurned, for indeed it has been impossible to work out the synthesis of a stream without introducing into its design many components whose function has only been discovered by actual observation of natural streams, and at times it has been necessary to use natural examples to demonstrate relationships, one such being the alluvium profile of the Nafayi. Nonetheless it seems a just claim that every stage in the argument has been invariably founded exclusively on understanding and nowhere on relationships indicated by observation alone.

The 'structure' of a stream, as illustrated by its characteristic diagram (see Figure 8 page 76), is essentially an abstract concept. But henceforward we shall be studying real streams, observable either in the mind's eye in the case of the synthesised stream now to be created, or directly in the case of the natural streams we shall thereafter be examining and comparing. The primary object will be to test theory against observation, and a measure of success will be the difficulty in keeping the two kinds of image separate.

We will now retrace all the steps of the argument in the one act of synthesising a particular stream as seen at a particular floodplain-belt cross-section. The data used will be the fundamental properties of its drainage basin such as have no direct reference to the stream itself, so ensuring that the raw materials of the process will be as elemental as we can make them. We hope to end up with a 'synthetic' portrait of a natural stream, sufficiently credible for us to match it with an actual situation. However, at the outset, I should confess that the exercise is based broadly on my own observations of the River Dart drainage on the granite mass of Dartmoor in Devon, already referred to in the last chapter. The trail of deduction is summarised in Figure 10.

We consider a highland mass of granite which had once been part of a wide area elevated to some 500 metres above a near sea. Soft flanking sedimentary rocks have been stripped away by erosion leaving the resistant centre of

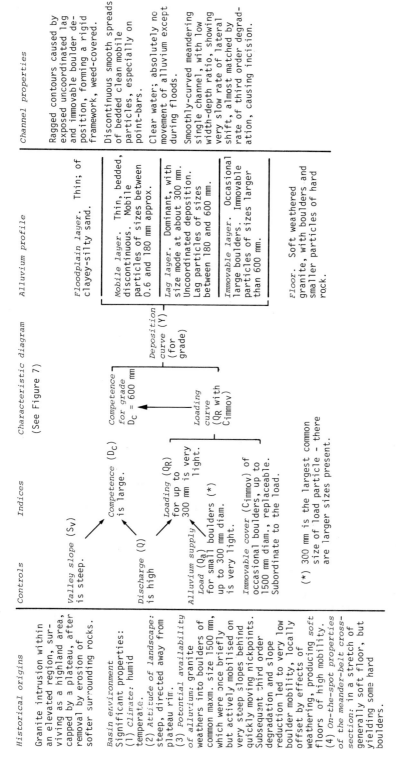

Historical origins	Controls	Indices	Characteristic diagram (See Figure 7)	Alluvium profile	Channel properties
Granite intrusion within an elevated region, surviving as a highland area, capped by a plateau, after removal by erosion of softer surrounding rocks. *Basin environment* Significant properties: (1) *Climate:* humid temperate. (2) *Attitude of landscape:* steep, directed away from plateau rim. (3) *Potential availability of alluvium:* granite weathers into boulders of common maxm. size 1500 mm, which were once briefly but actively mobilised on very steep slopes behind quickly moving nickpoints. Subsequent third order degradation and slope reduction led to very low boulder mobility, locally offset by effects of weathering, producing *soft floors of high mobility.* (4) *on-the-spot properties of the meander-belt cross-section:* in a stretch of generally soft floor, but yielding some hard boulders.	*Valley slope (S_V)* is steep. *Discharge (Q)* is high *Alluvium supply* *Load (Q_a)* for small boulders (*) up to 300 mm diam. is very light. *Immovable cover (Cimmov)* of occasional boulders, up to 1500 mm diam., replaceable. Subordinate to the load. (*) 300 mm is the largest common size of load particle – there are larger sizes present.	*Competence (D_C)* is large. *Loading (Q_R)* for up to 300 mm is very light.	*Competence for grade D_C = 600 mm* *Loading curve (Q_R with Cimmov)* *Deposition curve (Y) (for grade)*	*Floodplain layer.* Thin; of clayey-silty sand. *Mobile layer.* Thin, bedded, discontinuous. Mobile particles of sizes between 0.6 and 180 mm approx. *Lag layer.* Dominant, with size mode at about 300 mm. Uncoordinated deposition. Lag particles of sizes between 180 and 600 mm. *Immovable layer.* Occasional large boulders. Immovable particles of sizes larger than 600 mm. *Floor.* Soft weathered granite, with boulders and smaller particles of hard rock.	Ragged contours caused by exposed uncoordinated lag and immovable boulder deposition, forming a rigid framework, weed-covered. Discontinuous smooth spreads of bedded clean mobile particles, especially on point-bars. Clear water; absolutely no movement of alluvium except during floods. Smoothly-curved meandering single channel, with low width-depth ratio, showing very slow rate of lateral shift, almost matched by rate of third order degradation, causing incision.

Figure 10. Summary of processes involved in the synthesis of a stream from knowledge of its basin environment (See Chapter 9)

granite still largely intact, capped by a plateau. We
shall examine a stream flowing down one of the steep sides
which considerations of simple geometry inevitably produce.

The 'basin environment' is the expression we have
already used to denote in the widest sense the properties
of all the ground both upstream of and including our point
of reference at a floodplain-belt cross-section. In
Figure 9 above, we recognised that certain of these properties were significant in determining the behaviour of
the stream at the cross-section, and these are now specified.

(1) The *climate* is humid temperate.

(2) The *attitude of the landscape* is steep, directed
away from the plateau rim.

(3) The *potential availability of alluvium* has
changed with time, because it is a function of the changing
competence of the stream. The jointed granite weathers
into boulders of common maximum size about $1\frac{1}{2}$ metres in
diameter. The first effect of the stripping away of the
highland flanks had been to produce within this and every
one of the principal drainage basins an extremely steep
stretch along the side of the highlands, bounded at its
head by a prominent nickpoint. By virtue of its great
competence, the main stream was once able to mobilise the
boulders, abundantly available, and transport them as load
particles down a very steep graded profile. Rapid erosion
at the head of the stretch pushed the nickpoint forward
until the geometry of the situation halted it somewhere on the plateau, whereupon all the loads quickly
decreased. Resultant third order degradation (but probably
following a brief episode of aggradation) brought down the
value of the competence everywhere to smaller than the
critical mobility size of the boulder-floor and all processes slowed down drastically, as erstwhile load boulders
became immovable boulders. All loadings then became much
lighter.

(4) *On-the-spot properties* at the floodplain-belt
cross-section are not necessarily common to the basin as a
whole. Differential weathering may have locally caused
floors to become soft, as has happened *at this cross-
section*, although residual cores of hard granite maintain
a supply of boulders up to the maximum size dictated by
the jointing.

From these properties we can deduce the values of the
controls. First, we know that the declining *valley slope*
is still as steep as need be to keep a gravel of small
boulders mobilised. The *discharge* is high, inevitable
within an area of high relief in a humid climate. Because
of the generally soft floor, there are few potential
immovable particles available and most of the cover for
grade can only be provided by load particles, as already
available in adequate quantity (which need only be small)
for particles up to the size of the small boulders, say
up to 300 mm diameter. Small boulders therefore provide
the significant portion of the *load*, although in very
small quantity. The load of finer gravel and sand would
of course be decidedly heavier, but not by so much as to
affect appreciably the equilibrium.

Plate 5.   The *lightly-loaded gravel stream* of the Bagoué
River near Papara, in the north of the Ivory Coast.
The high banks display only the floodplain layer,
composed of silt-clay, whilst the water conceals a
thin lag-cum-immovable layer of vein-quartz gravel.
A thin and discontinuous mobile layer of fine gravel
or pebbly sand of common maximum particle size about
25 mm was not seen at this site.   Competence is of the
order of 80 mm.

Now we translate these data into the usable forms of
the two *indices*.   The combination of an inherited steep
valley slope and a high discharge assures the possibility
of a large *competence* for the stream at grade if required
by the loading.   The combination of a light boulder load
(as permitted by the large inherited competence) and the
high discharge produces a light boulder *loading*.   There
will also be some *immovable cover*.
The *characteristic diagram* can now be drawn for the
stream at the cross-section, which will certainly be flowing at grade because of the soft floor.   The diagram is
shown in Figure 7 (above, page 74), whose construction has

already been discussed. A reasonable estimate of the
competence for grade is *600 mm*. It is this value which
will determine so many of the first order characteristics.
     From consideration of the *deposition curve* so obtained
we can construct the *alluvium profile,* as shown in Figure
10, by applying to it the two critical competence ratios,
which we know to be roughly 0.3 for the *critical lag
ratio* (D_l/D_c) and 0.001 for the *critical mobile ratio*
(D_m/D_c). For a competence of 600 mm, the *critical lag
size* is therefore about 180 mm and the *critical mobile
size* about 0.6 mm. We discover that the alluvium profile
is dominated by the *lag layer,* as is characteristic of a
lightly-loaded gravel stream. The lag particle population
displays a boulder mode of around 300 mm, representing the
largest common size in the loading. The other two channel
layers, the *mobile layer* and the *immovable layer* are
thinner, both being discontinuous. The *floodplain layer*
is not represented by the deposition curve of the characteristic diagram and although we have not yet examined its
formation, already we can deduce that it has here a sandy
and relatively non-clayey composition, as dictated by the
large competence.
     Next, we look at the *channel*. Its contours tend to be
ragged. This is because of the mostly complete exposure,
to both scour and view, of the larger immovable and lag
boulders, whose movement, if any, is both extremely slow
and uncoordinated. The smooth spreads of the smaller
mobile particles, displaying fluent, coordinated bedding
structures, are only occasionally seen in the channel,
covering the boulders. Clear pools mark the sites of scour
holes which, in the intervals between floods, become
regions of stillness. At low water there is no stirring
of alluvium anywhere. The boulders protruding from the
depths form a rigid open framework within which smaller
particles in transit quickly find shelter from the current
and thereafter nothing is free to move, a state that can
continue even at moderate flood, when still no erosion is
possible anywhere and the water remains clear. Weeds
flourish on the boulders, in marked contrast with feeble
growths on the smaller cobbles, and the usual bare surfaces
of finer particles. Channel shift is obviously very slow,
although we have evidence of it in rare sweeps of gleaming,
well-scrubbed mobile gravel and sand and in the reciprocal
focuses of erosion, the marks of very high floods only.
Some boulders are seen to have been disturbed, even transported, showing fresh surfaces unusually free of weed,
indicating that the lag particles are being nudged downstream, although possibly the main spur to movement is
breakage, initiated by weathering, into the smaller
particles that are more easily removed.
     Lateral movement of the channel may be so slow that
vertical movement perceptibly competes with it in a clear
demonstration of third order degradation at grade. Before
ever the floor could become flat and flush with the floor-
plane, further appreciable diminution of the already light
boulder loading, probably in both size and amount, will
have caused the stream to degrade - in third order time -

by just so much as is required to replenish its stock of
alluvium and maintain the cover for grade. The result is
incision of the channel.

The processes are not conducive to the development of
braiding. Change in the status quo is possible only very
locally, where the stream can muster its strongest force.
This is where at the same time the depth of flow is
greatest and the level of the bottom of the flow is lowest.
Here erosion in depth continues, provided the floor remains
erodible. Elsewhere there is no effectual erosion, and
there may be deposition. Thus the principal thread of flow
maintains itself, whilst subordinate ones are self-
extinguishing. The result is one channel, meandering.

The portrait of a particular stream has been sketched.
With the additional knowledge of the type of vegetation
characteristic of a neighbourhood, we can well imagine an
actual locality. I admit to any charge of hindsight, as
my mind returns to the West Dart River, and in particular,
as illustrated in Plate 4 (page 72), to a two kilometre
stretch located between Two Bridges and the foot of the
gorge at Wistman's Wood, some six kilometres from the
source on the plateau. The valley slope is about 15 m per
km. The conditions described apply continuously along
this stretch, except where, in curiously broken short
intervals, moderately-loaded and even heavily-loaded
regimes are to be recognised, each displaying an appropriate increased steepness. We shall see later (page 138),
in a discussion of changes in stream properties 'along the
stream', that such seemingly incongruous conditions are
to be expected along lightly-loaded gravel streams supplied
with coarse gravel from the floor, for the reason that the
dominant lag particles travel so extremely slowly that the
particle size distribution of the gravel deposition along
the stream is inevitably very irregular. Certain processes
exploit this situation, locally creating sharp nickpoints
whose migrations upstream maintain short steep stretches
of active degradation, possibly braided. Other short
steep stretches may of course result from hold-ups by
locally inerodible bedrock floors.

Chapter 10

THE CHANNEL PROPERTIES OF GRAVEL STREAMS

The stream 'synthesised' in the last chapter is a particular example of a lightly-loaded gravel stream. In this
section we shall consider gravel streams generally, an
undertaking we now realise to be not difficult, for we
are familiar with the very few controls that significantly
govern the working of any kind of stream.

For streams at grade (more or less), these controls
resolve themselves into the single 'index' of the *loading*,
as expressed by both the size and the amount of the
alluvium. Variation in the *size* is already recognised in
the sharp distinction which exists between gravel and sand
streams, but beyond this we shall not use it as a basis of
classification. Variation in the *amount*, refering only to
the gravel loading, will be seen to provide a better scale
against which to examine and compare all the variations
possible in gravel stream behaviour.

The classification of graded streams presented on
page 77 distinguished three classes of gravel stream specified by this variable of the amount of the loading: these
classes were the heavily-loaded, the moderately-loaded and
the lightly-loaded gravel streams. Whilst the characteristic diagrams (see Figure 8, page 76) obviously cannot show
class boundaries, fortunately it happens that progressive
change in the amount of the gravel loading, considered
over the whole range of values possible, produces, in
turn, two fairly sharp changes in the behaviour of a
stream, therein providing convenient visual criteria for
each of three even divisions of the range. These divisions
we will identify with the three classes just mentioned,
and discover the criteria (summarised in Table 2, page 94)
as we go along in this enquiry.

We have seen (pages 62-66) how the loading of a stream
determines the competence required for the establishment
of grade, which, provided the floor is sufficiently
erodible, can be brought about promptly in second order
time by the operation of the competence-degradation interaction. The heavier the loading, the larger is the
competence for grade. The relationships are easy to
visualise from the basic cover formula $C_{load} = k.Q_R/U$,
where $U = \phi(1/(D/D_c))$. To maintain the load cover C_{load}
at the value suited to grade for a given value of the
loading Q_R, the travel velocity U is adjusted by regulation
of the competence D_c (effected through the interaction) to
give the required value to the parameter Q_R/U for all
sizes of the alluvium. When the gravel loading Q_R is
heavy, both U and D_c assume relatively high values; when
Q_R is light, both U and D_c assume relatively low values.
These are the important relationships from which we can

easily deduce the characteristics of any graded stream's
first order equilibrium.

We will begin with the *heavily-loaded gravel streams*,
assumed to be at grade or near to it. As just indicated,
the competence has to be relatively large and is certainly
much larger than any common size of particle in the alluvium supply. This means that there can be no (or very few
indeed) immovable or lag particles and that the channel
deposition consists virtually exclusively of the *mobile
layer*, showing the coordinated bedding structures we would
expect where particles of all the sizes present can be
picked up and transported by the stream at comparatively
low discharges from many sections of the channel pattern
at frequent intervals of time. Except at very low water,
the stream is for ever eroding and depositing. No bank is
safe for long; the large absolute values of the competence
assure frequent strong currents able, when armed with
gravel in transport, to cut through any clayey matrix
binding the gravel, and the universal low competence ratios
(D/D_C) imply that the currents can also shift easily even
the largest particles. The collapse of a bank means both
the release of load particles into the current and the
widening and consequent shallowing of the flow, which together promote deposition. A chance hold-up of a bunch of
larger particles launches the growth of a bar, causing
disturbance elsewhere. The result of the continuous and
ubiquitous instability is *braided flow*, and this is the
criterion of the heavily-loaded gravel stream.

Sorting is poor. The competence ratios (D/D_C) of all
sizes D are well below unity and consequently the travel
velocities U of all sizes are *proportionally* far less
disparate than they would be for a light loading and
smaller competence D_C, as is clear from consideration of
the formula $U = \phi(1/(D/D_C))$ in the case where D/D_C approaches unity. Thus the larger sizes do not monopolise
the deposition, which shows an even representation of a
wide range of sizes, as shown in Figure 8a (page 76). This
fairly even mixing is still evident on close inspection of
small portions of the deposition and there is little sign
of any segregation of the alluvium into beds of restricted
size-range, as may be conspicuous in more lightly loaded
streams. However, one effect of the braiding may be to
produce partings of *much* finer alluvium, maybe of fine sand
alone or even silt and clay, which represent deposition in
slow-moving or still water impounded by cut-offs in
anabranches. We should also note that the distinction
between a heavily-loaded gravel stream and a heavily-loaded
transitional stream (as will be examined in Chapter 12)
may not be obvious, because the very wide range of sizes
represented in the evenly mixed depositions may include an
unobtrusive but yet substantial proportion of sand
(Plate 6).

Enough properties have been described to specify a
kind of stream that is both distinctive and familiar.
Together the properties are so well known that there is no
call to match each one against a separate piece of evidence,
and it is enough to cite the well known examples of the
Rhône tributaries the Ardèche and Durance, as described by

Table 2.   Properties of the three classes of graded
gravel stream.

Property	Gravel loading (amount) (Q_R)		
	Heavy	Moderate	Light
Competence (D_c)	Relatively large	Relatively moderate	Relatively small
Competence ratios (D/D_c)	Low	Moderate	High
Travel velocities ($U = \phi(1/(D/D_c))$)	High	Moderate	Low
Dominant channel layer	Mobile	Mobile	Lag
Channel form	Braided	Meandering	Meandering
Width-depth ratio (W/H)	High	Moderate	Low
Critical features	Braiding (high mobility)	Single channel, showing features characteristic of the mobile layer (pool-and-riffle configuration and wide point bar).	Single channel, with features of mobile layer absent or poorly developed. Lag layer usually wholly submerged. Canal-like aspect.

Doeglas (1962), and the small glacial stream on Mount
Rainier, Washington (state), as described by Fahnestock
(1963). The fundamental cause of a heavy gravel loading
is simply an abundant gravel supply that is both available
and, because the valley slope is steep and the competence
consequently large, accessible. As the examples bear out,
this dual requirement can only be met on a continuing
basis by the combination of ground readily erodible into
fairly durable gravel and a high and steep topographical
relief, as in Alpine valleys. But the same relationships
also produce heavy gravel loadings, although only briefly
and locally, on generally much more lightly loaded gravel
streams behind even modest nickpoints, as we have already
recognised (pages 23 and 91) and will further investigate
later (pages 137-138). It is interesting to note that
many placid English gravel streams exhibit short braided
stretches characterised by small islands called aits or
eyots, where the presence of a weir and a lock testifies
to local steepening.
    Heavily-loaded gravel streams of the kind that rise in

mountain areas cannot of course persist indefinitely downstream of the gravel sources, because of the readiness of
the gravel particles to waste into sand and finer materials,
and they are replaced first by more lightly-loaded gravel
streams and ultimately, if their courses are long enough,
by sand streams. We noted earlier (pages 59-60) that the
rate of wastage of gravel of any uniform composition is
governed principally by the competence ratio (D/D_c) of the
particle size, so that the smaller the particle relative
to the competence, the slower the wastage with distance
along the stream. We have just recognised that heavily-
loaded gravel streams are characterised by both large
competences (D_c) and low competence ratios (D/D_c) even for
the largest particles travelling, and therefore we conclude
that their gravels must all waste relatively slowly with
distance along the stream. This accords with Tricart and
Schaeffer's (1950) finding that heavily-loaded periglacial
streams show a relatively low rate of pebble rounding with
distance. By the same token we are not surprised to read
of andesite boulders still being conveyed as mobile
particles 50 miles from their mountain source, as described
by Mackin (1948) for the Shoshone River at Cody in Wyoming.
  Nonetheless the Shoshone gravel has wasted so much
that the gravel loading at Cody is no longer heavy enough
to enforce a braided course, and the stream flows in a
single meandering channel, classically at grade over a
floor of 'unresisting' sandstone. We will now investigate
the properties of this kind of stream, whose considerably
lighter loading qualifies it for the title of *moderately-
loaded gravel stream*. Applying the same reasoning as for
the heavy gravel loading, we infer that both the travel
velocity U and the competence for grade D_c possess relatively 'moderate' values. The competence is still much
larger than most of the gravel of the alluvium supply and
the mobile layer remains dominant. For a stream such as
the Shoshone at Cody, far removed from the sources of the
gravel, there would not be any lag particles in the deposition, whose presence there, as we shall appreciate
later (pages 139-140), could only presage a 'regime change'
to a sand stream at some short distance downstream, which
is not the case. On the other hand, if there were an
immediately local source of the gravel, there could certainly be a lag layer and maybe an immovable layer also.
In any case, only the mobile layer is visible in the
channel. But it is very much less mobile than in a
heavily-loaded gravel stream. The competence ratios (D/D_c)
are higher for all the gravel particles and now the deposits can only be shifted at times of at least fairly
high flood and then only in restricted parts of the
channel pattern. The flow has resolved itself irreversibly
into a single thread. Any subordinate channel, however
formed, is bound to disappear, because the flow within it
is too weak to extend it quickly and cannot compete with
the relatively much more effective action achieved by the
main flow. Here, assuming a readily erodible floor, the
current is both strongest and deepest, and in every way
holds the initiative. The more quickly shifting main
channel progressively captures the subordinate ones,

eventually standing alone and unchallenged. Thus in this usually obvious distinction between the braided and the single channel we can welcome a convenient critical distinction between our classes of heavily and moderately-loaded gravel streams.

The main feature of the single channel is the smooth coordinated deposition of the mobile layer, disposed in the lengthwise cyclic pattern of the well-known 'pool and riffle' configuration. Riffle bars are formed of the coarsest mobile particles thrown out of the deeper scour holes at time of flood, as described on page 33. These holes appear at the outside of the meander bends, which form (or sometimes only try to form, if prevented by an inerodible floor or other impediment) along the channel at regular intervals, probably as dictated by purely hydraulic considerations, and the riffles grow just downstream of them, as smooth, even-sized, imbricated pavings composed of these largest mobile particles temporarily immobilised by reason of their position, but enjoying too short a rest to become more than slightly covered by the weeds. The surfaces of the riffle bars fall away steeply and regularly in the downstream direction into the next pool, whose deepest point will be the scour hole feeding the next riffle. There is little action at low water, except for the winnowing away of fine alluvium from the riffles by the steep but shallow flow tumbling down the riffle sur-face and its deposition in the deep still pools. But at high water the combined linear and vortical flow scours the pools, reinforces the riffles with large particles and carries the finer ones forward, some of which settle on the next point bar. At the same time there is tendency for the whole channel to shift laterally by a little amount (as further discussed presently).

There are many excellent descriptions of pool and riffle streams, particularly by members of the U.S. Geo-logical Survey. Papers especially relevant to the present work are those by Wolman (1955), Hack (1957) and Wolman and Leopold (1957), whose observations of Appalachian streams clearly define the phenomenon. Of special interest also is Nordin and Beverage's (1965) description of pool and riffle features on the Rio Grande in New Mexico at the Otavi gauging station. Here the first order equilibrium is determined exclusively by the moderate, cobble-sized gravel loading, regardless of the fairly heavy sand loading whose influence is only going to be felt downstream after the elimination of most of the gravel by wastage (see page 113). Plates 2 and 3 (pages 37 and 52) depict examples in Europe.

The mobility of the channels of moderately-loaded gravel streams can of course vary between wide limits, depending on the actual amount of the gravel loading. At one extreme, where the loading is relatively heavy, we have the very mobile condition, close to the limit at which braiding occurs, recognisable by quickly eroding banks and wide bright clean spreads of newly deposited mobile gravel on point-bars. The competence is still large enough to maintain rapid retreat of the concave banks, unmatched however by any equally strong impulse in the opposing

point-bars to advance. The development of these bars is
in fact continuously restrained by the governing effect of
the competence, always adjusted, *in a graded stream*, to
maintain the 'thickness' of the alluvium cover (C_{load}) -
of which the point-bar is an expression - at the same
value, *regardless of the amount of the gravel loading*.
Thus the movement of the concave banks alone sets the
pace of lateral migration, in this case a fast one, and
the relatively sluggish advance of the trailing point-bars
produces the characteristic equilibrium state for this
kind of stream of a *wide channel*. As will be discussed
further on pages 103-106, this implies a *high width-depth
ratio*.

At the other extreme within the range of moderately-
loaded gravel streams, we approach the condition of a
light gravel loading and find that the channel is beginning
to become rigid under the influence of larger competence
ratios (D/D_c). The mobile layer is still continuous and
the point-bars remain important features, but except close
to the water the look of continuous activity has gone, as
soil and weeds encroach. The opposing banks have generally
weathered smooth and grey with time and possibly harbour
colonies of birds in holes dug evidently in recognition of
the small risk of imminent destruction. The ability of
the stream to erode is obviously much reduced and the concave banks retreat much more slowly, but the conspicuous
point bars emphasise the continued ability of the stream
to maintain a constant alluvium cover (still mainly of
mobile particles) by the adjustment of the competence to
suit the lighter gravel loading. With the advance of the
point bars now *relatively* brisk compared with the retreat
of the banks opposite, the result is a narrower channel
and a lower width-depth ratio.

As the gravel loading becomes even lighter and the
competence ratios (D/D_c) even larger, so the status of
the load particles changes. Mobile particles become lag
particles, because they are now of size larger than about
$0.3D_c$. Henceforward the extremely slow moving lag particles furnish most of the alluvium cover, as the mobile
particles become too sparse even to provide a continuous
mobile layer and are no longer sufficient to display the
conspicuous, fluent features characteristic of the
moderately-loaded gravel stream. We now have the *lightly-
loaded gravel stream*, whose very different properties we
can deduce. The width-depth ratio has decreased even
more. The result, for a relatively fine-particled gravel
loading and a perennial stream in a humid climate, is the
almost complete permanent submergence of the channel bed,
now little more than a flat, thin layer of generally
inert (lag) particles, beneath a continuous sheet of
water. The stream has the appearance of a featureless
canal, narrow, regular, steep-sided, betraying its natural
origin only by any smooth meanders inherited from a previous moderately-loaded state, and the occasional appearance above the water of small banks and narrow point bars,
composed of mobile gravel.

We have already considered an example of the lightly-
loaded gravel stream in the case of the boulder stream

'synthesised' in Chapter 9 and identified with a section
of the West Dart River on Dartmoor (see Plate 4). This
example is unusual in that it shows a combination of small
stream size (only 6 km long) and large particle size (into
the boulder range), with the consequence that the predominant lag particles, which are boulders, are necessarily
very conspicuous in the channel, often standing out of the
water. Normally however, the lag sizes are much smaller
and as described in the last paragraph, so that the predominant lag deposition can only be a very thin layer
resting on the floor, permanently hidden from view beneath
the deep water of the narrow channel. Such streams are
common in humid West Africa (Plate 5 page 89), where the
only gravel may be durable vein-quartz (eroding unaltered
from otherwise completely decomposed bedrock), and there
the apparently gravel-free 'canals' may extend long
distances. On several occasions in different regions I
have seen the lag gravels of these lightly-loaded streams
retrieved from the middle of their channels either by
diving or mechanical means, their lag status indicated by
comparison with similar gravels displayed in full alluvium
profile in the flanking floodplain, exposed by excavation.

We shall see later (Chapter 15, page 139) that in areas
where the floor of the lightly-loaded gravel stream is
unable to replenish it with lag particles, then the condition is unstable with respect to distance along the stream.
The lag particles travel so slowly that only a short
distance further on there has to exist a point, as shown
in Figure 24 (page 154), where they have not yet had time
to arrive from upstream, and thus the maximum particle
size (D_{max}) decreases quickly with distance on account of
the 'non-arrival' of the largest particles. The process
is accelerated by the simultaneous rapid decrease in the
competence (D_c), whose value is governed by D_{max} if the
stream is at grade, and this assures that the largest
particles travelling continue to be very slow moving lag
particles, whatever their absolute size. The process
terminates suddenly in a change to a sand regime along a
short stretch of the longitudinal profile, to be referred
to as a 'regime break'. An example of such an unstable
lightly-loaded gravel stream is a part of the Adour River
in southern France, described on pages 156-158.

We can now with more certainty recognise the principal
criteria distinguishing moderate from light gravel loadings, and one from another of the two classes of graded
stream they represent. The moderately-loaded gravel
stream is recognised by the dominance of the mobile layer,
clearly exhibiting itself in the pool-and-riffle configuration and the wide point bars. The lightly-loaded gravel
stream is recognised by the subordination of the mobile
to the lag layer, usually wholly submerged, and the notable
absence or meagre development of the features of the mobile
layer, often giving the channel the aspect of a canal.

We have now examined the complete spectrum of the
gravel streams graduated according to variation in the
amount of the controlling gravel loading. On this basis
three classes have clearly presented themselves, heavily,
moderately and lightly-loaded gravel streams, whose
critical properties are summarised in Table 2.

Chapter 11

THE CHANNEL PROPERTIES OF SAND STREAMS

Although the variations to be observed in the channel
properties of sand streams quite closely resemble those
of the gravel streams just described, there are significant
differences in the processes involved. In sand streams
the competence ratios (D/D_c) of all the common sizes of
the alluvium particles are invariably small (as discussed
presently) and we have to look for other immediate cause
than the relative mass inertia of the individual particles
to explain the variations in the general mobility of the
channel forms. This other cause is the *cohesion* of the
deposited alluvium as created by its silt-clay or 'mud'
content, considered in relation to the first order *erosive
force* of the stream. Ultimately we can identify the
causes of the variation in mobility in both gravel and
sand streams with the single property of the *erodibility*
of the deposited alluvium, complement of the floor erodibility considered earlier (page 83). We shall discover
(see Figure 12) that for all streams at or near to grade,
regardless of the processes involved, its value is controlled simply by the competence (D_c) of the stream as
related to and determined by the ruling loading (Q_R), of
sand or gravel, as the case may be.
  In the case of sand streams, we might suppose that an
equally important and quite independent influence would be
the *silt-clay loading* (Q_m), whose value must govern the
silt-clay deposition (Y_m) to some degree in that obviously
there can be no silt-clay deposition without at least some
silt-clay loading. Nonetheless, we shall see that, apart
from the essential condition of an 'availability' of silt-
clay in the system, the only significant control of the
value of the silt-clay deposition (Y_m) for the *graded* sand
stream is, paradoxically, the *sand* loading (Q_R). This
curious relationship is perfectly understandable, because
it is the sand loading (Q_R) which exclusively determines
the competence for grade (D_c), which itself determines
whether there should be *any* (or virtually any) silt-clay
deposition in the channel *regardless of the amount of silt-
clay loading*, and also broadly the proportion of silt-clay
deposition in the floodplain layer.

11.1   Bank erodibility

Erodibility is defined as the facility, high or low, with
which a stream erodes a specified material, in first order
time. It is a measure of the *relative* instability of the
material, as determined by its properties as they relate
to the first order erosive force of the stream. It would

be possible, if need be, to find appropriate physical
units to express this idea, but the argument does not
require such action because the quantitative value is, for
our purpose, adequately expressed in a word, with added
qualification if needed. As we have seen, the erodibility
of even a boulder deposit may be 'high' where the stream
flow is powerful; by contrast we now recognise that the
erodibility of mere clay may be 'low' in a gentle sand
stream. It will be apparent at once that a principal
control of erodibility in any circumstance is the competence.

Our present concern is the *bank erodibility* (E_b) because undoubtedly it is the response of the channel banks
to scour that principally determines a stream's first order
behaviour.

For *gravel* streams we saw that the bank erodibility
depended on the competence ratios (D/D_c) of the common
gravel sizes of the channel deposition and that these
ratios in their turn depended on the gravel loading (Q_R)
for these sizes, as being the determinant of the competence
for grade (D_c). Thus, in the end, the bank erodibility
of a graded gravel stream is governed solely and simply by
the gravel loading (Q_R).

However, for *sand* streams the competence ratios (D/D_c)
are invariably very small, reflecting both the small size
of sand particles and the unfailing ability of all sand
streams to maintain at least fairly large competences for
grade, rarely ever falling below about 40 mm. They owe
this ability to the fact that streams of competence smaller
than this value are in process of becoming incapable of
sustaining further third order degradation on account of
rapidly increasing deposition of silt-clay particles in
the channel and the development there of this very cohesion we are considering. The weak stream can no longer
readily erode and lower its floor and eventually the time
comes when there can be no further evolutionary decline
in values of either the slope or the competence. Thus we
have to recognise the existence of a lower limiting value
for the competence of all streams normally evolving, which
we can call the *critical minimum competence*. Later we
shall see how its value is probably about 30 mm. The
important conclusion now is that for virtually all streams
for which there is channelled flow, the competence ratios
(D/D_c) for the sand particles are always very small, never
approaching anywhere near unity.

It follows that if the competence ratios were the only
criterion of the bank erodibility of sand streams (as they
are for gravel streams), all sand streams would be in a
permanently unstable condition. As this is patently not
so, we look for another control and find it in the *cohesion*
of the particles composing the material forming the channel
banks, due to the binding action both of the moisture
within it and, more importantly, of the silt-clay there.
As Hjulstrom (1935) has demonstrated in a well-known diagram (e.g. see Scheidegger, 1961, page 135), solid particles of size smaller than about 0.1 mm require, with
decreasing size, an *increasing* critical flow velocity (and
therefore shear force) for initiation of their movement,

which is significantly the opposite of the corresponding
relationship for particles larger than 0.1 mm. It is
evident from this that the cohesion of deposited alluvium
varies both with the amount and (inversely) with the
particle size of its *silt-clay content*.

We now need to examine the constitution of the bank
material of sand streams. Only the two upper layers of
the alluvium profile are involved, which are the floodplain
layer, formed essentially outside the channel, and the
mobile layer, formed within the channel. It happens that
their silt-clay contents are usually very different, that
of the floodplain layer being substantially the greater.
However, the erosive force of the stream is stronger at
the lower level of the mobile layer, where moreover the
flow is armed with the erosive tools of transported bedload material. Nonetheless in sand streams the upper
floodplain layer does manage to contribute considerably -
and very likely predominantly - to the resistance of the
banks through the shield provided by collapsed masses of
this layer as they lie temporarily immovable at the foot
of the bank (as illustrated, for a gravel stream, in
Plate 3). Walker (1957) suggests that in the case of the
Ohio River this shield is so effective that it even seals
the mobile layer under the floodplain against entry of
the river water. Thus, when considering the resistance of
the stream banks to erosion, we must take into account the
differing silt-clay contents of both the layers, floodplain and mobile. We shall denote these two quantities
by the symbols M_f, for the floodplain layer, and M_m, for
the mobile layer, the values being regarded in each case
as the percentage of silt-clay. We will now investigate
the control of their values.

We saw earlier (pages 71-73) how the deposition Y of
particles of size D is regulated according to the basic
deposition formula $Y_{load} = Q_R.\phi(D/D_c)$. It is in accord
with this relationship that the *critical mobile size*
($D_m = 0.001D_c$) varies directly with the competence D_c, so
that as D/D_c decreases towards the critical value of
approximately $0.001D_c$, so Y_{load}, also decreasing, approaches, and beyond this point assumes, a *zero value*.
The size of the largest silt-clay particles is 0.06 mm
and we can calculate that this measure is also the
critical mobile size (D_m) for a competence of 60 mm.
Consequently M_m, the silt-clay content of the mobile
layer, is of appreciable value only for competences smaller
than about *60 mm*.

Although strictly the Y formula relates only to the
deposition in the channel, it is also relevant in some
degree to the formation of the floodplain layer outside
the channel, where an 'effective competence', smaller and
much less distinct than the channel competence (D_c), must
strongly influence the amount of the different sizes of
'fine' particles deposited in this layer. It is now
generally accepted that this deposition takes place
principally on the shoulders of point bars from fairly
swiftly flowing water, although it is certainly supplemented, if only through infiltration, by subsequent deposition of fine mud from slowly moving or stagnant water

The stream realised

on the floodplain proper. But the Y formula broadly
applies everywhere and we find that, whereas for competences (i.e. channel competences) smaller than this same
value of 60 mm .the floodplain layer consists exclusively
of silt-clay particles, for competences larger than this
the silt-clay content (M_f) of the floodplain layer
gradually diminishes until, probably at about *120 mm*,
corresponding with the onset of braiding (as discussed
later), it falls steadily towards a zero value, copying
the trend of the silt-clay content (M_m) of the mobile
layer at 60 mm.   Other influences are relevant, especially
of course the silt-clay loading (Q_m) without which there
can be no silt-clay deposition, but they cannot normally over-
rule the primary control exercised by the competence.
     Thus we recognise the existence of two critical values
of the competence governing the silt-clay content in sand
stream deposition, one about 60 mm for the mobile layer
and the other about 120 mm for the floodplain layer.   As
each of these values is exceeded, the value of one or
other of the silt-clay contents, M_m and M_f, falls
toward zero, *regardless of the silt-clay loading.*   The
supposed relationships are shown diagrammatically in
Figure 11, the details of which are based on evidence
that will be discussed presently.   It may be observed
that the graph for M_m shows that the silt-clay content of
the mobile layer never falls absolutely to zero, presumably because of the two subordinate processes of subsequent
infiltration of silt-clay into the voids between the sand
grains and also of the limited silt-clay deposition possible locally at low discharges, especially in the minor
channels of braided flow.
     We shall see shortly how these conclusions conform
with the field evidence, including especially the valuable
quantitative relationships established by Schumm (1960,
1963) for streams on the Great Plains of the United
States.
     Meanwhile, we may provisionally accept that the silt-
clay content and therefore also the *cohesion* of any part
of the channel bank of a sand stream is broadly controlled
by the competence (D_c) alone, as dictated in the graded
stream by the sand loading (Q_R).
     However, the bank cohesion is only one of the two
controls of the bank erodibility (E_b). The other (page 99)
is the *erosive force* of the stream in first order time,
as directly expressed by the competence.
     We now have:

     (1) bank cohesion = $\phi(1/D_c)$

(as just demonstrated), and

     (2) erosive force = $\phi(D_c)$.

Now bank erodibility

     $E_b = \phi(\text{erosive force}, 1/\text{bank cohesion})$

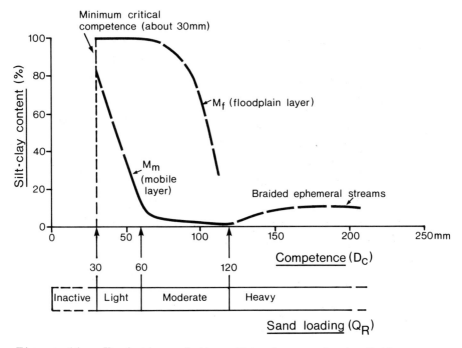

Figure 11. Variation of the silt-clay content of the
    mobile and floodplain layers with the competence and
    sand loading of sand streams.
    Note. The graphs are only diagrammatic.

(by definition). Therefore the bank erodibility

$$E_b = \phi(D_c).$$

For a graded stream, D_c is determined solely by the sand
loading (Q_R). Therefore the bank erodibility

$$E_b = \phi(Q_R).$$

This last expression is the same as the one for gravel
streams, although obtained differently. The separate processes involved for gravel and sand streams are shown diagrammatically in Figure 12.

11.2   The width-depth ratio

The width-depth ratio for the channel of a stream is an
important property which for us possesses the special
merit of being easily perceived and measured. Moreover,
study of it will provide insight into the control of
other properties of sand streams. We have seen (pages 96-
97) that for graded gravel streams the width-depth ratio
is determined by the bank erodibility alone and we shall

103

The stream realised

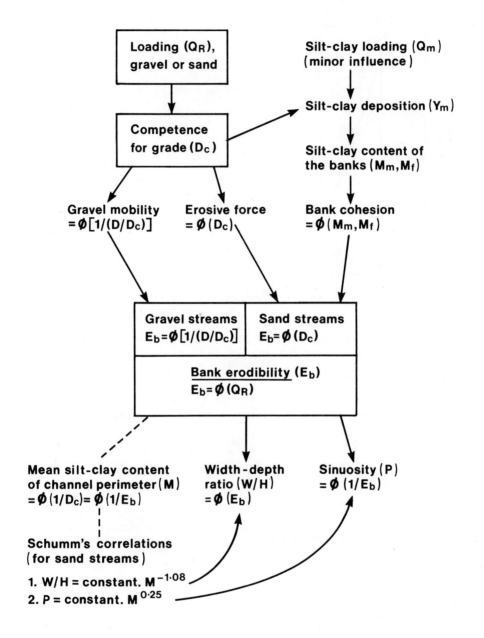

Figure 12.   The control and influence of bank
     erodibility (E_b).

now examine this same argument, rather more closely, for both gravel and sand streams.

In this context, the values of the *width* and the *depth* are those that relate to the bankfull discharge. W is the simple width so indicated and H is the mean depth to the channel bed in the stream centre, that is to say excluding the steep sides of the channel bottom rising to the banks. These definitions usually permit ready assessment from drawings of channel profiles, as well as rough estimate by inspection in the field. They also agree closely with Schumm's definitions (1960, page 18).

The width-depth ratio (W/H) relates to the discharge (Q) in the equation WHV = Q, where V is the velocity of flow. All quantities are the first order characteristics. The range of possible values of V (compare page 51 for a similar argument) is proportionally very limited in comparison with that of the product WH. Thus $\dot{V}$ is no more than a modifying influence and for our argument may be disregarded except as a constant.

Therefore, effectively,

$$WH = constant.Q,$$

whence

$$W/H = constant.W^2/Q.$$

Thus W/H varies directly with the channel width squared per unit discharge, and consequently at any one meander-belt cross-section (where Q is constant) we need only examine the single variable of the *width*, which, by virtue of the power function, is evidently a sensitive index. For these circumstances we can write $W/H = constant.W^2$.

We begin the argument by recognising that the width of the channel represents the balance between the two very different influences which respectively tend to shift laterally one or other of the opposing banks at a bend in the channel. For the retreating *concave* bank, receiving the brunt of the stream's force, the rate of shift is governed by the bank erodibility (E_b); and for the advancing *convex* bank, the rate of shift is governed by the rate of accretion to the point bar that flanks it. It must be appreciated that we are now expressly considering only streams that are *at or near to grade*. For this condition, although the bank erodibility (E_b) - relevant only to the concave bank - is governed directly by the stream's competence (D_c), ultimate control of this property is exercised by the amount of the *ruling loading* (Q_R), of gravel or sand as the case may be. On the other hand, the rate of accretion - relevant only to the convex bank - merely represents maintenance of the alluvium cover (C), which, for a stream at grade, is of a more or less fixed value *regardless of the amount of the ruling loading*. This is because its value is continuously sustained at the value of the cover for grade (C_p), in which little variation is possible, by continuous second-order adjustment to the competence (through the competence-degradation

The stream realised

interaction). Thus, for the stream at or near to grade, the only one of the two balancing influences able to vary appreciably is the one affecting the retreating concave bank, as controlled by the ruling loading (Q_R). Consequently, in the process of bank migration, the only pacemaker is the concave bank, and where it goes, eventually the convex bank passively follows. This it is obliged to do, because the retreat of the concave bank tends to widen and shallow the channel, and thus also to reduce the competence and increase the rate of deposition at the point bar. However, any adjustment required is not brought about at once and if, because of high erodibility, the pacemaking concave bank collapses very easily, then the other bank tends to lag behind and the channel width is permanently greater. Conversely, where the concave bank is only very slowly eroded, the point bar opposite is always at least nearly fully established and the channel is narrower. Thus the immediate control of the width of a graded stream is the erodibility (E_b) of the concave banks, which itself, as we have seen, is determined by the ruling loading (Q_R).

Accordingly, we have, for a given value of the discharge Q and for all graded streams,

$$W = \phi(E_b).$$

It has been shown that

$$W/H = \text{constant}.W^2,$$

and

$$E_b = \phi(D_c) = \phi(Q_R).$$

Whence,

$$W/H = \phi(E_b) = \phi(D_c) = \phi(Q_R).$$

Thus the width-depth ratio of a graded stream (or one nearly at grade - this practical qualification is always important) is determined ultimately by the amount of the ruling loading. In other words, for heavily-loaded streams W/H is relatively large, and for lightly-loaded streams it is relatively small. This is a simple relationship, but we note that it can only be *understood* by consideration of fairly complex interactions, linking both physical and geometrical processes (because competence adjustments require slope adjustments - see page 47) and both the first and second orders of fluvial time.*

The validity of the relationship will be demonstrated presently in reference to actual streams. Meanwhile it will be useful to examine the intermediate link, relevant only to sand streams, between the width-depth ratio (W/H) and the silt-clay content of the banks, as determined primarily by the value of the competence for grade (D_c). We shall see whether our theoretical conclusions conform with one of Schumm's (1960) empirical correlations relevant to them. He showed convincingly (see Figure 13) that, for

*See Postscript, page 192.

many sand streams on the Great Plains in the United States, $W/H = constant.M^{-1.08}$ approximately, where M is the mean percentage of silt-clay in the channel perimeter, calculated according to the usual weighting formula for such a geometrical situation, $M = (W.M_c + 2H.M_b)/(W + 2H)$, where M_c and M_b are the corresponding percentages (silt-clay contents, as previously considered, but to slightly different particle size specifications) for the *channel bed* and the *banks* respectively.

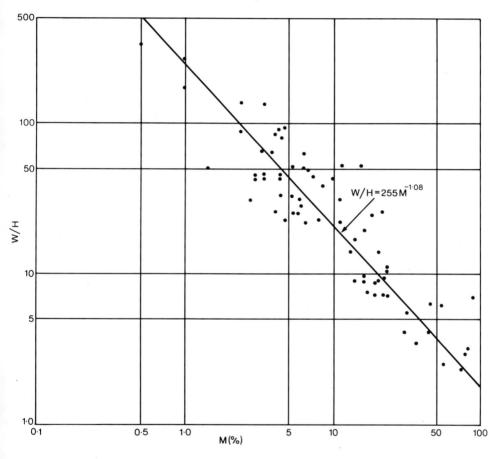

Figure 13. Schumm's correlation between the width-depth ratio (W/H) of the channel and the weighted mean silt-clay content in the channel perimeter (M), as discussed in Section 11.2. After Schumm, 1960, Figure 8.

This may be written in our notation

$$W/H = \phi(1/M) - \phi(1/M_c, \ 1/M_b).$$

Let us now compare these empirical equations with the theoretical equations derived previously. We have

The stream realised

(1) $W/H = \phi(1/M) = \phi(1/M_c,\ 1/M_b)$ (empirical)

(2) $W/H = \phi(E_b) = \phi(D_c) = \phi(Q_R)$ (theoretical)

As demonstrated in Figure 11 and discussed on pages 101-102,

$$M_m = \phi(1/D_c),$$

where M_m is the silt-clay percentage of the mobile layer, and

$$M_f = \phi(1/D_c),$$

where M_f is the silt-clay percentage of the floodplain layer.
    Now $M_c = M_m$, because the channel bed is part of the mobile layer, and M_b = a weighted mean of M_m and M_f (weighted by the thickness of each layer exposed in the channel bank). Whence,

$$M = \phi(M_c,\ M_b)\quad \text{(equation (1) transposed)}$$

$$= \phi(M_f,\ M_m)$$

$$= \phi(1/D_c).$$

The two formulae, empirical and theoretical, are thus seen to be at least consistent with each other. But we can also demonstrate a broad correlation.
    Where D_c is less than 60 mm, M_m is of appreciable value, increasing as D_c decreases, and M_f is 100%. Therefore M is high and we would expect W/H to be low, which it is.
    At the other end of the range, where D_c is greater than about 120 mm, both M_m and M_f are low, and therefore so also are M_c and M_b, and M. We would therefore expect W/H to be high, which it is.
    In between, where D_c increases from 60 mm to 120 mm, M_m is low throughout and decreasing, and M_f first decreases slightly and then falls steeply towards zero. Thus M decreases in value across the range, but it is important to note that the rate of decrease is governed by the independent reaction of M with W/H caused by the weighting formula already quoted (page 107). For example, low W/H gives extra weight to M_b in the formula, and thus boosts M where D_c is small. Consequently there is a tendency for values of M to decrease *regularly* across a wide proportional range as D_c increases from 60 mm to 120 mm, so procuring the regular decrease in the M values which Schumm records across the whole range of his measurements, as shown in Figure 13.
    Thus we have an understanding of Schumm's correlation and at the same time a confirmation of the validity of our approach. We can build on this, because Schumm (1963) also demonstrated that this same quantity M relates to the channel sinuosity (P) in a corresponding formula $P = \text{constant}.M^{0.25}$. This suggests a link between the sinuosity

and the bank erodibility (E_b), as will be investigated later (page 117).

11.3 A review of graded sand streams

The agreement just demonstrated between theoretical and empirical formulae for the width-depth ratio W/H of graded sand streams simply corroborates our earlier conclusion (page 106) that the value of this ratio is governed ultimately and exclusively by the sand loading (Q_R), as fully expressed in the simple statement $W/H = \phi(E_b) = \phi(D_c) = \phi(Q_R)$. Thus the sand loading (Q_R) *alone* is the arbiter of the principal characteristics of the first order equilibrium and must provide a sound basis for a systematic review of graded sand streams in general. Clearly, for this purpose we may repeat the kind of procedure already applied to gravel streams, of systematically traversing the complete range of all possible *sand loadings* (Q_R), from heavy to light. Again we shall discover criteria for distinguishing three similarly titled classes, which are (as indicated in Table 3, page 121) the heavily-loaded, the moderately-loaded and the lightly-loaded sand streams.

11.3.1 Heavily-loaded sand streams

The heaviest sand loadings are found in steep ephemeral streams in semi-arid regions, where large quantities of sand may be transported during brief and infrequent flash flows. In such streams these events are the normal expressions of first order behaviour and their logical outcome is the establishment, if the general attitude of the landscape permits it, of steep valley slopes adjusted to provide the large competences needed to maintain grade. The word grade is used advisedly. Although no settled equilibria are possible, for either the first order steady state or the second order grade, nonetheless the values of all first order properties, including that of the competence, will fall within ranges narrow enough to demonstrate the statistical validity of such equilibria, despite frequent considerable departures from the mean value. Thus we have no difficulty in recognising with certainty the salient characteristic properties, such as the very large competence (maybe exceeding 300 mm, as discussed presently), the high bank erodibility, high width-depth ratios (probably exceeding 100 at all discharges), braiding and other consequences of high mobility.

The properties of ephemeral streams will be further considered in the next chapter, where we shall see that they frequently belong to the generally uncommon 'transitional regime', for which both gravel and sand particles are evenly represented in the deposition. For them obviously the competences for grade may be very large indeed, as governed primarily by the gravel sizes. But we are now considering streams distinguished by a general lack of gravel particles and for these it is only the amount of the sand loading that maintains the large competences.

The stream realised

The values of these competences may be assessed very approximately by gauging the critical mobile size (D_m), which, as the smallest common size in the mobile layer, we know to be approximately $0.001D_c$, where D_c is the competence. Leopold and Miller (1956) published particle size distribution figures for the beds of ephemeral streams in New Mexico, which indicate that this size is often as large as 0.25 mm, suggesting competences of about 250 mm, a measure consistent with the occurrence of cobbles in the 64-128 mm size range, though not necessarily the largest sizes transportable. The modal size of the sand deposited ('sand' as defined in the qualitative sense discussed on page 58) is about 1.0 mm, understandably a coarse size, although as close to the critical mobile size, 0.25 mm, as it would be reasonable to expect. Exceptions to these conditions are however not uncommon, as already mentioned, because of local deposition of silt-clay in minor secondary channels. But characteristically the sand is very coarse, as I can certainly confirm from my own observations in semi-arid areas in both Namibia and Western Australia.

Typical of sand streams possessing a rather less heavy sand loading is the former Platte River in Nebraska (before human intervention changed its equilibrium), fancied to be 'a mile wide and a foot deep'. The properties of this stream are essentially the same as those of the ephemeral streams just discussed, though more regular because of the perennial flow. The braided condition is conspicuous, apparent both in the formation of anabranches and the complex tracery of the minor threads of flow seen at low water, ceaselessly shifting sand.

11.3.2   Moderately-loaded sand streams

The smaller competences for grade required by moderate sand loadings provide a reduced bank erodibility no longer able to maintain braided flow. As already recognised for gravel streams, effective erosive power is now restricted to a single major thread of flow which, as it shifts its position sideways and downwards, captures every other flow and establishes a well-defined single channel for itself.

However, the competence may still be large enough to ensure at least a fairly high mobility, as may be seen in the Mississippi River downstream of the Ohio River entry. Concave banks retreat readily and the point bars, necessarily (though tardily) advancing in pace with them, are conspicuous in their fresh aspect, free of soil or vegetation cover.

The bedforms display a considerable variety of styles, mostly of ephemeral origin, as we would expect where the competence ratio of the particles of alluvium is so small. Shapes are determined by the fleeting conditions of the hour at the particular location in the channel, as determined by the temporary and local values of both the 'competence' and the 'loading'. But the *ranges* of these values are the expressions of their first order values and vary within the appropriate limits. For example, where

the first order sand loading is heavy and the resultant
competence (D_c) is large, the widest possible choice of
bedforms is offered, including the plane beds and anti-
dunes of the so-called 'upper regime'; conversely, lightly-
loaded sand streams of small competence are permanently
restricted at all times to the ripples and dunes of the
'lower regime'. At low water there is the same choice of
bedforms for all streams, with universal low mobility of
the bed. There is then a tendency for the much reduced
flow to concentrate into a well-defined and relatively
stable 'thalweg channel' of small width-depth ratio, which
may become (if the first order loading is not too heavy)
an established, miniature 'lightly-loaded stream', meandering inside the high-water channel, but, of course, only
pursuing its separate existence at low water.

The alternating processes of *cut and fill* at a cross-
section of the channel are the same as for gravel streams.
The scour holes excavated in meander bends at times of
high water are refilled with sand at times of low water,
and at the intervening bars the reverse process takes
place. The *net* discharge of sand along the channel is
directly expressed by the sand loading, which, as we have
seen is continuously able to regulate the unequal amounts
transposed in the separate actions of cut and fill, through
its control of the competence for grade. Also we should
note that the characteristic riffles of moderately-loaded
gravel streams cannot form because of the low competence
ratios of the sand particles, although the rigidity of the
riffle bars may be reproduced in some degree in the more
lightly-loaded sand streams, in the cohesion of the bar
surfaces resulting from a slight silt-clay content in the
deposition.

The competences of such streams probably range between
the two critical values of approximately 60 mm and 120 mm
discussed earlier. Within this range (see Figure 11 above)
there is virtually no silt-clay in the channel bed (the
mobile layer) and virtually nothing else but silt-clay in
the upper bank (the floodplain layer). As discussed
earlier, the value of M, Schumm's weighted mean silt-clay
content for the channel perimeter, is moderate but decreasing as the competence (D_c) increases. Thus values of W/H
are moderate but increasing with the competence, varying
say between 10 and 100.

The competence may be gauged both from assessment of
the critical mobile size (D_m) as indicated by quotations
of particle size distribution and also from study of
records of the basal lag and immovable layers, the formation of which the smaller competences naturally facilitate.
Fisk's (1944) cross-sections of the Lower Mississippi
meander-belt, as drawn from borehole information, locally
show these characteristically closely-packed basal gravels
lying, appropriately for a channel of depth generally 20
to 25 m, at a fairly steady 40 m below the floodplain
surface, as often as not resting on a floor of the same
alluvial material previously deposited under a different
regime. The largest particles commonly recorded in the
overlying mobile layer of gravelly sand are 1 inch (25 mm)
(see especially Fisk's Plate 6B, showing a section

south-west of Memphis), from which we conclude that the competence of the Mississippi here may be rather less than 100 mm (from $D_1 = 0.3D_c$). This value, however, is not universal, because channel steepening at meander-neck cut-offs may raise the competence to at least 200 mm and intro-duce $2\frac{1}{2}$ inch (say 65 mm) cobbles freely into the mobile layer. But Carey (1969), over a long acquaintance with the channel, only twice ever saw 4 inch (100 mm) cobbles and then only where the circumstances were exceptional.

Nordin and Beverage (1965) provide particle size distributions for the bed material of the Rio Grande in New Mexico, downstream of Bernalillo, which suggest a critical mobile size (D_m) of about 0.1 mm. This stream is well known to carry a very heavy silt-clay loading (Lane (1940) quotes a concentration of no less than 21% by weight at San Marcial) and yet rarely is there record of signifi-cant silt-clay content in the channel bed. The largest particles frequently belonged to the 16-32 mm size range and in one sample to the 32-64 mm range. We might assess the competence here also at 100 mm, suggesting that the sand loading is not particularly heavy, as already recog-nised by Lane and Borland (1954) from study of the rate of deposition of sand downstream in the Elephant Butte Reservoir. Appropriately the stream keeps to a single channel and its width-depth ratio is of the order of 100.

Further mention is here required of the sand streams of tropical West Africa discussed earlier. On pages 28-30 and 38-39 my records of the Nafayi River in Sierra Leone were used to demonstrate the properties of a complete alluvium profile. These together indicated a competence value of about 80 mm, higher than for most of the streams in the region because of a rather heavier gravel loading, and indeed the Nafayi should be classed a transitional

Plate 6. Heavily-loaded transitional stream deposition seen in cliffs of aggradational New Red Sandstone behind Oddicombe Beach, Torquay, Devon. The wooden rule in the photograph is 100 mm long. Although the stream flow had evidently been strong enough to trans-port the limestone cobbles as mobile particles, it could not prevent plentiful deposition of sand along with the gravel, signifying a very heavy sand loading. The result is a typical transitional bimodal particle size distribution.
The segregation of the cobbles into bunches suggests that their competence ratio (D/D_c) had been fairly high, although, because of their mobile status, less than the critical lag ratio (D_1/D_c) of 0.3. From this we may infer, assuming the size of the largest of the cobbles to be 150 mm (intermediate diameter), that the competence (D_c) of the stream had been of the order of 600 mm. In relation to this high value, it is under-standable that the sand and finer gravel particles are evenly mixed, because their travel velocities (U), governed by their competence ratios (D/D_c), must have been almost equally rapid.

stream. The common range of competences was 50-80 mm.

It will be understood that all these estimates of
competence are very approximate, mainly because of the
paucity of the quantitative evidence on which they are
based. Their principal significance lies in the relative
magnitude of the values one to another, together with the
understanding that they represent determinate absolute
values which undoubtedly are capable of much more accurate
measurement.

11.3.3   Lightly-loaded sand streams

Lightly-loaded sand streams require small competences for
the maintence of grade, and the result is low bank erodibility. These are the products of well-watered gravel-
free areas of generally low topographical relief, where
the gentle slopes restrain the generation of alluvium
(low 'accessibility') and ensure that the run-off is discharged in perennial streams. This latter circumstance
and the small width-depth ratio of the single channel
together result in the permanent drowning of the narrow
channel bed beneath deep water; at the same time the low
bank erodibility and the slow lateral shift of the channel
allow the establishment of thick vegetation to the water's
edge at both banks. The situation is identical with that
of the lightly-loaded gravel stream, whose aspect we
described as that of a featureless canal. It may even
happen that there is absolutely no visible sign of bed
alluvium by which to tell whether we are looking at a
gravel or a sand stream.

The competences producing these characteristics must be
smaller than about 60 mm, below which value we have recognised that appreciable silt-clay deposition commences in
the channel. The floodplain layer already consists almost
entirely of silt-clay and the combined erodibility is so
low that the W/H ratios may be as little as 5 and under,
as certain of Schumm's (1960) examples show, with corresponding values of M, the mean silt-clay content of the
channel perimeter, as high as 80%. Schumm's records also
show clearly, especially those for the Smoky Hill-Kansas
River stream (1960, page 25 and related diagram), how both
the higher M values and the lower W/H values correspond
with marked flattenings of the stream slope, signifying
the decreases in competence which are the immediate causes
of these trends.

Now we can examine more fully the concept of the
critical minimum competence of the normally evolving sand
stream as it slowly lowers its floor and decreases its
slope in the continued process of third order degradation
at grade. Very weak streams cannot erode very muddy
channel beds and so at last the evolutionary process has
to stop. Of course there are abnormal situations in which
the competence may be independently established at a very
low value indeed, the best known of which are the backwater
stretches of streams just before they reach a fixed base-
level such as the surface of the sea, although here the
tides introduce other controls. An example of another

kind is the nearly flat Illinois River (Rubey, 1952), which is the almost completely unloaded overflow channel of Lake Michigan. These *inactive streams*, possessing *sub-critical competences*, do not however belong to the normal evolutionary process, which is the main concern of this study.

The critical situation can best be examined at the very head of streams rising on topographic plains (see Figure 30, below, page 177) and eventually, by reason of geometry, no longer able to maintain active headward erosion. Here, after the bulk of the eroded sand and gravel has disappeared downstream, is a situation in which virtually no further supply of these materials is available (as discussed more fully later on pages 176 and 184-185). Slow degradation continues for a time, but stops when the competence reaches the critical minimum value. Eventually the channel is filled in by encroaching hillside deposits, supported by vegetation, which the weakened stream flow is powerless to remove. In West Africa (Sierra Leone and Guinea) I have seen pits dug into such ill-defined source areas and have noted the preservation by burial of complete alluvium profiles resting on soft floors, testifying not only to the prior existence of channelled flow but also to the actual value of the critical minimum competence reached.

The characteristic alluvium profile is shown on the left hand side of the first diagram of Figure 14. A notable feature is the absence of any gravel particles at all except in the deeply buried, very thin basal gravel, combination of the lag and immovable layers. Its detrital origin was always beyond doubt in my experience, because of the occurrence of worn pebbles and heavy minerals similar to those seen in the residual accumulations at the surface. Silt-clay is the principal constituent, mixed with some sand in the mobile layer. The critical lag size (D_1), indicated by the smallest size of pebble in the basal gravel, is both small and distinct, probably around 10 mm, although I have never specifically measured it. However, I can be more sure about the penultimate condition frequently preserved in terrace deposits a short way downstream, rather more distinctly preserved moreover because of the presence of slightly greater quantities of sand and gravel, the latter showing minimum sizes of between 10 and 15 mm. From all the evidence I suggest that a reasonable estimate of the critical minimum competence is about 30 mm, consistent with a critical lag size (D_1) of about 10 mm ($0.3D_c$). The true value may vary somewhat because of the modifying influence of the variable silt-clay loading, but this is only speculation, and in any case the measure of 30 mm can be considered a fair approximation of the mean of the range as a whole.

11.3.4   Variations in the alluvium profile of sand streams

To complete our study of the alluvium profile of sand streams we need to consider the *profile height*, which is the difference in elevation between the floodplain surface

The stream realised

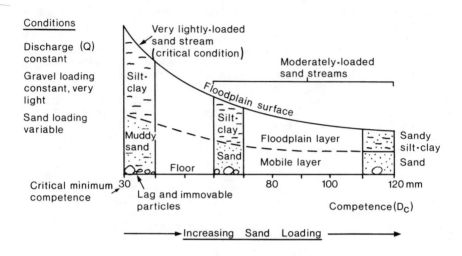

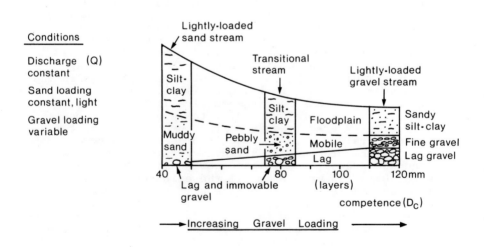

Figure 14.   Alluvium profiles of sand streams for varying
             conditions.

and the floor.

The profile height (H') must vary directly with the channel depth (H), and we know (pages 105-106) that H is governed by two formulae:

WH = constant.Q, approximately,

and

$$W/H = \phi(E_b) = \phi(D_c) = \phi(Q_R).$$

From these we have

$$H = \phi(Q, 1/E_b),$$

and therefore also

$$H' = \phi(Q, 1/E_b).$$

Thus, for a constant value of the discharge (Q)

$$H' = \phi(1/E_b) = \phi(1/D_c) = \phi(1/Q_R).$$

This relationship, combined with the others we have established, enables us now to construct the alluvium profiles of sand streams for all possible variations in both the sand and the gravel loadings. Examples for certain ranges of each of these quantities are illustrated in the two diagrams of Figure 14. This completes our review of sand streams, leaving only the very significant property of the channel sinuosity to be examined in the next two sections.

11.4   Channel sinuosity

Channel sinuosity (P), defined by Schumm (1963) as the ratio of the channel length to the valley length, can vary between a value of 1.0 for a straight channel up to one of 2.5 and over for a very sinuous one. The property is of special interest because it is a first order characteristic which can exceptionally change its value in first order time (i.e. without change in the elevation of the floor) and cause fundamental disturbance to the first order equilibrium. This happening is examined in the next section under the heading of 'stream metamorphosis'.

The key to an understanding of the control of sinuosity is Schumm's (1963) empirical correlation $P = constant.M^{0.25}$, as established for unconstrained sand streams in the Great Plains and later confirmed by other evidence. The quantity M is the same weighted mean silt-clay content that we considered on page 107, recognising it as a fairly accurate index (inverse) of the erodibility (E_b) of the channel banks, and with it the competence (D_c) and the sand loading (Q_R).

So, apparently,

$$P = \phi(1/E_b) = \phi(1/D_c) = \phi(1/Q_R).$$

The stream realised

We will consider first a fairly heavy sand loading (Q_R), for which the competence (D_C) is correspondingly large. The stream is braided, or near to it, and the banks are everywhere unstable. This means that long *strips* of the banks are being eroded at any one time, resulting in such rapid downstream shift of any nascent meanders that they never have opportunity to develop laterally. Here P is always low, never removed far from unity (see Figure 15 for a summary of conclusions).

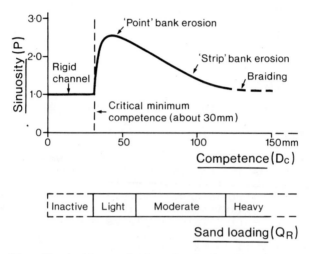

Figure 15. Variation of the channel sinuosity (P) with the competence (D_C) and the sand loading (Q_R) in sand streams.
Note. The graph is only diagrammatic.*

Next we turn to a light sand loading (Q_R), for which the competence (D_C) is small. The bank erodibility is now low, in fact so low that effective erosion can only take place, even at high discharge, at rare *points* distributed along the banks, located at the sharpest bends in the single channel. The process of the development of the meanders as a result of this circumstance has been described by Hickin (1974) for the 500 km long Beaton River in British Columbia, Canada, from an analysis of ridge and swale patterns which show how the paths traced by the roving points of fastest erosion possess components of direction that are significantly lateral to the valley axis. The process begins slowly, whilst the radius of curvature of the channel is still relatively large and the rate of erosion small. Eventually, however, the radius locally decreases beyond a critical value, r_m, for which $r_m/w = 2.1$ (where w is the channel width), and then, as a result of a sudden change in the flow characteristics which we need not consider, the local erodibility increases greatly, permitting local accelerated bank retreat. The existence of this critical value was first recognised by

*See Postscript, page 192.

Leopold et al. (1960). Henceforward, the effective erosion
is entirely concentrated at these few *points* of relatively
great instability, whose wanderings *along* the stream's
concave banks generate the fluent curves characteristic of
streams of high sinuosity.

Finally, we consider the abnormal 'inactive streams'
which flow at competences smaller than the critical minimum
competence, whose value we have assessed at about 30 mm
(page 115). Such weak flows are not possible in streams
that have evolved normally by third order degradation, but
can only be the result of independent events, as in the
cases (already mentioned) of the Illinois River, overflow
of Lake Michigan, and the lowest 300 km of the Mississippi
River where the slope is reduced by the backwater effect.
The banks of these streams are virtually inerodible and
there is no possibility of the development of meanders.
P is always near to unity, unless a greater value has been
inherited from a time when the conditions were different
in some way. We may also conclude that their other channel
properties, such as the width-depth ratio and the constitution of the alluvium profile beneath the floodplain, are
also not genetically related to the existing passive
hydraulic circumstances.

These conclusions on sinuosity are partially confirmed
by Schumm and Khan's (1972) experiments, in which many of
the loading-competence associations discussed in the
present work were reproduced by adjustment of the alluvium
feed (the load) and the 'valley slope' to permit the
establishment of grade. Regrettably however, the tests
may not have been run over long enough periods for the
channel to attain the much greater sinuosity values (P)
which the photographs suggest might have been eventually
reached, the maximum value recorded being only 1.26. I
also believe that the assignment of the so-called 'meandering thalweg channel' to the status which this title implies
may not be justified, in that the wholly submerged trough
which was so identified may be equally well regarded as
the normal and complete channel of a stream flowing at a
discharge continuously exceeding the bankfull discharge,
whilst the experiment's intended channel provided the
flooded floodplain. This interpretation is consistent
with that advanced by the authors for the subsequent
'suspended-sediment tests', in which the alluvium feed
contained 3% of 'suspended sediment' and the same trough
could accommodate all the water. This suggests, as further
discussed on page 175, that the previous submergence had
been the consequence of the *complete lack* of *fine* particles
(silt-clay alone in this situation) essential for the
deposition of a floodplain layer (see also pages 35 and
36). These tests were all very relevant and if they could
be repeated over much longer periods of time could perhaps
reproduce, with the appropriate controls, the highly
sinuous channels seen in nature.

Meanwhile we have enough data to show the broad
relationships, which are illustrated in Figure 15.

11.5   Stream metamorphosis

We now come to the special influence the sinuosity (P) exercises over a stream's first order equilibrium, deriving from its simple control of the channel slope (S_c) through the geometrical association $S_c = S_V/P$, where S_V is the familiar valley slope, the first order control, invariable in first order time. We have recognised that P may vary between unity and more than 2.5 and consequently must expect the same wide proportional range in the values of S_c.

Schumm and Lichty (1963) described the dramatic effects of sudden changes of these values, from one end of each range to the other, in the Cimarron River of Kansas, because of which the stream assumed a fundamentally different first order equilibrium. The *metamorphosis*, as Schumm (1969) styled it, even caused such considerable change in the sand loading (Q_R) as we normally associate with the passage of a nickpoint, and in fact the two kinds of disturbance have much in common. But the important distinction of the metamorphosis is that there is no change whatever in the valley slope (S_V). The authors cited other examples of this phenomenon, also on the Great Plains and observed by other writers, showing that it is by no means exceptional, and more recently Burkham (1972) has described an almost identical chain of events in a stream in Arizona.

The history of the Cimarron River metamorphosis is briefly as follows. In the zone of interest in south-west Kansas, the stream is about 250 km long. In 1902 it was described as a 'meandering, looping stream of uniform width, clear and deep', perennial and about 15 metres wide, the image being that of a very sinuous, lightly-loaded sand stream. In 1914 the greatest flood on record changed it abruptly into a braided stream which in 1939 registered a channel width of over 360 metres, from which details we recognise a straight, heavily-loaded sand stream. Since then the width decreased to 170 metres, as measured in 1954, possibly presaging a gradual return to the original meandering condition. Undoubtedly meteorological and vegetational changes have influenced the events, but as there has been no question of change in the climate or other aspect of the basin environment comparable in intensity with the observed change in the behaviour of the stream, we need to look for primary explanation to the functioning of the stream itself. In fact the process can be well understood in the light of the present theory.

During the great flood of 1914, the water flowed straight down the whole width of the valley bottom, initially very lightly-loaded and therefore the better able to erode. The temporary and absolutely exceptional 'competence' of the steep flow would have been so large that the old floodplain surface, evidently sparsely protected by vegetation, suddenly became highly erodible and the resultant widespread erosion both destroyed the old meander pattern and generally exposed the less cohesive alluvium concealed beneath the floodplain surface. There could be no immediate return to the old style of flow and

Table 3. Properties of the three classes of
graded sand stream (and of the inactive streams).

Property	Sand loading (amount) (Q_R)			Inactive streams
	Heavy	Moderate	Light	
Competence (D_c) (approx.)	>120 mm	60-120 mm	30-60 mm	<30 mm (subcritical)
Channel form	Braided	Single channel	Single channel	Rigid single channel
Silt-clay contents: - mobile layer (M_m) - floodplain layer (M_f)	<10% (Low)	<10% Variable, high	Variable, high 100%	High 100%
*Width-depth ratio (W/H) (approx. ranges)	High (>100)	Medium (10-100)	Low (<10)	Low
Sinuosity (P)	Straight (braided)	Moderate	High	Very low
Critical features	Braiding and high mobility	Single channel, with conspicuous, new-formed bed features.	Narrow, deep single channel. Absence of visible bed features.	Straight channel, whose form has not changed since establishment of the inactive stream.

after the flood had subsided the new stream continued to
flow straight down the valley. Because of the steepened
channel slope, the competence was now larger. This
initiated degradation along the course, which at once
supplied the substantially heavier sand loading needed to
re-establish grade, which could henceforward be maintained
by a suitably accelerated third order degradation. The
channel remained appropriately very wide until a chance
spell of several years of continuously restrained meteorological conditions and temporarily reduced discharge
encouraged the building of a new floodplain (as described
by Schumm and Lichty) and provided the reduced bank
erodibility (E_b) needed to induce the channel to become a
little narrower (W/H = $\phi(E_b)$).

Hereafter we have to follow the process into the
future, assuming no recurrence of the great flood. The
new, narrower channel begins to meander slightly, marking
the start of a gradual reverse metamorphosis. Increasing
sinuosity means decreasing channel slope, causing decreasing competence and a tendency for aggradation, at once

*See Postscript, page 192.

countered by third order decrease in the loading. Because
of this the channel continues to narrow, giving more space
for the increase in sinuosity demanded by the decrease in
competence and decrease in the channel slope. The lower
bank erodibility prescribes 'point erosion' of the banks,
which is the necessary inducement for the increase in
sinuosity. Every action tends to maintain the momentum
of the process of change in one direction, which, if undisturbed, continues until the reappearance of the sinuous,
narrow, lightly-loaded sand stream. Sooner or later,
however, all will be suddenly reversed by another great
flood.

Almost certainly this cyclic alternation of streams of
high and low sinuosity is a phenomenon only possible in
fairly arid, or maybe glacial, climates unable to provide
the vegetation cover needed on the floodplains to withstand
the rare but inevitable great floods, for there seems to be
no record of such events in streams of comparable size in
either humid-temperate or humid-tropical regions. On the
other hand, meandering streams in these regions do sometimes show evidence of their prior existence as straight
braided streams when the climate had been different.
Examples are the Lower Mississippi, well know to have been
braided during the last glaciation, and the Murrumbidgee
River in New South Wales, whose interesting history has
been pieced together by Schumm (1968). In these cases,
however, we need to recognise that the final and evidently
irreversible change to a meandering stream was not necessarily immediately caused by the change to a more humid
climate, whose effect rather had been to convert a phase
of cyclic alternation of meandering and braided flow into a
phase of exclusively meandering flow.

It is interesting that a given basin environment is
not always disposed to produce only one kind of stream.
As is not uncommon in nature, one set of data may admit of
two possible solutions.

11.6   A classification of sand streams

Having now recognised the amount of the sand loading (Q_R)
as the undoubted single primary control of all the major
properties of graded sand streams, we can confidently
adopt a scheme of classification of sand streams based
upon the three-fold division of the whole range of possible
values of this variable already followed in the 'review'
of Section 11.3 (page 109). As with gravel streams, which
were similarly classified, the criteria identifying the
three classes of heavily, moderately and lightly-loaded
sand streams are generally distinctive, as shown in Table
3, logically linked, as has been shown, to the two critical
competence values of approximately 60 mm and 120 mm
illustrated in Figure 11.

The table also includes reference to the abnormal class
of the 'inactive streams', whose competences are smaller
than the critical minimum value of about 30 mm. We have
noted that these streams are not formed in the course of
normal stream evolution through third order degradation,
but are the products of independent circumstances.

Chapter 12

THE CHANNEL PROPERTIES OF TRANSITIONAL
STREAMS

As the title implies, a transitional stream is a cross
between a gravel and a sand stream, recognised by the presence of roughly equal amounts of gravel and sand particles
in the deposition.

However, an even mixture of the ingredients is rarely
seen in close view, because the tendency for polarisation
into either mainly gravel deposition or mainly sand deposition (as discussed on pages 61-62) persists locally.
Folk and Ward (1957) described an example of this phenomenon in a bar on the Brazos River of Texas, observing
that usually the sediment contained either no gravel at
all or about 60% gravel, and that regardless of the proportions of gravel and sand the principal modes were nearly
constant at either 8 mm or 0.25 mm. This clear evidence
of either one or the other of the two populations of alluvium particles persistently dominating the deposition demonstrates in miniature the contrast between gravel and sand
regimes. Where the temporary and local values of the
'competence' are low, the current transports and deposits
only the sand and very fine gravel, and there, because the
supply of sand is so much heavier than that of fine gravel,
the resultant deposition is nearly all sand. Conversely,
where the temporary and local values of the 'competence'
are high, the sand and very fine gravel do not settle
(except as filling between the coarse gravel particles)
and the resultant deposition is nearly all the coarser
gravel.

The polarisation is very marked where the evenly-
matched (though not equal, as emphasised on pages 60-61) gravel
and sand loadings are not too heavy, implying that the
competence for grade is small enough to permit the formation of a well-defined lag layer. In this situation the
whole possible range of mobile sizes, from $0.001D_c$ (the
critical mobile size) to $0.3D_c$ (the critical lag size) is
fairly evenly represented in the mobile layer and there is
maximum disproportion between limiting values of the
competence ratios (D/D_c), i.e. between 0.001 and 0.3. An
example is the Nafayi River (pages 28-30), where, as
appropriate for the small competence of 80 mm, the mobile
layer contains a considerable quantity of slowly-travelling
pebbles of size just smaller than 25 mm, the critical lag
size. These pebbles are scarcely ever other than in an
inert state and consequently tend to segregate, *within* the
mobile layer, into 'residual' bands and clumps of almost
pure gravel deposition. But the bulk of the loading is
sand of size smaller than 1 mm (we can disregard the minor
mode of 2-4 mm sizes prominent in the deposition), which,
being constantly picked up and dropped by modest currents,

separately segregates into fluent spreads of almost pure sand deposition. The aspect of the mixture of incompatibles, like streaky bacon, is illustrated in Figure 3 (page 32).

However, there are also the very heavily-loaded transitional streams, always ephemeral and already briefly mentioned when we were considering the class of heavily-loaded sand streams (page 109), both styles being typical of steep landscapes in semi-arid regions. Here the sand loadings are so very heavy that, despite accompanying gravel loadings which alone are heavy enough to require large competences for grade, there is as much sand as gravel in the deposition. Often, especially in larger streams carrying alluvium mostly drawn from some distance upstream, the competence is much larger than the size of even the largest gravel particles travelling, so that the range of values of the competence ratio (D/D_c) is restricted to from 0.001 (the critical mobile size) up to say only 0.03, which is significantly far removed from unity. This means that all the alluvium is highly mobile, both sand and gravel, and the resulting deposition, of a limited range of sizes, is seen mostly as an even mixture of sizes, rarely showing any marked polarisation. Streams of this kind occur in granitic regions supplying fairly durable fine gravels of granite debris, the common particle sizes in the deposition ranging between about 0.5 mm and 15 mm (conforming with the limiting D/D_c values just quoted). A striking example with which I was once closely familiar is the Omaruru River in Namibia, an ephemeral stream 200 km long, which, every once in a while, flows steeply (at about 6 m/km) across the down-warped continental margin through the Namib Desert to the sea, some 70 km north of Swakopmund: I have noted almost identical circumstances along the continental margin in Western Australia.

Frequently also, especially near the gravel sources, the gravel feed to the very heavily-loaded streams is of very coarse size, and then the whole possible range of mobile sizes up to, or at least near to, $0.3D_c$, the critical lag size, may be evenly represented in the channel deposition. Then of course polarisation into bands of either very coarse gravel alone or the mixed fine gravel and sand just discussed may be very evident, features which are particularly well displayed in New Red Sandstone breccias (Plate 6, page 112).

As already recognised (page 109), the first and second order equilibria of such streams are never distinctly established except as statistical mean states and it must be open to question whether a true, continuous lag layer is ever physically established; nonetheless the approximate critical values of D/D_c as distinctly recognisable in the other classes of stream must still broadly apply and we can assess quantitative data accordingly. Leopold and Miller provide such data in the paper already quoted (1956), an example being the third-order (in reference to the hierarchy of stream size) Arroyo Caliente in New Mexico. The size distribution for the sample discussed on page 110 shows that the finest 33% of the alluvium all fell within the 0.5-1.0 mm size range (i.e. with none finer than 0.5 mm) and the coarsest 4% within the 128-256 mm range. This suggests a critical mobile size of say about 0.6 mm and a competence of 600 mm. The gravel mode, not marked, lay in the 32-64 mm size range, the comparatively low competence ratios of which (about 0.05-0.10) causing a general even mixing of sand and gravel within the channel deposition.

In other respects the properties of transitional streams are mostly simple blends of those of gravel and sand streams. Often, of course, the properties are the same for both regimes, braiding, for example, being common to all heavily-loaded streams, and we have noted that it can be difficult to differentiate lightly-loaded gravel and sand streams at first sight because in both of them the alluvium is not visible beneath the deep water of the channel. But even though there are other properties, especially such as relate to bed forms, which are characteristic of only one or other of the two regimes, nonetheless it is sometimes possible for them *both* to be exhibited at the same time in a transitional stream. For example, in the Arroyo de los Frijoles in New Mexico, an ephemeral, heavily-loaded transitional stream, Leopold et al. (1964, page 209) recognised fairly permanent surface accumulations of coarse gravel deposited periodically along the channel 'strikingly reminiscent of the occurrence of pools and riffles in perennial gravel streams'. We may suppose that they were formed in just the same way as the riffles of gravel streams, the large particles having been thrown up by vortical action out of scour holes sited just upstream of the occurrences at time of high flood, where they remained stranded until able to slip out of sight when eventually undercut by erosion. The significant difference from the process in gravel streams is the simultaneous smothering of the distinctive gravel stream bedforms by the large sand component of the deposition, so producing distinctive hybrid features.

Thus the behaviour of transitional streams does not seem to merit close separate treatment, and in any case we note that transitional streams are uncommon in comparison with gravel or sand streams. For these reasons we will not further classify them, although this could be done (as with the gravel and sand streams) on the basis of variations in the 'ruling loading', which is here the combination of the separate gravel and sand loadings.

Part IV

ASPECTS OF STREAM EVOLUTION

Chapter 13

THE LONGITUDINAL PROFILE OF EQUILIBRIUM

Until now we have been considering the properties of
streams as restricted to individual points on the stream,
or more exactly - according with our first order concep-
tion - to floodplain-belt cross-sections. Henceforward we
shall investigate these same and other properties as they
vary continuously *along* the stream. The most significant
expression of this new perception is the *longitudinal
profile*, which, unless indicated to the contrary, we shall
regard. as the profile of the *floor-plane* along the floodplain-belt.
    We have seen that the sense (up or down) and the speed
of displacement of the floor-plane at any one cross-
section both depend directly on the mutual relationships
of (1) the loading (Q_R), which determines the competence
for grade, (2) the actual competence (D_C), which may or
may not be the same as the competence for grade, and
(3) the floor erodibility, which, in a degrading stream,
is the immediate arbiter of the very possibility of change.
Ultimate control is vested in the combined properties of
the basin environment as a whole, and we saw from the
example of the 'synthesised' stream (illustrated in Figure
10) how a rudimentary knowledge of these properties enables
us to assess all the quantities just mentioned. From the
same kind of information we shall now investigate how the
system reacts *along* the stream, in both the short and the
long term.
    This extra dimension of length along the stream and
the capricious nature of change in the physical environment
in this same sense together introduce new complexity into
our enquiry and obviously we can consider only very
generally the different situations possible. On this
condition the situations resolve first into the *normal
profile of equilibrium*, and then into the only two marked
deviations from it, which are the mutually opposing forms
of the *nickpoint* and the *regime break point*.
    Little need be said about the *normal profile of
equilibrium*. It is the ideal, regular shape conceived by
W.M. Davis, to which all longitudinal profiles ultimately
tend, but which few attain, because the processes of
evolution may be so hindered by obstacles that they are
unable to complete their work before the whole system is
upset by some 'independent disturbance'. The shape of
this normal profile is the concave-upwards curve, whose
radius of curvature decreases upstream, and the explanation

for it lies in consideration of the combined normal
tendencies of (1) downstream *increase* in the discharge (Q)
and (2) downstream *decrease* in the size and amount of the
loading (Q_R), as caused by wastage of the alluvium into
progressively smaller and fewer particles in the effective
gravel and sand size ranges. As a result of the downstream decrease in loading (Q_R), the competence (D_C) of
graded streams also tends to diminish downstream, which,
considered in relation to the corresponding downstream
increase in discharge (Q), on two counts ensures that the
valley slope (S_V) tends to decrease downstream. Of course
there is always distortion of the normal profile below the
entry of any major tributary whose loading is different
from that of the main stream, but this merely demonstrates
a compromise between the normal requirements of the two
feeds and poses no problems.

Nickpoints are essentially points on the longitudinal
profile where the slope suddenly steepens in the downstream direction; whilst *regime break points* are points
where the slope suddenly eases in this direction. Although
the origins of these points are very dissimilar, these
simple opposing definitions would seem to be invariably
appropriate for streams generally at grade.

The 'nickpoint' definition appears to accord with
normal usage for streams, except that deliberately no
reference is made to the feature's origin. But the 'regime
break point' is a new name for a phenomenon which is less
well known, except in relation to hillslopes, where it
identifies with Ruxton and Berry's (1961) 'piedmont angle'.
On streams it is the site of Yatsu's (1955, 1959) slope
and particle size 'discontinuities', which will be discussed (page 151 et seq.).

Chapter 14

NICKPOINTS

Ultimately there is only one reason for the existence of
any nickpoint, which is the *independent* relative lowering
of the floor at a point downstream, so creating a new
spatial relationship over the intervening stretch. As
shown in Figure 16, the new profile consists of three
elements, (1) (assuming no 'independent disturbance') the
completely unaffected and therefore easy slope upstream,
(2) a steep middle stretch changing its form rapidly, and
(3) the new easy slope somewhere downstream. The cause of
the lowering of the floor downstream is primarily physical,
as examples considered later will show, but its effect,
the steepening in the middle, is by contrast essentially
geometrical in quality, the simple result of an independent
relative displacement, in the vertical sense, for whatever
reason, of two points on the longitudinal profile, only
one of which has appreciably moved. But of course the new
geometrical state initiates physical reaction, which may
be lively.

To see how the situation changes, we will follow the
course of events as they affect any point A, as shown in
Figure 16, on the steep middle stretch, assuming now that
the floor is readily erodible along the whole profile for
all competences obtaining. The steepness creates a large
competence, which causes rapid second order degradation at
the point, resulting, possibly after some further steepening, in eventual decrease in the slope there. The same
thing is happening just upstream (but still within the
middle stretch) and the erosion causes a heavy loading to
develop at the point, where grade soon establishes,
governed by a competence and a slope still showing high
values. There is a second order tendency for this grade
to establish everywhere, but of course, in third order
time, the consequent relaxation in erosion causes decrease
in the loading and third order degradation. As we have
seen, the two tendencies are compatible in the process of
third order degradation at grade, in which the loading,
the competence and the slope all decrease as the floor at
the point continues to fall.

Somewhere upstream lies the limit B of the unaffected
profile. The continued lowering of the floor at the point
A implies continued change in the geometrical relationship
of A to B, resulting in further steepening of the stretch
joining them. This must go on, because any pause in the
degradation at A results in reduction in the loading, which
only induces more degradation. Thus whilst upstream of
B everything stays exactly as it has always been and no
influence from that side can appreciably change the elevation of the floor there, immediately downstream of B the

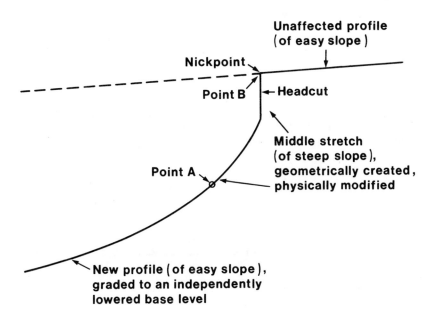

Figure 16.   The elements of a stream's longitudinal
    profile at a nickpoint.

slope is increasing continuously and may even eventually
produce a vertical, or near vertical, *headcut* in a process
examined on the next page.   The point B is now a *nickpoint*,
according to the definition (page 127).   The situation is
unstable and in due course the floor on the upstream side
of the nickpoint *collapses*, entirely as a result of action
from the other, downstream side, which may even have been
undercutting it if the floor upstream should have been
relatively inerodible.   In this way the nickpoint moves a
short distance upstream.   The immediate result is a temporary respite in degradation, first because the change in
the geometry of the situation provides an easier slope
below the nickpoint, but also because the collapse boosts
the loading.   But of course eventually the loading must
decrease and the cycle of action repeat itself.
    Back at Point A the process of third order degradation
at grade continues, but always more feebly, as the level
of the floor gradually descends towards the new base level
and the slope necessarily eases.   As the nickpoint recedes
upstream, the situation left behind it is one of gradual
return towards the pre-existing conditions.   Although the
loading immediately below the nickpoint may be relatively
heavy, it is only a local surge whose force is progressively absorbed downstream by the effects of the decreasing
slope on the competence and the travel velocity, which also
decrease.   Often temporary aggradation may result, especially in the early stages, when the upstream length of
stream actively degrading, both in the mainstream and in
tributaries, is still *proportionally* rapidly increasing,

but of course the longer term tendency is for third order degradation. In any case, because of the continuous acquisition by the stream of new alluvium from somewhere upstream, the loading is everywhere bound to be at least a little heavier than it had been before the nickpoint had passed, especially if the new alluvium particles are both large and durable. Thus inevitably the new slope must remain at least a little steeper.

The distinction of a *headcut* is that the slope has become so steep that the stream floor collapses under its own weight in an essentially non-fluvial process which has merely been initiated by stream scour. There is in fact a drastic change in 'regime', the physical aspects of which, governed by the particular composition and structure of the floor, we need not examine, the only feature now significant being the sudden great increases in the slope and the alluvium mobility. In consequence, provided the floor is readily erodible, the headcut is a focus of instability and remains so throughout a clearly defined *first, rapid stage* in nickpoint migration. For it cannot continue to exist indefinitely. Because of the general steepening of the stream slope downstream of a nickpoint, as just mentioned, the height of the headcut decreases as it *retreats* upstream, as shown in Figure 17a. The level of the floor at the foot of the headcut rises vertically more quickly than the floor of the unaffected stream at the top of the headcut, and eventually meets it, so eliminating the headcut. But the nickpoint remains, although no longer so sharp a feature. Moreover it still continues moving upstream in a *second, slow stage* of nickpoint migration, the speed of which is now dependent entirely on the rate of *decline* of the profile slope behind it through normal third order degradation. Finally, the two slopes above and below the nickpoint become indistinguishable and the nickpoint vanishes.

Examples of the first, rapid stage of the process are not easy to find in nature in localities where the floor is continuously readily erodible, because this stage is so quickly brought to a finish. Also, because the downstream independent lowering of the floor may happen slowly over a long period, as where the cause is a gradual fall in sea level, its effects on the upstream profile may keep pace with it, so that a headcut is never formed. Thus the whole process can usually only be witnessed where the independent lowering has been sudden, following some distinct geomorphological event such as a river capture, a sudden lake-draining, a meander cut-off (Crickmay, 1960), earthquake action (Morisawa, 1968, pages 108 and 110), or human intervention (Daniels, 1960). There have also been revealing laboratory reconstructions, especially those of Lewis (1944), Brush and Wolman (1960), Leopold et al. (1964, page 442) and Schumm and Parker (1973), though some of these tend to exaggerate the role of aggradation because of the unnaturally high proportion of potential mobile particles (of sand) contained in the artificial floors eroded. All the observations described, however, of both natural and simulated processes, accord with those we have been considering.

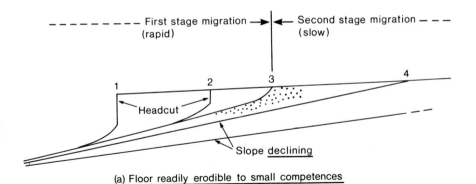

Figure 17. Nickpoint migration along graded streams: the two basic situations.

   We may also note that headcuts deep enough to have reached the *sources* of streams are somewhat more stable, because they are no longer directly activated by concentrated channelled flow. Nonetheless examples are only too well known as the causes of devastation in badland topography and donga erosion.
   However, the discussion so far fits only one of *two general situations*, for the process is different in several respects where the floor material possesses a large *critical mobility size* (D_b), as in the case of the bouldery Dartmoor granite considered earlier (see Chapters 8 and 9), for which the value of D_b is between 1 and 2 metres. The processes involved have already been examined briefly, when we noted that effectively the stream can only degrade at all immediately below the nickpoint, where alone, very briefly and very locally, its competence ever exceeds the critical mobility size. Downstream of this stretch, after the competence has fallen to become equal to this critical

value, further effective degradation ceases and the nickpoint leaves behind it, as shown in Figures 17b and 18, an
inerodible channel possessing a 'frozen', constant, very
steep *critical mobility slope*, flanked by even steeper
gorge sides also 'frozen' as a result of an analogous hillslope process. As the headcut of the nickpoint retreats,
the steep straight profile rises quickly behind it,
eventually intersecting the original profile as the headcut vanishes and the whole system becomes rigid. The nickpoint is still a prominent feature but is now virtually
stationary, and we can call it an *arrested nickpoint*.

In this situation continued third order degradation is
only very slowly effective, because potential alluvial
particles contained within the floor are mostly immovable
particles or large lag particles. Initially a very
slightly greater rate of degradation may be possible
through the winnowing away of the smaller particles, but
the effects are, except for *local* irregularities, evenly
disposed all along the steep slope and cannot result in
any overall slope decline. The same reasoning applies to
the slow removal of boulders through weathering and subsequent breakage into smaller, transportable sizes, and thus
we recognise that any change in this situation can effectively only come about, as for headcuts, by the *retreat* of
the steep unchanging slope and not by its decline.

Figure 18 also shows that these arrested nickpoints
must usually be compound, by reason of the prior weathering
of the old surface to which the original profile belonged.
Commonly, especially if produced when the climate was
tropical, the weathered zone changes in depth abruptly
into hard rock at a defined but irregular basal surface
(Ruxton and Berry, 1959), the effect of which, as is clear
from Figure 18, is to expand the nickpoint into a *stepped
profile* consisting of short steep stretches of hard floor,
where the slope is the same as downstream in the gorge
(i.e. equal to the critical mobility slope), lying between
generally longer flat stretches of soft floor, where the
alluvium supply is of much smaller particle size.

All these features may be seen in the Dart River drainage on Dartmoor, as represented, for example, in the profile of part of the upper East Dart shown in Figure 19.
In the gorge here, shown in Plate 7, the critical mobility
slope is 70 m per km, whilst in a similar gorge 12

Plate 7. Part of the East Dart River gorge shown in the
profile of Figure 19. The stream is very slowly
lowering the 'frozen' floor profile defined by the
critical mobility slope (here about 24 m/km on average),
established following the incision of the gorge by the
passage upstream of a highly erosive nickpoint headcut,
able to mobilise the boulders (see Figure 18 and pages
131-132). Interference by the one-time introduction
from the valley sides of additional boulders mobilised
by periglacial solifluction has only slightly modified
the outcome of the main, fluvial process. The stream
here is about 5 metres wide.

Stream evolution

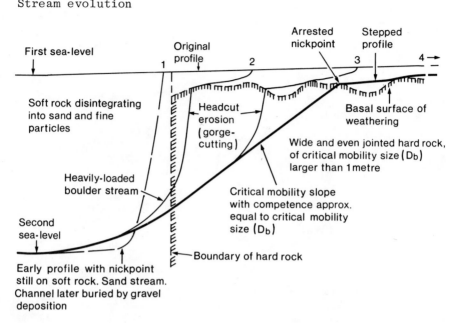

Figure 18.   Diagram illustrating the migration of a nick-
    point up a stream rising on wide-jointed hard rock
    highlands.

kilometres downstream (where the discharge is greater) it
is 24 m per km.   An explanation for the separation of the
gorges would involve a considerable discussion of the
episodic geomorphological history of Dartmoor which we
cannot embark on here, but we may note that a probably
contributory cause of the very marked stepping of the
profile above the gorge (as illustrated in Figure 19) is
an early (mid-Tertiary) regional tilt whose component in
the direction of flow (south-east) is about 8 m per km,
first recognised by Green (1949).   The present stream is
thus picking its way across elevations of the basal surface, initiated long ago under tropical conditions, and
later tilted.
    The phenomenon of the stepped profile may also be the
result of differential weathering having effect subsequent
to the formation, downstream of a gorge of the kind just
considered, of the still fairly steep, graded profile which
had been required by the stream when carrying away the
copious products of the still active gorge incision.   This
stream, heavily loaded with coarse gravel, would have been
highly erosive and it would have readily cut itself, even
through a fairly tough floor, the smooth steep profile
required for continuous grade.   We now suppose that after
the final 'freezing' of the gorge, the loading quickly
became much lighter, so that general degradation ensued
along the whole profile.   Beneath the coarse gravel valley-
fill the degrading stream would likely have encountered an
alternation of more and less weathered bedrock, which
locally may even have been completely rotted and devoid of

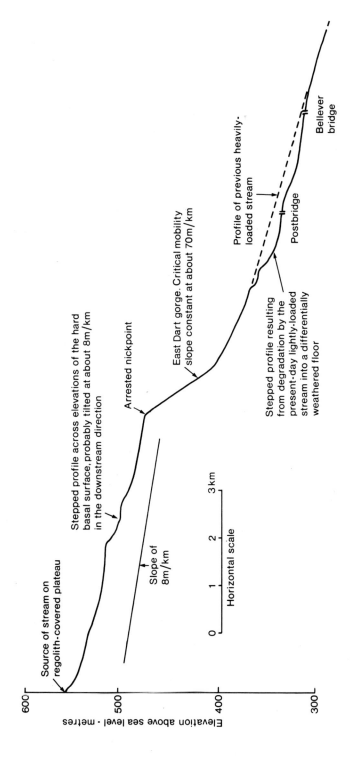

Figure 19. Profile of the upper East Dart River on Dartmoor. (Drawn from information on H.M. Ordnance Survey 1:25 000 map.)

gravel-sized particles. Here degradation could have proceeded as rapidly as the second order equilibrium called
for, the only significant control now being the rate of
disintegration, *without possibility of replacement*, of the
original, much travelled, coarse gravel into smaller
particles. As both the size and the amount of the loading
continued to decrease, the degradation would have proceeded
unchecked into the locally soft floor, the local slope
would have declined, the competence decreased and the
larger particles changed status from the one of mobile
particle, which travels briskly, to the one of lag particle,
which scarcely moves. Thus would have established at
grade a much more gently-sloped, lightly-loaded and
generally inert gravel stream characterised by smaller
gravel particles, very different indeed from its former
state. But it is only a local phenomenon, because there
are also the stretches where the weathering had not been
so intense and, we suppose, the bedrock had disintegrated
into closely-spaced hardrock boulders. Here degradation
could not proceed rapidly if only because the disintegrating coarse alluvium could replenish itself with lag and
immovable particles from the floor, more or less as required. The result here would have been the development
of a lightly-loaded boulder gravel stream perhaps similar
to the 'synthesised' example of Chapter 9, and the profile
of the stream today would be virtually the same as the
original one.

The shape of the whole profile resulting from these
two effects depends on the along-valley distribution of
the weathered and unweathered stretches. Geometry requires
that the newly flattened portions are separated from the
steeper, unaltered portions by short, very steep stretches,
whose slope in these circumstances assumes the 'critical
mobility slope' (see page 132) appropriate to the floor
granulometry. If the unweathered stretches are narrow, a
giant stairway develops (as shown by many streams in West
Africa, where weathering is intense); but where the
weathered stretches are narrow, the effect is rather that
of a series of indentations in the old smooth profile, one
of which is demonstrated clearly by the East Dart River in
the neighbourhood of Postbridge (see Figure 19).

However there is another process which is likely to
render the flat stretches even flatter, even to the point
at which a sand stream establishes. Where the meander-
belt is able to wander easily within soft ground (see
Figure 20), it may stray right away from the edge of the
old *gravel train* (Wooldridge and Linton's (1955) useful
term) into a more or less gravel-free area. Here the
almost immobile lag particles cannot follow and consequently the loading is now suddenly restricted to the
smaller mobile particles, which of course are satisfied by
a smaller competence for grade. The new competence is
readily achieved by yet further degradation and flattening
of the profile (through the competence-degradation interaction), stopping only when the larger mobile particles
are themselves stranded as new lag particles. Thus establishes a lightly-loaded gravel stream of even smaller
gravel size, or maybe even a sand stream with a gravel lag

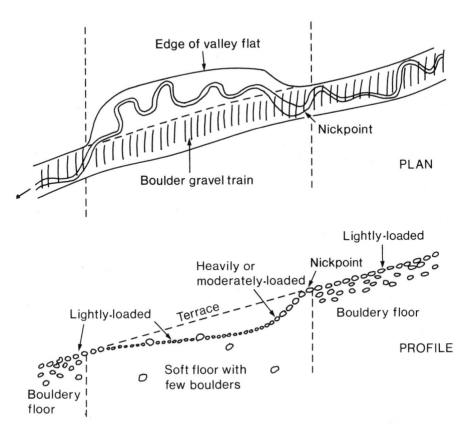

Figure 20. Stepped profile the result of differential
weathering of the floor along a lightly-loaded boulder
gravel stream.

layer. The abandoned gravel train is now a *terrace*, which
does not however prevent the gravel train and the meander-
belt merging at a common elevation somewhere downstream,
as Figure 20 demonstrates. Upstream the stretches of old
and new profile can only be linked by a nickpoint, where
a short steep stretch of *moderately-loaded* or even *heavily-
loaded* gravel stream must develop, showing a wide mobile
channel, possibly braided, certainly quickly shifting
laterally and providing striking contrast with the channel
generally.

A good demonstration of this process may be seen in
the wide flat of the West Dart just downstream of Two
Bridges, indicated by very marked local sinuosity along an
otherwise long, straight stretch of the stream probably
artificially created during alluvial tin-mining operations
abandoned a few hundred years ago. The channel, shown in
Plate 8 (page 148), remains straight where the relatively
flat, canal-like, lightly-loaded, inert gravel regime
persists, with maximum common size no more than 80 mm and

137

competence even smaller. But at intervals, just downstream of wherever the channel crosses depositions of
coarser gravel (of maximum common size about 150 mm),
there is a much steeper slope below a nickpoint and the
stream freely displays all the conspicuous properties of a
moderate loading, including (especially over one stretch,
shown in Plate 3, page 53, about 0.5 kilometre downstream
from the bridge) some very pronounced meandering. I have
also seen the effects of the process in a very different
context in the Yengema diamondfield in Sierra Leone, where
often the stream had locally abandoned its vein-quartz
gravel train left high and dry as a terrace, to become
entrenched *beside it*, through completely decomposed bedrock, in the process of acquiring the more gentle slope
needed for its new, almost gravel-free loading. The
terrace had gravel and perhaps diamonds; the floodplain
deposit had only barren sand.

Stepped profiles are certainly typical of lightly-
loaded, coarse-particled gravel streams replenishing
their gravel loading from the floor. For them both the size
and the amount of the feed of rock fragments from the
floor are almost invariably uneven along the stream
and the travel velocity of the dominantly lag gravel is so
slow that the larger particles do not move far enough
from their points of origin to smooth out the inevitable
irregularities in the loading. The patchy occurrence of
prominent immovable particles adds to the disorder.
Stretches of *fine lag* gravel may incongruously *succeed*
stretches of *coarse mobile* gravel, locally sharply
steepened by the geometrical effects we have been considering to produce conspicuous nickpoints and unexpected wide,
braided reaches. All this takes place with the stream
remaining more or less at grade, unless patches of inerodible floor obtrude. Again the Dart River shows these
features extremely well, as in the stretch upstream of
Two Bridges upon which the portrait of the synthesised
stream of Chapter 9 was based (Plate 4, although not
within the view of this photograph). It is interesting to
consider that the ragged longitudinal profile seen here is
the outcome of an *advance* in Davis's cycle of erosion,
which paradoxically in an earlier stage would have shown
the classically smooth profile of a continuously heavy or
moderate loading and a fluent, fast-travelling boulder
gravel train (sure evidence of which is the common
occurrence of small *boulders* which are 'mobile-rounded',
as considered later in Chapter 16).

Chapter 15

GRAVEL TRANSFORMATION ALONG THE STREAM

Regime break points, which are the geometrical opposites
of nickpoints, are associated with abrupt reductions in the
maximum particle size of alluvium deposited along the
stream. The question introduces the wider subject of the
self-induced transformation of alluvium along the stream
as affecting both the size and the composition of the
particles and we will consider regime breaks merely as one
feature observed in this broader view.

We have already recognised that sand, especially
durable quartz sand, is relatively unaffected by these processes of transformation. This is so not only because of
any innate resistance to wear, but also because a smaller
competence ratio (D/D_c) imparts a lower rate of wastage
with distance along the stream. The explanation for
this relationship has already (page 59) been briefly
examined and we shall look at it now more closely as we
restrict our attention to the more conspicuous trans-
formations which affect gravel particles alone.

We begin by distinguishing the two principal causes of
gravel *size reduction* along a stream. One is *wastage*, as
just mentioned, by which is implied the gradual disintegration of larger particles into smaller ones, a process
that continues whenever gravel is transported. The other
cause, effective only in streams flowing outside the
gravel source areas, is the possible *non-arrival* of the
largest gravel particles because of their slower travel
velocity (U), as governed by the formula $U = \phi(1/(D/D_c))$.
This latter cause, however, may only *begin* to take effect
a long way downstream, because in heavily-loaded gravel
streams flowing outside the gravel source areas even the
largest particles are travelling quickly and at any point
of observation on such a stream it is usually certain that
all the particles that began the journey, regardless of
size, have been passing by for a long time already. In
fact it is the wastage which *indirectly* initiates the non-
arrival of the largest particles. Because of wastage the
heavily-loaded stream may be transformed, *along the stream*,
into a lightly-loaded stream, whereupon the largest
particles assume lag status and begin to travel very
slowly indeed. Inevitably they are progressively left
behind, to be replaced by smaller 'largest particles'.
But of course, for the stream at grade, the competence is
also, for this reason alone, becoming smaller and the
travel velocity (U) of these new 'largest particles' is
just as slow as those they have replaced. The situation is
therefore unstable and the values of the largest particle
size, the competence and the valley slope together fall
quickly towards zero, only to be arrested before reaching

it when the sand loading imposes its own independent
equilibrium in the establishment of a stable sand regime.
In this way a regime break is formed.

Thus the process of size reduction along a stream
divides into *two stages*:

(1) an upstream stage of *gradual* size reduction brought
about by *wastage alone,* and

(2) a downstream stage of *sudden* size reduction caused
by start of the *non-arrival* of the very slowly travelling
largest particles.

The division is so distinct that we will base upon it our
general enquiry into gravel transformation along the
stream, considering the two stages in turn. Our eventual
conclusions are summarised in Figure 27 (page 160).

15.1   Stage 1 gravel transformation: size reduction
        through wastage alone

Before considering closely any process of gravel transformation, we need to select appropriate units of size
reduction.

Size reduction can be regarded either as *decrease in
the absolute particle size*, which may be represented by a
small measure of length δD, or as *decrease in the proportional size*, represented by a corresponding dimensionless measure $\delta D/D$. Either measure may be assessed in
relation either to *time* (t) or to *distance* (z) along the
stream. There are thus four basic quantities. We already
recognise (in the concept of competence ratio (D/D_c)) that
proportional sizes are generally more significant as indicators of behaviour than absolute sizes, and we shall therefore consider only the two 'proportional' quantities:

(1) *Rate of proportional size reduction with time*, denoted
by I_t and defined in the equation $I_t = (dD/D)/dt$.

(2) *Rate of proportional size reduction with distance*,
denoted by I_z and defined in the equation $I_z = (dD/D)/dz$.
It may be noted already that I_z is identical with the
'coefficient of size reduction' a, appearing in the equation of Sternberg's Law, $D = D_o e^{-az}$, here expressing variation of the size D with distance z beyond a datum where
$D = D_o$. We shall return to this relationship on page 149.

We begin the enquiry by supposing that the gravel
consists exclusively of material of uniform composition
whose rate of size reduction with *time* (I_t) is constant,
regardless of variation in D. Thus

$$I_t = (dD/D)/dt = \quad - \text{constant.}$$

Next we suppose there exists on the stream course a
defined last point of supply of gravel-size particles and
that the distance of any point downstream from it is z, as
measured along the floodplain-belt. This introduces the
other basic quantity, the rate of a size reduction with
distance (I_z), which relates to I_t in the equation

$$I_z = I_t/U,$$

where U is the now familiar travel velocity of a particle of size D.

Before investigating variation in I_t, we shall reconsider the important concept (introduced on page 60) of the largest particles travelling, whose size is the *maximum common size* (D_{max}). To study the Stage 1 size reduction, we must first suppose that the loading (Q_R) of the gravel leaving the last point of supply is *heavy*, implying that the competence ratio (D_{max}/D_c) of the maximum common size is comparatively low and that the travel velocity (U) for the size D_{max} is rapid. The purpose of this is to preclude the possibility of the 'non-arrival' of the largest particles and to ensure that D_{max} decreases downstream through wastage alone.

The causes of variation in I_t are many. Much experimental work involving tumbling barrels and similar equipment has been done on this aspect of the problem, as reviewed by Pettijohn (1956, pages 533-538) and Kuenen (1956, 1959), who specify a number of immediate causes. Fortunately the significant primary influences are few, as the following analysis attempts to show.

(1) A most important influence is obviously the *durability* of the particle, signifying its capacity for resistance to wastage by virtue of its hardness, soundness and shape. We shall examine these properties presently, but meanwhile may write, assuming other things being equal, $I_t = \phi(1/J)$, where J is a measure of the durability and is deemed to be increasing with increasing durability in the sense just specified.

(2) Another important influence is the *frequency of movement of the particle in any direction*, whose first order value is clearly controlled inversely by the competence ratio D/D_c for the particle's size D. This frequency, which will be denoted by F', is not the same as the frequency F, previously considered on pages 51-52, conceived as the frequency of motion in the downstream direction only. We shall have to compare the two frequencies presently, but meanwhile may note that, other things being equal, I_t is, for obvious reasons, directly proportional to F'.

(3) The *competence* (D_c) and the *maximum common size* (D_{max}) together govern the violence or, as Wentworth (1922) called it, the *rigour* of the treatment endured by particles in their physical encounters one with another. An index of rigour would be the maximum energy possessed by the largest particles moving, as determined both by their individual mass, which is a function of D_{max}, and by their maximum instantaneous velocity, which is a function of the competence D_c. Other things equal, the rate of size reduction with time is governed by the rigour so gauged and we may write $I_t = \phi(D_c, D_{max})$. This relationship may be simplified, because the ratio D_{max}/D_c is usually fairly constant along the stream, with D_c dependent on D_{max}, and in this context its variation could not be significant. Thus the single index of D_{max} usually adequately represents the influence of variation in rigour and we have simply $I_t = \phi(D_{max})$.

(4) The *absolute size* (D) of a particle is significant

because larger particles are necessarily more likely to be flawed than smaller ones, and it may even be that unflawed particles are only found abundantly in sizes smaller than a critical absolute size, linked, as we saw on page 84, to a critical mobility size. But this consideration, like that of the particle's soundness and shape (to be considered presently as aspects of the durability), is significant only near the gravel sources. We need to take note of this influence, but can generally ignore it as merely modifying.

(5) Finally, we need to note Kuenen's (1959) and other investigators' conclusions that the rate of size reduction of gravel particles is much greater if the bedload particles are *principally* of gravel rather than of sand. We already recognise that these two alternatives are respectively characteristic of gravel and sand streams, and in view of our present concern only with gravel streams we can ignore this otherwise important factor.

The conclusions drawn in this analysis are summarised in the simple statement

$$I_t = F'.\phi(1/J, D_{max}),$$

and we also have

$$I_z = \frac{F'}{U} . \phi(1/J, D_{max}).$$

On page 51, we saw that U = V.F, where V was the mean 'velocity of motion relating only to periods of actual displacement downstream', and F the corresponding 'frequency of motion in the downstream direction only'. We also saw that the range of values of V was so restricted proportionally in comparison with that of F that we could regard V as a constant and U as approximately proportional to F.

So we have

$$I_z = \frac{F'}{F} . \phi(1/J, D_{max}).$$

We will call the parameter F'/F the *motion frequency ratio* and note that its full definition reads

$$\frac{\text{frequency of motion of particle in any direction (F')}}{\substack{\text{frequency of motion relating only to periods of} \\ \text{permanent displacement downstream (F)}}}.$$

Although these specifications of F' and F are not quite explicit, they adequately express the essential distinction between the two frequencies. We shall later find the parameter useful when we further explore the effects of the so-called 'movement in situ', the phenomenon already recognised in our enquiry into vortical action in scour holes or 'ephemeral potholes'. This showed that for limited periods of time within small defined areas there may be much movement of particles for no net displacement (as for a ship swinging at anchor), so that F' must then be very much greater than F.

Both F' and F are functions of D/D_c, the competence ratio for the size in question D, and therefore F'/F is also a function of D/D_c. To discover the sense of this function, we will consider its value for certain critical values or ranges of D/D_c. First, when D/D_c is less than the critical mobile ratio (about 0.001), the particle is virtually permanently in suspension, being transported almost entirely by the along-stream linear component of the stream flow. In this range therefore F' and F are both nearly equal to unity and their ratio F'/F is itself approximately unity. As D/D_c increases, so the particle becomes more inert and more ready to stay 'anchored' to a scour hole rather than be swept out into the linear flow. Within the scour hole it may either be tossed independently of the other particles present or, if relatively large, be intermittently tumbled as the material beneath it is cut away. We shall also see (page 168), on evidence provided by Schumm and Stevens (1973), that the large mobile particles may also merely vibrate in situ. In any case it is clear that for increase in D/D_c, whilst movement in situ must continue, there is increasing reluctance for any attendant downstream displacement, and so F'/F increases with increase in D/D_c. When D/D_c exceeds the critical lag ratio (about 0.3), although any kind of motion becomes much less frequent, F'/F still increases until we reach the limiting case where D/D_c is equal to unity. Here we may suppose that the particle may still occasionally be moved in situ, but never displaced downstream, so giving a theoretically infinite value to F'/F. We have now considered the whole range of possible values of D/D_c, and there can be no doubt that $F'/F = \phi(D/D_c)$, according to our mathematical convention. It is also evident that the proportional range of values of F'/F is great, if not infinite.

Although this conclusion is based on deduction, there is good field evidence for it in the fluvial rounding of durable quartz pebbles, as will be described in the next chapter. But now, on the assumption that our understanding of this motion frequency relationship is correct, we may state the *basic wastage formula* as follows:

$$I_z = \phi(1/J, D_{max}, D/D_c),$$

in which $I_z = (dD/D)/dz$ and is the rate of size reduction with distance, J is a measure of the particle durability, D_{max} is the maximum common particle size, in this context acting as an index of the rigour endured by the particles in transport, and D/D_c is the competence ratio for the size D, acting as an index of the motion frequency ratio F'/F.

Presently (page 147), we shall discover how this formula accords with Sternberg's Law, for which I_z is constant in the situations for which it is relevant.

Meanwhile we shall investigate how the durability (J) may vary and apply the formula to cases of 'differential wasting' along the stream.

There are two principal determinants of the *durability* of a gravel particle, which are its hardness and its

soundness. The shape also has influence, in that sharp
corners are obviously more vulnerable to wear than blunt
ones, but this factor is not of far-reaching importance and
can be disregarded except near the gravel sources. On the
other hand, the particle's *hardness*, an expression of its
composition, permanently determines its resistance to
abrasion; and its *soundness*, by which is implied its
freedom from structural or textural weakness or flaws,
either innate or induced, determines its resistance to
breakage. In the event of deficiency in either of these
properties, the particle wastes quickly in almost any
circumstances and it is evident that the durability J is
a most important control of the value of I_Z, matched in
effectiveness only by variation in F'/F, the motion frequency ratio, just considered.

The most durable particles are thus obviously those
that are both very hard and perfectly sound, a combination
of properties to be found par excellence, as we shall see,
in unweathered gravels composed of well-worn vein-quartz,
from which any unsound elements have long since been
eliminated by repeated mechanical action. However, all
gravels waste rapidly when they have only recently been
released from their primary sources, for this is the time
when the effects of past weathering prove critical, and
any weaknesses already induced in the particle *outside* the
stream, as affecting either its composition or physical
structure, ensure its early disintegration. It is debat-
able to what degree the more intense biochemical weathering
processes are still effective within the floodplain-belt,
but the most vulnerable location for gravel-sized particles
in this respect is probably within the mobile layer of a
moderately-loaded gravel stream, where alone (see pages
95-97) the particles can rest for at least reasonably long
periods undisturbed *above* the permanent water level.
Indeed evidence for this may be seen on point-bars, where
the undersides of exposed rock gravel particles often show
signs of incipient weathering that are absent from their
exposed surfaces. Nonetheless we should expect that any
actually broken weathered pebble seen on a bar is one that
has only recently been released from an environment right
outside and above the floodplain-belt, where alone sustained
weathering could have taken place. Thus it is probable
that the processes of wastage within the floodplain-belt
itself are always mainly mechanical, either direct acting
or exploiting, as occasion allows, any weaknesses previously induced by the possibly far more effective bio-
chemical processes that function outside it.

Fortunately the relative importance of the different
processes of wastage need not concern us closely, for we
shall make no attempt to define the durability J as a
quantity except by its effect, relatively considered for
each material, on the value of I_Z, the rate of proportional
size reduction with distance, given that the other variables are constant. This accords with Kuenen's (1959)
expression of his experimental results, wherein he showed
that *silica gravels*, by which term we now mean those whose
particles are mostly composed of free silica (such as
quartz, flint, chert, etc.), are generally much more

durable than all others, which we can broadly refer to as
rock gravels. In the field we can only recognise the
essential condition of the constancy of the 'other variables' over the short stretches where the same value of
D_{max} applies to both of any two materials being compared,
for only then will the travel velocities U be identical.
Here the test is simple, for the less durable material
will appear to become relatively less abundant downstream,
yet not so much because it is disintegrating more quickly
but because its particles are smaller, and are therefore
travelling faster, and are for this reason providing a
smaller deposition.

A typical situation will now be described which
illustrates the whole process of gravel transformation by
differential wastage. We suppose that there are two
different kinds of gravel moving downstream from a common
last point of supply. There is (1) a heavy loading of a
granite 'rock gravel', fairly durable, of maximum common
size (D_{max}) 1000 mm, and (2) a moderate loading of quartz
'silica gravel', very durable when worn, of maximum
common size about 250 mm. The floor is everywhere readily
erodible and consequently the stream flows continuously at
grade. The processes we shall follow are illustrated in
Figure 21.

At the start the competence is large, as required for
grade by the heavy granite boulder loading. The quartz
gravel, of smaller size and lighter loading, has no influence on the equilibrium at this stage, as it hurries
inconspicuously along a channel dominated by gravel
boulders. However, the wastage formula $I_z = \phi(1/J, D_{max}, D/D_c)$ shows that this relationship will not continue
indefinitely, because the value of each of the three
governing parameters is higher for the granite gravel than
for the quartz gravel, and consequently the granite gravel
is wasting much the more quickly in respect to distance
along the stream. In fact the quartz gravel, as soon as
it has parted with its unsound components and had its
rough edges knocked off, is moving along the stream almost
intact, in marked contrast to the more vulnerable granite.
In consequence, not only does the maximum particle size
(D_{max}) in due course become the same for both gravels, as
shown in Figure 21, but also, at this same point along the
course, their loadings (Q_R) very likely assume the same
'moderate' values, so producing a 1:1 mixture of granite
and quartz particles in the deposition.

However, the difference in durability persists and, as
the mixed gravel continues down the stream, the roles of
the two constituents change places. The quartz carries on
virtually unchanged in size, whilst the granite continues
to waste relatively rapidly. Henceforward the tough
quartz gravel controls the equilibrium, so that the rate
of decrease of the competence (and of course the valley
slope with it) with distance is much less than previously.
The competence ratios (D_{max}/D_c) for the largest quartz and
granite particles become increasingly disparate and this
is reflected in their respective travel velocities (U).
The quartz henceforward travels slowly, and indeed it
decelerates as its value for D_{max}/D_c increases in response

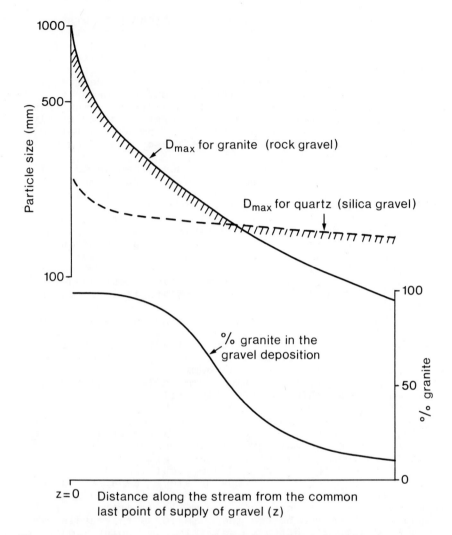

Figure 21.   The transformation of a mixed gravel deposition
    along a stream: the Stage 1 process.
    The hachured line shows the maximum particle size
    (D_{max}) of any kind of gravel - which is the principal
    control of the stream's equilibrium.

to the decrease in the combined loading through wastage;
whilst the granite *accelerates* as it becomes smaller
relative to the competence.   So, if only because of the
increasing difference in travel velocities, the granite
gradually disappears from view.
    The gravel deposition has become completely trans-
formed - in size, amount of loading, and composition.   The
primary cause is seen to have been the difference in the
durability of the two materials, whose effects, however,

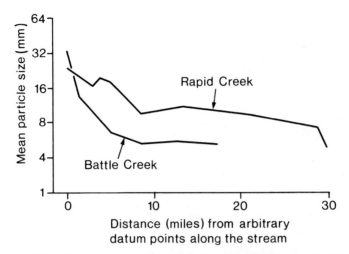

Figure 22.   Change in the mean particle size of the
    deposition along two gravel streams draining the
    Black Hills of Dakota.   After Plumley (1948).

have been systematically exaggerated by the resultant
differential rates of change with distance in the *size* and
amount of the loading of the two constituents.
    A well-known record of the process is Plumley's (1948)
account of the changes he observed along terrace deposits
of two streams (a third one examined is less relevant,
though its properties are consistent with the argument)
draining isolated occurrences of granite and metamorphic
rocks respectively in the Black Hills of Dakota.   He
showed (see Figure 22) that upstream near the gravel
sources in each case there was a rapid reduction in the
mean size of the coarse-particled, predominantly rock
gravel deposition with distance along the stream, followed
by a quite sudden steadying of the mean size (at values of
10 and 6 mm respectively) as silica gravels became more
abundant.   Measurements for the 16-32 mm particle size
range showed (if some allowance is made for contamination
from local gravel supplies) a consistent downstream increase in the amount of silica particles from about 40%
to nearly 90% in the one case and 30% to over 70% in the
other.   Although these records do not directly relate to
the gravel deposition as a whole, there is no doubt that
the trends are consistent with the process just described
and illustrated in Figure 21.
    As Plumley recognised, in neither case does the mean
particle size decrease exponentially along the stream, as
Sternberg's Law requires, and for which the graphs of
Figure 22 would be straight lines.   Before considering the
reason for this, we will enquire into why Sternberg's Law
is certainly valid in some situations, for instance the
one he himself examined, as described by Barrell (1925)
and Leliavsky (1955).
    Sternberg recorded both the maximum common size (D_{max})

and the mean size of the well-worn, fairly durable rock gravel deposition of the Rhine along 200 kilometres of its course between Basle and Mannheim. Along this graded stretch, into which no tributaries enter, D_{max} decreased from 160 mm to 80 mm, and the mean size from 40 mm to 20 mm. The constancy of the ratio of D_{max} to the mean size is consistent with the continuous heavy loading all the way, signifying that the proportional decrease in the effective loading (Q_R) had been limited and consequently that the *shape* of the deposition size frequency curve (Y) had scarcely changed, although of course it had shifted sideways along the particle size axis (cf. Figure 8a on page 76).

If we look at the wastage formula $I_Z = \phi(1/J, D_{max}, D/D_C)$ as it relates to this situation, we note first that J is constant and then that as D_{max} (the index, of rigour) decreases, so, in quite independent compensation, D/D_C (the index of the motion frequency ratio F'/F) for the largest particles increases (in that D_{max}/D_C increases with decrease in Q_R). Thus it is possible to accept that I_Z, the rate of size reduction with distance, is constant, as Sternberg's records showed it to be. This is Sternberg's Law.

The correlation between I_Z (the rate of proportional size reduction with distance) and the usual statement of Sternberg's Law is demonstrated as follows.

Let the value of I_Z be $-a$, a constant, whose sign correctly is negative. Thus

$$(dD_{max}/D_{max})/d_Z = -a,$$

by definition, or

$$a.dz/dD_{max} = -1/D_{max}.$$

Integrating with respect to D_{max},

$$a.z = -\log_e D_{max} + c,$$

Plate 8. A straight reach (perhaps an ancient artificial diversion) of the West Dart River, just downstream of Two Bridges, on Dartmoor, as discussed on pages 137-138. The stream here flows at a very gentle slope as a *lightly-loaded gravel stream* of competence probably no more than 60 mm. The stream bed is composed of inert lag and immovable particles of granite and vein-quartz of maximum common size about 80 mm. A deposition of silty sand is accumulating in the grass in the middle distance, the lack of more conspicuous deposition being consistent with the negligible mechanical erosion taking place anywhere in the upstream drainage because of the present universal boulder immobility. This photograph was taken only 200 m downstream from the very localised situation of Plate 3, where the competence was much larger (and the slope steeper).

where c is a constant. Let $D_{max} = D'_{max}$ where $z = 0$. Therefore

$$\log_e D_{max} = \log_e D'_{max} - a.z.$$

This is perhaps the more readily comprehensible form of Sternberg's Law, which, however, is normally written

$$D_{max} = D'_{max}.e^{-az}.$$

For Sternberg's data, as just quoted, we obtain

$$I_z = -a = 0.0035 \text{ per kilometre.}$$

Sternberg's Law has also been shown to apply to the results of experiments using abrasion barrels (see, for instance, Krumbein (1941a)), for which we note that J is constant (as soon as the corners have been knocked off the particles), F'/F is constant at unity (or near to it) and D_{max} as an index of rigour is apparently effectively constant over the narrow ranges of size considered (for instance, in Krumbein's well-known experiment with lime-stone fragments the particle diameter decreased only 20% over the whole range for which the graph of log size against distance appeared to be a straight line).

However, the 'law' does not apply to Plumley's results, except over short stretches. In the light of the imaginary case we examined on pages 145-147, the reason is apparent. The graphs (Figure 22) each divide into sections, as ideally reproduced in Figure 27 (see page 160). Upstream near the gravel sources, the value of J, the durability, increases rapidly with distance, as the weaker particles are eliminated and the sharp corners are blunted. Thus, in Figure 22, the graphs over the stretches 0-8 miles are concave upwards. At 8 miles, just as we might suppose J to be approaching the kind of constant value for rock gravel which Sternberg met on the Rhine, the rock gravels are replaced by silica gravels, introducing a sharp increase in the value of J for the controlling larger sizes, and the curves flatten out. Thereafter the graphs are fairly straight, following Sternberg's Law, although it would appear that one of the streams (Rapid Creek) might be approaching a regime break at 30 miles. This is the feature to be discussed in the next section.

15.2   Stage 2 gravel transformation: size reduction
        through the non-arrival of the largest particles
        travelling, resulting in the formation of regime
        break points

Although, as we have just seen, the results of gravel transformation by wastage may be far-reaching, they appear only gradually along the stream. By contrast, the equally impressive results of the process now to be considered appear *suddenly* - in respect to distance, of course, and not to time.

The phenomenon of the *regime break* was first recognised

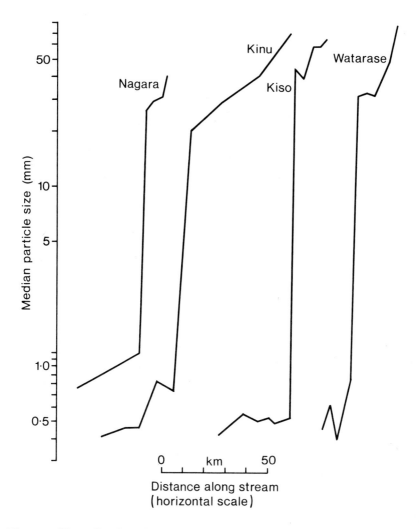

Figure 23. Regime breaks on streams in Japan. The graphs
   show variation in median particle size for the channel
   deposition with distance along the stream. After
   Yatsu (1959).

and described by Yatsu (1955), who noticed that along
several graded streams draining the Japanese highlands
there existed short stretches, generally less than
3 kilometres in length, across which the slope of the
stream sharply decreased in the ratio of 3:1 and, as shown
in Figure 23, the median diameter of the channel bed
alluvium decreased from about 30 mm to less than 1 mm. In
other words he had seen gravel streams suddenly become
sand streams.
   In the simple situation considered in the last section,

a heavily-loaded gravel stream passed beyond a clearly
defined last point of supply of gravel. Stage 1 represented the first stretch of the stream below this limit,
within which particles of any size travelling had had
enough time to move to beyond any point on the stretch,
because of their relatively rapid travel velocities (U).
Eventually however, as we move further downstream, we
reach a critical point, as shown in Figure 24, where the
largest particles, whose loading is now *light*, are only
just arriving at a very slow travel veloʒity indeed, so
that downstream of this point they are not to be found at
all. This is the start of the Stage 2 stretch, within
which the process of size reduction is caused primarily by
the *non-arrival* of the largest sizes.

The position of the critical point dividing the two
stretches is governed by the basic equation $z = \int U.dt$,
where z is distance travelled in time t at a variable
travel velocity U. The important variable is U because
its proportional range of values is enormous for particles
of the controlling maximum common size D_{max}. For example,
where the amount of the gravel loading (Q_R) is heavy at
the start .of Stage 1, the travel velocity (U) for this
size can be very rapid (maybe even of the orders of tens
of metres a year, though the actual value is immaterial
in study of such disparate orders of magnitude). But
eventually, towards the end of Stage 1, where Q_R is light,
we can suppose the travel velocity U to be so slow that
the largest particles do not travel 10 metres in
thousands of years. Thus there must exist some point
where, for the first time, the largest particles have not
yet arrived, so marking the beginning of the unstable
Stage 2, where the situation is further aggravated by the
continuing efforts of the stream (through the competence-
degradation interaction) to maintain *grade* by causing the
ever diminishing gravel to travel ever more slowly. A
useful analogy is that of a valley glacier which, although
at the valley head travelling at a very appreciable rate,
somewhere slows to a halt at a stationary line.

We will examine the process more closely. As the
gravel wastes along the stream in Stage 1, grade is continuously maintained by decrease in the competence (D_c)
through the operation of the competence-degradation interaction described earlier. The role of the competence is
to regulate the travel velocity (U) of the different sizes
of alluvium - according to the formula $U = \phi(1/(D/D_c))$.
- so as to provide the constant *cover* (C) needed to prevent
either degradation or aggradation. We have seen (pages
61-62) that normally this cover is provided either almost
entirely by gravel particles, when we have a gravel stream,
or almost entirely by sand particles, when we have a sand
stream, as demonstrated in the formula $C = k(Q_{Rg}/U_g +
Q_{Rs}/U_s)$. We are now considering a gravel stream, by which
we understand that the travel velocity of the sand (U_s) is
so rapid that the sand cover parameter (Q_{Rs}/U_s) is of
negligible value. The relevant formula is now simply
$C = k.Q_R/U$, where the variables Q_R and U relate exclusively
to the 'larger gravel particles' travelling, ranging in
size from D_{max} down to an unspecified size below which the

cover of the increasingly quickly travelling particles is not appreciable.

The relevance of the cover to the argument is that for a stream continuously at grade, its value remains fairly *constant* along the stream - we may visualise a constant 'thickness' of cover - and this is so despite decrease in both D_c and the absolute sizes of the 'larger gravel particles'. Therefore

$$C = k.Q_R/U = constant \ along \ the \ stream.$$

In this equation the controlling variable is the loading Q_R of these 'larger particle sizes'. As the gravel wastes along the stream, so Q_R decreases and there-fore U correspondingly decreases, by continuing adjustment in the competence through the operation of the competence-degradation interaction. *Thus U is proportional to Q_R.*

These quantities relate to the 'larger gravel particles', of which D_{max}, the maximum common size, is representative, and therefore the travel velocity of the *largest* particles is approximately proportional to the gravel loading (Q_R) (of the 'larger gravel particles'), *regardless of absolute size.*

The effect of wastage on Q_R is great. This is so if only on account of wastage by abrasion, ignoring the effects of breakage. For example, a reduction in particle diameter to 25% of its previous diameter implies a reduc-tion in volume to $1\frac{1}{2}$% of its previous volume. If Q_R decreases in this proportion, so does U. Thus, as the gravel wastes, eventually we reach a point along the stream where Q_R is very light and here the extremely slow moving largest particles are the vanguard of all the particles of their size travelling and *none* are to be found downstream of them.

Where this happens, Stage 2 begins and there is an immediate marked increase in the value of I_z, the rate of size reduction of the largest particles with distance, but now having nothing directly to do with wastage. The non-arrival of the expected largest particles implies decrease in D_{max}, although not necessarily also decrease in the new significant amount of the loading Q_R. This amount now relates to the narrow size range of the newly qualified, slightly smaller 'largest particles' and is likely to be appreciably greater than the corresponding amount of the loading of the 'largest sizes' that have just failed to arrive. However it is only the decrease in D_{max} which renders these slightly smaller particles any more signi-ficant than previously and the net result is unquestionably decrease in the competence for grade D_c. Thus, although restrained to some degree by the heavier loading of the smaller sizes, the fast tempo of the new trend must continue, as expressed by the greatly increased value of I_z for the largest particles, and the situation continues to be unstable (with respect to distance). As the distance increases, so the values of D_{max}, D_c and U all fall quickly towards zero, accompanied by S_v, the valley slope, by whose adjustment the value of D_c is determined. Thus is initiated the *regime break*.

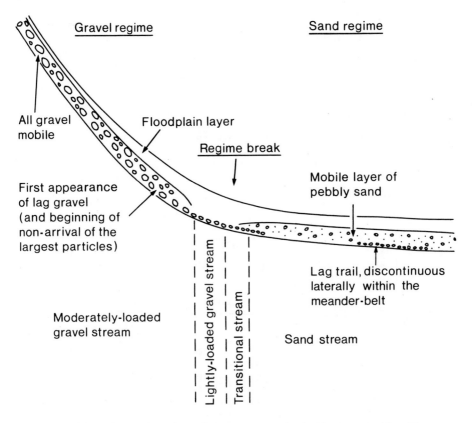

Figure 24. A regime break, represented diagrammatically by a cross-section along the meander-belt.

However, as shown in Figure 24, the process is never completed because of intervention by the independent *sand loading*, which until now has played a negligible role in the establishment of equilibrium. As the falling value of the competence D_C approaches about 100 mm, the sand begins to make its presence felt through the slowing down of its travel velocity (U_S) to such value that the sand cover $C_S = k.Q_{RS}/U_S$ begins to make a significant contribution to the total cover. As the competence continues to decrease, so the proportion of the cover provided by the sand alone increases, until soon it is maintaining the equilibrium almost unaided by the gravel residue. Now the situation stabilises, because the values of Q_{RS} and U_S are fairly high and there is no risk of the non-arrival of any of the sand particles. The gravel stream has become a sand stream - there has been a *regime change*.

The gravel residue is now a 'passenger' in a system over which it possesses negligible control. The new competence, probably of value about 100 mm, has been determined virtually by the sand loading alone. Initially

the largest size of the gravel particles will be well into
the lag range and we can visualise the new alluvium profile
as composed of a thick mobile layer of pebbly sand, in
which the comparatively few pebbles are of all sizes up to
about 30 mm ($D_1 = 0.3D_c$), overlying a lag layer of gravel
particles larger than 30 mm. The process of the 'non-
arrival' of the largest lag particles still operates as we
continue downstream, but now without any marked effect on
the competence, controlled almost exclusively by the sand
loading and only very slowly decreasing. Thus the maximum
particle size (D_{max}) gradually falls to a value smaller than
the critical lag size ($D_1 = 0.3D_c$), and then there are no
more lag particles.

In reality, however, this may not be the case, for we
must not overlook the possible longer-term process of the
upstream migration of the regime break itself (comparable
with the migration of the foot of a valley glacier).
Despite the continued downstream crawl of the largest
particles in the Stage 2 stretch, the migration is nonetheless more likely to be in the upstream direction, because of
decrease in the gravel loading (Q_R) at source in response to
third order degradation. As the regime break point moves
upstream, so it leaves behind it a trail of lag gravel (like
a glacial terminal moraine). Such a *lag trail* of residual
gravel, rich in the more durable silica components of the
original gravel train, may, if the residue should also
include valuable heavy minerals (such as gold and diamonds),
furnish profitable pay-leads or pay-streaks, specially rich
if for any reason the migrating regime-break should have
lingered for a time in one place. It is interesting to note
that these lag trails, possibly divided from the sources of
the heavy minerals by hundreds of kilometres of coarse-
particled, heavily-loaded rock gravel regime, in which no
concentration of the minerals is possible in the exclusively
mobile deposition, may be the *only* rich deposits of the
mineral (and I can cite spectacular examples of isolated
rich alluvial diamond deposits in West Africa that can only
- and perfectly satisfactorily - be explained thus).

The effect of this regime change on the shape of the
longitudinal profile is of course marked, because of the
sudden decrease in the competence to a nearly constant
value. The discharge will not have varied appreciably and
consequently any change in the competence is bound to be
accurately reflected in change in the slope (through the
competence-degradation interaction). Thus a regime break
is indicated on the profile by a conspicuous *regime break
point*, where the slope suddenly eases in the downstream
direction. As already indicated, the regime break point is
geometrically the opposite of a nickpoint, and we can now
see how the causes of each are very different indeed.

It is understandable that regime break points have
attracted less attention than nickpoints, for they are less
common. Rarely may we see more than one change from gravel
to sand along a stream (although the process can be reversed by a nickpoint) and frequently, especially in small
islands like Great Britain, gravel streams run into the
sea without change in regime (except to an independent
estuarine or marine regime). Moreover, as will be discussed

presently, there may be no sharp change from one regime to the other where the sand loading is particularly heavy, as illustrated by the 'transitional' streams of semi-arid regions (see Chapter 12).

Yatsu's accounts (1955, 1959) remain the most striking demonstration of the phenomenon, but equally sure cases are recognisable in the description by Vogt (1962) of the Adour River in southern France, by Nordin and Culbertson (1961) of the Rio Grande in New Mexico (between San Felipe and Bernalillo), and by Speight (1965) of the Angabunga River in Papua.

I have personally examined the Adour regime break, following Vogt's closely documented footsteps. The example is particularly interesting because it displays within a short stretch of about 20 kilometres, as shown in Figure 25, no less than *five* of our recognised classes of graded stream, beginning with a heavily-loaded gravel stream freely transporting mobile cobbles of size 180 mm (intermediate diameter) and ending with a fairly lightly-loaded sand stream. The gravel is a rather fragile, not very sound, dark grey quartzite whose immediate source is an uneven deposit of Quaternary 'fluvio-glacial' outwash derived from the nearby Pyrenees, across which the Adour upstream picks its way alternately as a braided, heavily-loaded gravel stream and a meandering, moderately-loaded gravel stream. Near Toulouzette, 10 km downstream from St. Sever, the Adour, now 150 km long, leaves this source area for the gravel-free coastal plain and our interest is in watching the quite rapid disappearance of its gravel load. Figure 25 shows how the decrease in the gravel loading along the stream provides this exhibition of the different classes of gravel streams, whose properties, described already in Chapter 10 and summarised in Table 2, need not again be discussed. Plate 2 (page 36) shows the moderately-loaded gravel stream at Mugron. The measurements and estimates of the significant quantities specifying some of the stream properties at the points shown should however be regarded as only approximate and they are quoted simply to indicate the trends of the changes, which are so striking that no great accuracy is needed for this purpose. Indeed there are good reasons why it is difficult to obtain accurate particle size data within the critical stretch of the regime break where the gravel loading is light. One reason is that channel alluvium is not easily found here above or even near to water level in the canal-like channel characteristic of this class of stream. Another is that it is essential to be able to distinguish between depositions of the mobile layer and the lag layer, whose largest particle sizes are of course not the same. Moreover, in the transitional stretch, there is the polarisation of the mobile deposition into distributions dominated by either gravel or sand, as described in Chapter 12 (page 123). Upstream there is no problem, where the gravel loading is moderate or heavy, because here the ubiquitous wide gravel bars all belong exclusively to the mobile layer and the largest particles seen on them undoubtedly correspond with the maximum common size (D_{max}) (see page 60) and are assumed to exclude any possible locally-derived lag particles.

Gravel transformation along the stream

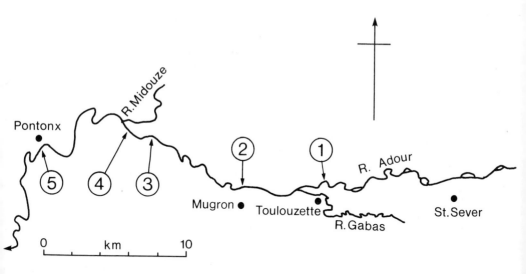

		5 Pontonx	4	3	2 Mugron	1 Toulouzette
Distance along stream from St.Sever (km)	z	32	24	23	15	10
Regime		Modtly.-loaded sand	Transitional	Lightly-loaded gravel	Modtly.-loaded gravel	Heavily-loaded gravel
Maximum common size (mm)	D_{max}	25	unsure	75	135	180
Median size (mm) (after Vogt)		sand	variable	20	40	50
Estimated competence (mm)	D_C	80		200	500	1000
Valley slope (m/km)	S_v	0.2	0.5	0.6	0.8	1.0

Notes (1) The sand regime begins at some distance upstream of Site 5.
(2) The values quoted are very approximative.
(3) The Midouze tributary is a lightly-loaded sand stream, of valley slope about 0.3 m/km. The Gabas tributary is a lightly-loaded (sic) gravel stream, entrenched in fine-grained sediment.
(4) D_{max} relates only to the mobile layer.

Figure 25. The regime break on the River Adour, in southern France.

Stream evolution

My visit to the Adour was also rewarded by an unexpected revelation of a lag trail. A dragline operating
in the channel a kilometre downstream of the bridge at
Pontonx and normally excavating the mobile layer of pebbly
sand had dug locally into the fairly soft limestone floor
and brought up good samples of the thin lag layer. This
was composed, as was appropriate, of particles of sizes up
to about 90 mm, consisting of well-worn quartzite and a
relative abundance of vein-quartz.

As mentioned earlier, there may be no regime break
where the sand loading is heavy. We have already seen
(Chapter 12) that in semi-arid regions a very heavily-
loaded transitional stream may conceivably show a substantial sand cover whilst the competence is still as large as
about 600 mm. In this situation the gravel loading is unlikely to be light and so the transition to a sand stream
would have begun before the drastic Stage 2 process of
size reduction through non-arrival of the largest particles
could have been initiated. As a result it would never operate,
and the whole transition would come about gradually, first
in a stable transitional stream, passing into a stable
heavily-loaded sand stream. The gravel would have disappeared through wastage alone.

By contrast, it is in the semi-arid environment especially where we can recognise very abrupt regime breaks at
the feet of steep gravel-covered *hillslopes*. Although the
present work is concerned specifically with streams, we may
note briefly the wider application of the theory we have
been using. Some hillslopes appear to be drained by generally parallel, graded streamlets, whose steep slopes are
maintained at constant values by very light loadings of
gravel particles. The competence of these streamlets is
equal to the critical mobility size (D_b) of the alluvium
(as discussed on pages 131-132). The sand loadings are
also very light, so that the gravel streamlets may be replaced, at the regime break junction with the pediment,
by 'sub-critical' inactive sand streamlets (of competence
smaller than about 30 mm), which are unable to maintain
channelled flow and consequently merge as sheetwash. The
gravel at the foot of the slope may waste quite quickly,
virtually in situ, because of its position in relation to
the water table, as shown in Figure 26b, and thus the slope
retreats. Any residue of silica gravel would survive as a
continuous lag trail flanking the hillslope, evenly covering the pediment as a 'stone line'. Alternatively, if the
residue of silica gravel is abundant, it may institute its
own silica gravel regime, so that the relatively steep
pediment would also be channelled by graded streamlets,
soon coalescing into proper streams. There would then be
room for another regime break downstream, as shown in
Figure 26a, where (if the silica durability were low
enough to permit it) the silica gravel streams would
abruptly change into sand streams, which, if very lightly
loaded and sub-critical, would merge into sheetwash as mentioned earlier. All such changes can be readily explained
by the theory.

Figure 26a also shows that there may be yet another
regime break above the rock gravel slope, dividing it from

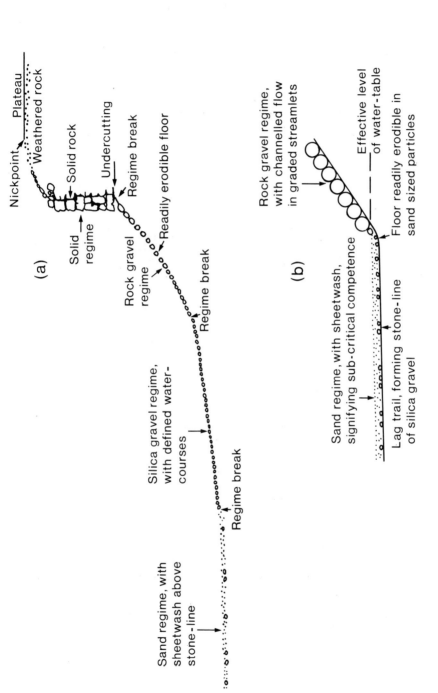

Figure 26. Regime breaks on a hillslope in a semi-arid environment.
(a) General view, with four regimes.
(b) Detail of a regime break dividing rock gravel and sand regimes, silica gravel being scarce.

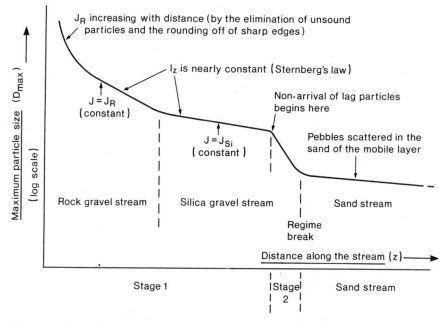

Figure 27. The stages of gravel transformation along a
stream, demonstrated by the graph of D_{max}, the maximum
particle size, against z, the distance along the
stream.
Stage 1 gravel transformation, through *wastage* alone,
controlled by variation in I_z, the rate of proportional
size reduction with distance.
$I_z = \phi(1/J, D_{max}, D/D_c)$.
J_R and J_{Si} are the respective durabilities of the rock
and silica particles.
Stage 2 gravel transformation, through the *non-
arrival of lag particles*, newly created as such by
decrease in the gravel loading by Stage 1 wastage.

a cliff of solid rock so compact that it behaves as if its
critical mobility size (D_b) were infinite. We can, of
course, often identify such a feature with the unstable
headcut that may form during any 'first stage' nickpoint
migration (see Figure 17), but where the vertical slope
is stable, both in streams and on hillslopes, it may be
more appropriate to regard it as the expression of yet
another kind of regime, the *solid regime*. As we have
already observed in headcuts, the vertical slope retreats
only by the independent process of collapse, initiated by
undercutting, and in this act provides the rock gravel
slope below with some or all of its loading of finite-
sized particles. Figure 26 attempts to illustrate most of
the processes that take place on hillslopes in semi-arid
areas. They may, of course, often be recognised in humid
environments, although overlaid and disguised by the
usually more important effects of other processes, such as
creep.

Finally, returning to streams proper, we can now compile *a general diagram of size reduction along a stream*, as shown in Figure 27. The graph relates to a graded stream unaffected by nickpoints and all the changes shown are the consequences of the purely 'evolutionary', uneven processes of gravel transformation along the stream.

Chapter 16

GRAVEL ROUNDING

A special aspect of the transformation of gravel along a stream is the progressive rounding of such particles as are both sound and tough enough to resist breakage. The process is interesting in its own right, because the property is conspicuous and distinctive, but an understanding of it can also be useful. We shall see that both the *degree* and the *kind* of roundness of a particle may make a statement about its history, especially evident if it is composed of material such as durable vein-quartz, able to act as a sensitive, long-lasting recording medium.

Primarily *roundness* is a measure of the accumulated effect upon the particle's shape of wastage suffered exclusively through progressive *wear* on its surface. Of course the wastage of fragile materials may be principally the result of obvious *breakage*, which is a different process, and where this happens the measure of any roundness achieved between acts of breakage is hardly significant. Now, however, we are specifically studying *the effects of wear on particles sufficiently durable not to break at all*, except into such minute fragments as are removed imperceptibly in the process of progressive wear, so that there can be *no limit* to the degree of roundness eventually attainable, consistent with the sphericity of the finished product. This condition eliminates many materials, such as certain kinds of limestone and chert, whose readiness to break into relatively large fragments may impose a low 'limiting roundness' quickly achieved; but it very surely includes some materials which ideally satisfy it, notably the quartz just mentioned.

Given that a gravel particle is durable enough to withstand sustained wear without breaking, we shall see that its *competence ratio* (D/D_c) is one of the principal controls of both the degree and the kind of roundness it attains for a given distance of travel.

Degree of roundness is clearly directly linked to the rate of proportional size reduction with distance (I_z), whose value we have already discovered (by the basic wastage formula, page 143) to be governed by the competence ratio.

Kind of roundness is a quality imposed on a gravel particle by the kind of wear it has endured, which itself is determined by whether the particle is of mobile, lag or immovable status. It is emphasised that this property has nothing to do with the property of sphericity, although it also, as we shall see (page 189), is in part governed by the particle's competence ratio. Broadly speaking, the kind of roundness is the effect which distinguishes, on the one hand, the wear of a *mobile particle*, whose

162

principal protuberances only are subject to relatively
heavy abrasion in a process in which the particle as a
whole is picked up and thrown around, from, on the other
hand, the wear of a *lag particle*, whose whole surface,
regardless of the detail of its shape (and including re-
entrant surfaces), is evenly worn and smoothed in a process
in which the generally inert particle is itself struck and
abraded, mainly by smaller particles. We also recognise
the wear of an *immovable* particle, differing from that of
a lag particle only in the existence of an unworn under-
side or 'sole'. There is of course a continuous gradation
of the effect across the mobile and lag ranges, governed
by the variation in the value of the competence ratio.
Examples of the different kinds of roundness exhibited by
vein-quartz gravel particles are shown in Plate 9 (page
173) and the distinctions are more closely discussed later
on pages 182-183. Now it is only important for us to
recognise that the degree and kind of roundness as broadly
understood are both governed by the competence ratio (D/D_c).

However, as we already know well, the competence ratio
itself is independent of an individual particle's absolute
size. As a consequence, we should expect sometimes to
find and recognise pebbles whose roundness has no genetic
relationship with the stream or deposit in which they are
observed, indicating that they must have been *inherited*
from an earlier deposit formed by a stream of different
competence. Similarly we should expect that the kind of
wear imposed on a gravel particle may change as it travels
downstream and its competence ratio changes, for whatever
reason.

We conclude that the process of gravel rounding in
natural streams is not easy to study systematically,
especially today within the geomorphologically disturbed
Quaternary period, when most gravel streams are transporting rapidly-wasting rock gravels. We saw in the last
chapter that this circumstance causes many important
quantities to be critically 'transformed' in value along
the stream, notably the competence ratio itself and with
it the travel velocity (U) of the gravel, and also the
very composition of the gravel. With such multiple variation in significant influences, it is only possible to
recognise broad trends and to seize upon certain *limiting
values* when they appear, as for example, considered more
fully later, Sneed and Folk's (1958) limiting roundness
value of 0.65 (on the Wadell scale, as will be discussed),
which they noted for quartz pebbles of a certain size
range after long distance of travel along the Colorado
River of Texas, which is undoubtedly a stream with a
complex history.

'Limiting values' of this kind are useful to the
enquiry because, regardless of how involved and obscure
may have been the detailed history of the operation of the
processes under consideration, nonetheless they provide
accurate quantitative records of certain *limitations* of
the processes and hence allow reliable assessment of
aspects of their mode of operation. Thus regarded, these
data can play an invaluable role in corroborating or
refuting any general conclusions reached about gravel

rounding, which, because of the complexities just mentioned, can perhaps *only* be conceived through a deductive approach. A theory originating in this way is described in the next section; and it will afterwards be tested against several isolated records of 'limiting values', which together support it.

Some of the most useful evidence for the theory comes not from today's streams, but from a reconstruction of the form and behaviour of the apparently extremely stable and uniform, moderately-loaded quartz gravel streams which once must have flowed across the Tertiary and early Quaternary erosion surfaces known to have developed upon certain of the world's stable landmasses, under humid tropical conditions. The main evidence is the almost ubiquitous occurrence today of large quantities of small, well-rounded quartz pebbles, showing a Wadell roundness of 0.8 and more, scattered over wide areas of ancient and mainly crystalline rocks in West Africa. These pebbles are undoubtedly of fluvial origin because in this region it is sure that there never have been the marine conditions which could have fashioned them. On the other hand they represent exactly the kind of really long-term product which, by application of the theory just mentioned, we might expect to have been created by the stable Tertiary streams. We seem to have evidence here of a realisation of the ideal circumstances required for the long-sustained wear, *at a near-constant competence*, of pebbles of composition ideally suited to record the wear. This evidence is described in Sections 16.2 (page 171) and 16.3. Meanwhile we shall consider the general theory.

16.1 A theory of gravel rounding

We have recognised that roundness is a measure of the accumulated effect on the particle's surface configuration of wastage by wear, which itself may be expressed, in respect to distance of travel along the stream, z, by the already familiar quantity, I_z, the rate of proportional size reduction with distance. Thus, if R is a measure of the roundness of a particle,

$$R = \int \phi(I_z)dz.$$

The wastage formula states that

$$I_z = \phi(1/J, D_{max}, D/D_c),$$

where J is the particle's durability, D_{max} is the maximum particle size, in this context acting as an index of the rigour endured by the particle in transport, and D/D_c is the competence ratio for the size D, acting as an index of the motion frequency ratio F'/F.

We will first define a simple situation. A moderately-loaded gravel stream is transporting very durable gravel of one kind and mainly of small particle size (say less than 100 mm) within a generally flat area in which the readily erodible floor is continuously able to supply the

same gravel in limited quantity evenly along the graded
stream. This applies to all particle sizes, including
some of immovable size, so that all the sizes are continuously represented along the stream. In this respect the
situation differs fundamentally from that of the last
chapter, which demanded a clearly defined last point of
supply of gravel. We will assume that the gravel's high
durability J is constant and that the competence D_c is
also constant, as it should be approximately in the
circumstances.

With J, D_c and D_{max} all effectively constant along the
stream,

$$I_z = \phi(D/D_c).$$

For any one value of D, I_z is *constant* and

$$R = \phi(z, I_z)$$

$$= \phi(z, D/D_c).$$

Let us now suppose that *a period of time t' has elapsed
since the event of rejuvenation* which established the
stream at its present general level and marked the beginning of the introduction of abundant fresh gravel into the
stream. In the shorter term this is inevitably a rather
vague concept and yet it is not so vague that the existence
of an approximate 'limiting' minimum value of t' cannot be
understood, implying that almost all the bedload alluvium
in the stream had entered it prior to at least a time t'
before today; and in the longer term, as we shall see when
we consider the evidence, this period is distinct, and
moreover can be regarded as an index of the 'maturity' of
the deposit. We shall of course, have to ignore any inherited gravel, assumed to be recognisable (which it often
is, by unmistakable contrast either in the degree of roundness or in the intensity of iron staining).

If z is now the *maximum* distance travelled by a
particle of size D since the event of rejuvenation,

$$z = U.t'$$

$$= t'.\phi(1/(D/D_c)),$$

where U, the travel velocity of a particle of size D, is
constant because D_c is constant. We are already very
familiar with the travel velocity formula $U = \phi(1/(D/D_c))$,
but need to remember that in this context it does not link
with the roundness equation just quoted, $R = \phi(z, D/D_c)$,
where $\phi(D/D_c)$ expresses the F'/F ratio.

However, at any point of observation along a stream a
limit is set to the possible value of z by *the length of
the stream z'* at this point.

Consequently there are two distinct situations to
consider, governed by the value of the competence ratio
D/D_c in its control of U, the travel velocity:

(1) For larger particles, where D/D_c is relatively
great, U is small and so also is z, which is a *variable*,

ranging in value from zero, where D/D_c is equal to unity or more, up to the maximum z', where D is of a critical value D_e.

(2) For smaller particles, where D/D_c is relatively small and D is less than D_e, the value of z is *constant* at z'.

We call D_e the *escape size* for reasons that will be apparent presently. D_e/D_c is the *escape ratio*. Both values are defined as those giving a travel velocity U such that $z' = U.t'$.

Returning to the roundness equation $R = \phi(z, I_z)$, we will henceforward distinguish R as R_m, the *maximum roundness* of a particle of size D at our point of observation, attainable only by particles that have been travelling for the longest duration of time possible in the circumstances, which of course will be less than t' if z' is less than $U.t'$. We also note that for such particles z = either $U.t'$ or z', whichever is the smaller.

The principal controls of maximum roundness have now been introduced, valid for all competence ratios and all ranges of t', the maximum possible duration of rounding, and z', the maximum possible distance of travel. The relationships of the controls are shown diagrammatically in Figure 28, in which are recognisable three distinct ranges in value of the competence ratio defining three distinct portions of the roundness graph:

(1) *Lag range*, where D/D_c is greater than the critical lag ratio (0.3). For lag particles, almost immobile on the floor, the travel velocity U is very slow indeed and therefore their maximum distance of travel, z, is very short and certainly shorter than z' except at the very head of the stream. Because the value of z is so small and despite the relatively high value of I_z for such sizes, R_m is low. Lag particles are invariably relatively poorly rounded.

(2) *Middle range*, where D/D_c is less than 0.3 but greater than D_e/D_c, the escape ratio. This is the range of greatest possible roundness, where the particles are small enough to belong to the exposed mobile layer and are therefore frequently disturbed by the stream flow, yet they are not so small that they are too quickly transported downstream beyond the point of observation. Within this range, as the graphs of Figure 28 show, as D/D_c decreases, I_z also decreases but z increases. Consequently the maximum roundness R_m, as governed by the formula $R_m = \phi(z, I_z)$, reaches its peak somewhere within this range (the argument cannot indicate exactly where) and may stay fairly constant within the range, as the straight line suggests.

(3) *Escape range*, where D/D_c is less than D_e/D_c, the escape ratio, and z is of constant value z', the length of the stream at the point of observation. In this range, as D/D_c decreases, I_z also decreases but without the compensation of any increase in z, and therefore the maximum roundness R_m decreases. As the value of D/D_c decreases towards the critical mobile ratio, whose value is about 0.001, the particles spend an increasing proportion of their time in suspension and the motion frequency ratio

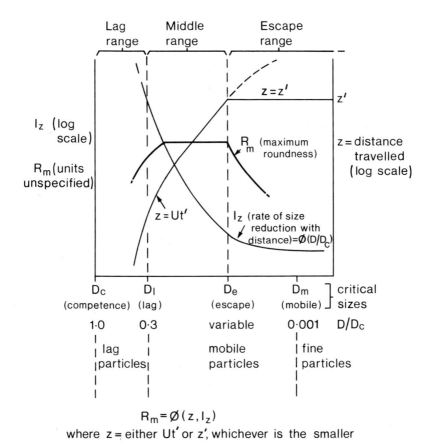

$$R_m = \emptyset(z, I_z)$$

where z = either Ut' or z', whichever is the smaller

Figure 28. The three ranges of maximum roundness R_m, for unbroken particles of gravel drawn from the floor all along the course of a stream of length z' after a duration of time t' since rejuvenation.

F'/F approaches the limiting value of unity, so producing a relatively low and constant value of I_z. In consequence the maximum roundness of the smaller particles after travel over a common and necessarily modest distance z' (this being a modestly sized world) is both low and fairly constant.

Of particular interest now is the *middle range*, where R_m can achieve its greatest value. This is where pebbles of a certain size continue to be agitated without being able to escape. We have already speculated on the phenomenon of ephemeral potholes in which particles of a certain size undergo violent attrition without leaving the pothole. There is no doubt in my mind of the efficacy of this milling process, for having frequently had occasion to examine the contents of permanent potholes cut in rock,

I have sometimes been impressed by the perfection of the rounding of *almost all* the quartz pebbles of some certain size within them, indicating that these pebbles had been trapped inside a pothole no longer receiving a fresh supply of pebbles. I have also seen diamonds recovered from Sierra Leone streams which amazingly have been worn nearly spherical and are almost visually unrecognisable as diamonds - the supposition being that there must have been two or more diamonds trapped in a permanent pothole together. Fundamentally the only difference between these permanent potholes and the ephemeral potholes is that in the latter the milling takes place over and over again in *different* places and at *different* times and for *all* the travelling particles of the critical size range. Thus, although extreme wear cannot be produced by ephemeral potholes, on the other hand nothing of the appropriate particle size range can escape them.

However this is not the only kind of situation able to produce rounding *in situ*, because Schumm and Stevens (1973) have provided striking evidence of another process, in which the particles are violently vibrated even within the very restricted confines of a bed of gravel structurally undisturbed. Their observations are so interesting, in regard both to this process and to activity in scour holes (which are ephemeral potholes), that we should consider them quoted in full:

'Experimental work involving rocks of cobble size was carried out in a large flume at the Engineering Research Center at Colorado State University, sponsored by the Wyoming State Highway Department as part of a study of riprap failure below culverts. The experimental pro-cedure was as follows: a cobble bed was formed by dumping rocks in a large outdoor flume. The surface was then leveled by hand. Water was then introduced through an 18-in diameter culvert onto the cobble bed, and the flow rate was increased until the bed failed. The condition under which failure occurred and the extent of the scour were then documented. Although all the results of these studies are not applicable to the problem of rounding and size reduction of rocks in streams, observations of particle motion prior to the failure of the bed are.

Motion pictures taken during the experiments show that the rocks began to move as velocity was increased. The following sequence was repeated during several experi-ments, utilising cobbles of different sizes and shapes. As velocity was increased to a critical value, cobbles vibrated in place on the stream bed, and collisions of vibrating rocks could be heard. This continued until at some higher velocity one of the particles (that one most susceptible because of its position, size, or density) was lifted or dragged out of the bed and trans-ported downstream. After a few rocks had moved, further increase in velocity formed shallow scour holes. Urbonas (1968) described conditions in the scour holes as follows: "Pressure fluctuations.... are high on the bottom of this hole. Apparently the scour hole reaches what could be called dynamic equilibrium, that is, a

point where the net scour is zero yet the bed particles
are in constant motion. During data taking, it was
observed that the particles in the bottom of the scour
holes are in constant motion continuously bouncing and
moving back and forth on the bottom. Average forces are
insufficient to lift these particles out of the hole.
Yet pressure fluctuations are great enough to cause
movement." '

There can thus be no doubt about the reality of gravel
rounding *in situ* in a gravel stream and now we need be
concerned only with discovering how the few variables which
control the process determine the position of this critical
'middle range' of competence ratios. So far we have
assumed that the two controls t' and z' are constant, which
of course they must be in any one observational situation.
But the values of t' and z' can vary greatly, and we will
investigate the effects of this variation by considering
two very disparate values of each of the quantities,
denoted t'_1 and t'_2 in the one case and z'_1 and z'_2 in the
other, the suffix 1 indicating in each case the greater
value. The roundness graphs for three of the four situations created are shown in Figure 29. The graphs are
easily drawn from consideration of the I_z and z graphs, in
relation to the formula $R_m = \phi(z, I_z)$. We see that the
values of the maximum roundness R_m are influenced only by
variation in t', being greater, for the middle range only,
where t' is greater. On the other hand, the value of the
escape size D_e is influenced by variation in *both* t' and
z', according to a relationship $D_e/D_c = \phi(t', 1/z')$.
Values of D_e/D_c, the escape ratio, may range from about
0.3, the critical lag ratio, for stream headwaters after a
long time has lapsed, to zero anywhere along the stream
whilst rejuvenation is still in progress. However, we
should not suppose from this that the high rate of rounding
with time associated with 'wear *in situ*' can take place
anywhere except within a zone close to the critical lag
ratio - say between 0.3 and about 0.07, as the evidence
will show later (page 178) - where alone the motion
frequency ratio F'/F is high enough, although of course
the question is only academic because the end-product of
high roundness is in any case barred to the relatively
small particles because they pass down and out of the
stream so quickly, whatever the length of the stream.

In the very long term, where t' is great, this downstream departure of particles of size smaller than the
escape size D_e must logically tend to become absolute, so
that a whole range of sizes disappears or *escapes* from the
stream as observed at the particular point along its
course where the value of D_e applies. The range of sizes
that have disappeared would not, however, extend to zero
because fine particles continue to enter the stream indefinitely from the valley sides by various means,
principally in suspension because the valley sides will
also have their escape ratios. Thus eventually, after the
act of rejuvenation has receded into the past as a distant
event, there should appear a nearly complete *hiatus* in the
size distribution, located between an upper limit equal to
D_e, the escape size, and a lower limit which should not be

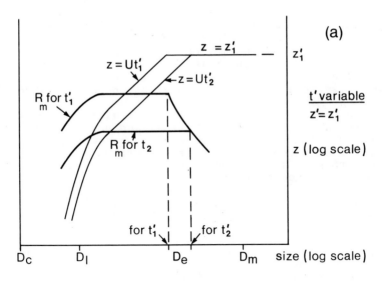

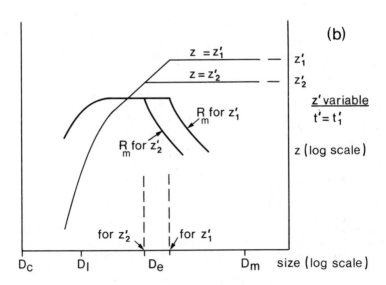

Figure 29. Roundness diagrams showing the effects of variation (a) in t', the duration of time since rejuvenation, and (b) in z', the length of the stream.

far from the sand-silt boundary at 0.1 mm. This hiatus must not, of course, be confused with the gap in the gravel-sand bimodal size distribution which we have recognised as typical of some lightly-loaded sand streams (page 75 and Figure 8) and transitional streams (page 123 et seq.), whose formation is independent of the passage of time.

We have now considered from a theoretical standpoint the main controls of the process of gravel rounding in a gravel stream *possessing constant competence*. As already indicated this condition is not commonly met in today's streams, so that often a very durable particle may begin its journey along a stream with a low competence ratio, as provided by the competence for grade demanded by accompanying larger, less durable particles, but end it, when eventually it has outstayed these weaker fellow-travellers, with a *high* competence ratio, perhaps even that of a lag particle. Initially this particle's round-ness, however measured, must have increased rapidly along the stream as the sharp corners and edges were blunted, but then would have come a possibly long stretch of stream where its competence ratio remained low and its rate of wastage with distance I_Z correspondingly low, and there the rate of increase of roundness with distance would have been slight. Further on again, paradoxically as the competence decreased and the rigour diminished, the value of I_Z must have increased in that more wear was imposed *in situ*, and then the rate of increase of roundness with distance would also have increased. Finally, with a yet further decrease in competence the mobile particle may have become a lag particle, which travels so slowly and so short a distance that no further change in roundness can be registered; and so must have ended a chequered but obviously common history.

Fortunately we do not have to rely entirely on observation of today's streams to judge the validity of the theory, for we can demonstrate very closely the simple situation upon which most of the argument has been based from the evidence of quartz gravels in certain tropical regions, considered not only in the short term as actually displayed by some of today's streams but also in the very long term of Tertiary streams reconstructed from some very special evidence which could not relate to today's streams. This will be examined now.

16.2   The rounding theory applied to quartz gravel in a humid tropical environment

Quartz is a form of free 'silica', which we recognised earlier to be the only material able to provide very durable gravel. However this property is only one of several which combine to make quartz the ideal medium for the study of rounding.

(1) Worn, sound quartz, which in the gravel range of sizes is normally vein-quartz, is indeed very durable. It is hard, compact and uniform in composition, not given to splintering (as is chert) and very resistant to biochemical alteration in fluvial environments.

(2) It is widely and at the same time often evenly distributed and may collect in streams in sufficient quantities to furnish on its own at least moderate gravel loadings. Although constitutionally and visually distinctive, its short-term behaviour in streams is identical with that of most kinds of rock gravel, whose densities

are approximately the same. Physically it differs significantly from rock only in the property of its superior
long-term durability.

(3) Because of its durability, a sound quartz particle
of gravel size can survive almost any amount of wear, and,
provided it is not caught in an actively weathering
environment, will continue indefinitely to express very
sensitively in its roundness both the total amount and the
kind of wear endured.

(4) Because of its durability, a quartz gravel can
maintain a stream at a fairly constant competence for grade
over a considerable distance, which rock gravels cannot do
because they waste too quickly.

(5) Finally, unlike some other forms of 'silica',
especially chert and flint, quartz is common in areas far
removed from the possibility of contamination by particles
rounded by marine action. We will see why this is important.

Remarkably, for our purpose, it is difficult to find
fault with quartz.

Before examining the evidence quartz provides, we
should note that the roundness values that will be quoted
belong to Wadell's scale of units, as measured by Krumbein's
(1941b) quick 'visual roundness method'. By this method
the roundness is estimated by comparing the shape of the
particle in silhouette with examples of corresponding
shapes shown on a chart whose values have been precisely
estimated by measurement. Reference will also be made to
Cailleux's first order scale (2r/L), values of which may
be converted into Wadell units by use of a table (see, for
instance, Cailleux and Tricart, 1964, page 117). Where
'well-rounded' particles are mentioned, it may be understood that the Wadell measure exceeds 0.70, the corresponding class-limit of Powers' scale (1953). Descriptive
estimates of lesser roundness are also quoted (such as
'subangular') and these similarly correlate with Powers'
scale.

We will begin by considering the situation of quartz
gravels on a Tertiary erosion surface, first noting that
even as quartz is the ideal medium for our study, so these
surfaces in certain parts of the world provide, equally
remarkably, the ideal environment. Our only regret can be
that the long-term stability of certain Tertiary times is
not reproduced anywhere in the world today.

As Thomas (1974) recognised, a high proportion of
tropical lands are underlain by old and relatively stable
landmasses composed mainly of crystalline rocks. Most of
their surfaces have remained above sea-level for a very
long time indeed, certainly since before the Gondwana dis-
persion of the continents, and as a result their features
are, as he put it, essentially 'functions of the duration
of weathering and the persistence of a low rate of denud-
ation consequent upon prolonged crustal stability'. In
the tropics the weathering has been intense, because here
a very thorough chemical alteration is possible of rocks
suitably placed in relation to the water-table (we need
not specify where), so producing *a clay-rich regolith
containing residual quartz* (ibid, page 40) and notably
devoid of hard rock.

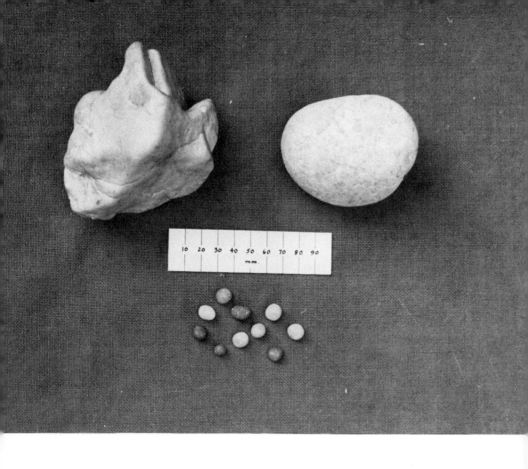

Plate 9. The wear and rounding of quartz gravel,
illustrated by specimens from Sierra Leone (see Section
16.3, pages 176 et seq.).
- Top left. Cobble showing *lag wear*. Although the
shape is very irregular, there are no sharp corners and
the surface is smooth, except across the wide *sole*
upon which it rests and which indicates that this had
been an *immovable particle*. The scale shows that the
competence of the stream must have been less than
100 mm. (From a terrace - gravier sous berge - of a
small stream near Sefadu.)
- Top right. Cobble showing advanced *mobile wear*. It
is well-rounded, the Wadell roundness being about 0.75.
The intermediate diameter is about 60 mm, from which
may be inferred that the competence of the stream had
been greater than $60/0.3 = 200$ mm (where 0.3 is the
universal critical lag ratio, D_l/D_c). (Inherited
gravel of the Tongo River, near Panguma.)
- Bottom. Small well-rounded pebbles, all of size less
than 10 mm and of Wadell roundness 0.8 and over,
inherited by today's stream from now wholly dispersed
'very mature' deposition on a Tertiary erosion surface.
(Bafi River, Yomadu, and typical of such pebbles to
be found right across West Africa.)

Stream evolution

The outcome of these special but often wide-ranging circumstances has been the formation of the great Tertiary erosion surfaces. The reader who has followed the 'evolutionary' arguments thus far (and especially the discussion of nickpoints (pages 128-134)) will have realised that the general theory is perfectly compatible with the concepts of 'cycles of erosion' and peneplanation. It happens that it is much easier to accept the concept of peneplanation in the tropics than elsewhere, because in the tropics not only are the surfaces more quickly formed but also they are *flat*, i.e. nearly horizontal, even in their earliest stages, so that variations in slope here are necessarily narrower and less readily perceptible and the 'peneplane' is more easily recognisable. The primary cause is the rapid, widespread formation of the soft tropical regolith, which creates a special erosional environment, affecting both streams and valley sides. Whilst the regolith is never very deep, almost everywhere it yields the same *fine-particled alluvium*, which is mostly silt and clay with some sand and little more than a trace of mostly pebble-sized vein-quartz, and consequently the competences of the graded, modestly-loaded streams it supplies are almost everywhere small and their *slopes are flat*. This in turn affects the geometrical associations, permitting the propulsion of nickpoints *far* upstream and the rapid permeation of large areas by flat streams, whose very flatness favours the further generation of the regolith which has initiated the condition. Of course hard-rock obstructions sometimes break the smooth continuities of the stream profiles, especially in the more deeply incised major streams, but the obstructions are usually only temporary and in any case the profile is flat between them.
The process of planation seems to work in two-phase cycles. When the climate is comparatively *arid*, lack of vegetation promotes accelerated valley-side erosion and the formation of pediments across the soft regolith, which of course are also relatively flat. But at the same time in the streams the heavier loads coupled with the lighter discharges produce heavier loadings, which cause either aggradation or at least, if the stream is still degrading, the cutting of rather steeper slopes. Later, when the climate becomes comparatively *humid*, the denser vegetation, by restraining valley-side erosion, conversely activates degradation in the streams which are now more lightly-loaded by reason of lighter loads and heavier discharges. Now the streams seek very flat profiles and keep degrading until either they achieve them or they are held up by hard rock, in which case marked stepped profiles result. But the rockbars are not often permanent barriers because they are easily by-passed through river-capture via short tributaries discovering and exploiting weathered zones which lead back into the main stream above the barrier, and in any case the hard-rock becomes vulnerable to bio-chemical weathering when buried during the subsequent arid phase. (As evidence of this I have seen, in Sierra Leone, large granite boulders, now completely rotted but perfectly delineated, with worn quartz gravel at their feet, deeply buried under arkosic arid-climate fill.) In

this way, in the alternation of arid and humid phases, the streams iron out hard irregularities and the whole landscape follows where the streams lead, gradually introducing a universal *flatness*. Even in the turbulent, most recent Quaternary, with repeated major disruption caused both by crustal uplift and tilt and by rapid alternation of the two climatic phases, we can still' see evidence of both processes having been in active operation, and we can observe the humid phase activity today. It is therefore not difficult to accept that during the long periods of crustal and climatic stability during the Tertiary and early Quaternary, wide areas of the old landsurfaces would have become very flat indeed, and of course there is sure testimony of this in the remarkably smooth planes clearly defined by the old surface remnants, although often now tilted.

We will now look more closely at such a landsurface during a humid tropical phase within the Tertiary period, in a wide area of deeply weathered granitic rocks sparsely but evenly penetrated by still intact quartz veins. The whole surface, excluding a few inselbergs of massive rock which have successfully run the gauntlet of chemical weathering, is graded to permanent base-level at the coast or an inland basin. Earlier, when the surface had been less even, a close network of minor streams collected mobile particles of the residual vein quartz from far and wide and discharged them into the relatively few major streams, of length say 50 kilometres or more, one of which we shall examine. It is a most interesting situation. The loading consists partly of lag particles of quartz, derived either from close at hand as a product of normal third order degradation of the floor or, if rather abundant, they may represent the lag trail to the regime break of a long since disappeared rock gravel stream (see page 155). But the principal component of the loading is provided by the mobile particles drawn from the tributaries and now present in sufficient quantity to give a moderate loading. The size of these particles is restricted to a narrow range, of which the lower limit is only a little smaller than the critical lag size (D_l = $0.3D_c$), whose corresponding travel velocity (U) is just slow enough for them still to be in the stream at all. This size is the *escape size* (D_e), discussed on page 169, below which the particles travel relatively so quickly that they have already escaped completely from the upstream drainage. For a long period of time there has been virtually no new supply of alluvium to the stream, except for fine suspended material, and thus the size distribution of the channel deposition (Y) cuts off sharply at this escape size, producing a very real hiatus.

The alluvium profile of this ancient stream can be reconstructed. There could be only a very thin floodplain layer, because the normal fine components deposited mainly from suspension would be scarce and indeed we might expect that the floodplain would be inundated with water even at moderate discharge. A near approach to this situation may well have been created by Schumm and Khan's (1972) experimental 'meandering thalweg channel' discussed on

175

page 119, where fine particles were also lacking. The
mobile layer would be a thick bed composed almost entirely
of the narrow range of sizes of the small quartz pebbles,
inevitably openwork in the channel but possibly filled
with fine particles (silt and clay) outside it. Under-
neath, resting on the soft floor would be a thin lag-cum-
immovable layer of the larger quartz particles.

If, in our imagination, we now look upstream to the
tributaries which supplied the mobile pebbles, we find
that these streams no longer exist. Here the maximum
distance of travel by alluvium (z') is short and all the
mobile pebbles have escaped, leaving only lag-cum-immovable
gravel. In this region we have said that the quartz veins
are not important and the lag-cum-immovable layer is thin
and probably discontinuous. In these circumstances of
negligible amounts of *both* sand and gravel loading, the
stream could have provided no effective cover of any kind
and the resulting degradation must eventually have introduced
a subcritical competence (of less than about 30 mm). Mud
and vegetation must have become established in the channel,
which eventually disappeared as such. The process, shown
in Figure 30, would be progressive downstream, creeping
along behind the rearguard of the slowly advancing train
of mobile pebbles, whose presence alone maintains the
channel. Gradually wide streamless areas appear, as the
headwaters are progressively extinguished.

However, back downstream again, where z' is greater,
the stream continues to be active, laden with the small
mobile quartz pebbles which, in this environment remaining
almost indestructible, can maintain indefinitely a surge
of moderate loading of these sizes, very slowly creeping
down the stream. The competence is ample, the stream is
'mobile' and the brisk lateral shift of the meanders pre-
vents induration of the floodplain by lateritisation, the
fate that is nonetheless reserved for it after the mobile
pebbles have mostly departed and the competence has diminished. But meanwhile there is endlessly repeated activity
in the meander-belt involving exclusively this 'middle
range' of particle sizes. The little pebbles are milled
in situ over and over again for a very long time and inevitably they become *well-rounded*.

16.3   Evidence from West Africa

The situation just described is necessarily conjecture,
because such stable streams are not to be seen today and
their deposits, after reworking by rejuvenated streams
and pediments, nowhere survive intact so far as I know.
Nonetheless there is abundant indirect evidence of the one
time existence of these streams.

The ancient landmass of West Africa, as situated
between Guinea and Nigeria, reproduces all the attributes
of the imaginary region we have been considering, including
the occurrence of wide tracts of ground continuously underlain by rocks, mainly granitic but also of sediments whose
original clastic properties have been eliminated by low
grade metamorphism, all of which have been penetrated

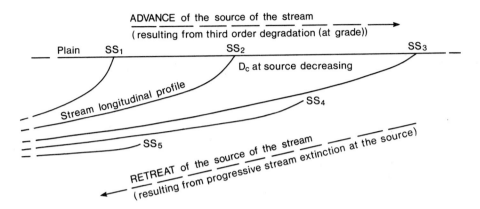

Figure 30. The advance and retreat of the source of a
   rejuvenated stream flowing at grade in a plain underlain by *fine-particled*, readily erodible ground.
   Successive positions of the source (the head of channelled flow) are indicated by the sequence of points
   ss_1, ss_2, ... ss_5. ss_3 is the furthest point of
   advance, where the competence D_c at the source first
   equates with the *critical minimum competence* (about
   30 mm).
   (In the case of a *coarse-particled* floor possessing a
   gravel-sized critical mobility size (D_b), the point
   ss_3 is an 'arrested nickpoint' (page 132) and the
   source will not retreat so long as D_b retains its
   value. The competence at ss_3 will, of course, equate
   with D_b, assuming that it is not less than 30 mm.)

sparsely but evenly by quartz veins. Local belts of land
are underlain by high grade metamorphic rocks, but they
differ significantly only in that they yield more vein-
quartz, and we shall see how this merely modifies the
evidence. The latest major planation is that of the Late
Tertiary erosion surface (which may have extended into the
early Quaternary, but this is not here significant), which,
after elevation and warping, providing a coastwise tilt at
the continent's edge, was deeply and comprehensively dissected by the flat but often stepped Quaternary streams in
a process that is continuing today. Lateritised remnants
of the Tertiary surface are preserved in the interfluves,
but only Quaternary stream terraces survive in the major
valleys. No remnants of undisturbed Tertiary major stream
deposits seem to have been recorded, although it is possible that they exist.
   Nonetheless, although dispersed, the old quartz
gravels are still preserved in great quantity all across
West Africa, especially in the major valleys, in the form
of well-rounded pebbles usually restricted to the size
range 7 mm to about 30 mm, together with larger, rounded
(but not well-rounded) pebbles, which are of notably
irregular shape. The roundness of the smaller pebbles is

commonly nearly perfect, showing Wadell values of 0.8 and
more, even for the smallest sizes in the range, as shown
in Plate 9. But there is an abrupt change at a narrow
critical size range. Diligent search may produce very
rare examples of marginally well-rounded pebbles of size
6 mm, but in my experience very surely none of size 5 mm
(intermediate diameter), for which the Wadell value of the
most rounded examples would barely attain 0.60. In the
course of travelling in West Africa I sought out and
measured the size of quartz pebbles of the escape size as
represented by the smallest well-rounded specimens discovered and moreover continued the habit when looking at
Late Tertiary quartz gravels in New South Wales, Australia,
which were evidently formed under comparable tropical
conditions. The results, including rough estimates of the
complementary *maximum* size of high roundness (as gauged
from scaled photographs), are set out in Table 4. It will
be noted that the Copeton (N.S.W.) minimum size of 6 mm
is slightly smaller than the usual limit, the explanation
for which is considered later.

The ubiquity of the little round quartz pebbles in
West Africa has naturally been well known to geomorpho-
logists working there, especially Vogt (1956, 1959, 1962),
who first recognised the spatial and temporal sequences
and common characteristics of the Quaternary terraces of
the major streams. He noticed, as I confirm, that the
well-rounded pebbles - which he referred to as 'billes'
('marbles') - bore no genetic relationship to their Quaternary stream environments, but had always been inherited
from higher terraces and that the highest terraces generally carried the highest proportions of the round pebbles.
At several localities in the Ivory Coast, his 'High
Terrace' showed median values of Cailleux's first order
roundness index of between 360 and 400, translating into
Wadell values of about 0.70, with between 10 and 15% of
the particles possessing values exceeding 450 Cailleux or
about 0.76 Wadell (Vogt, 1956). Nonetheless, impressive
though they are, these High Terrace values still belong to
a mixture of gravels, composed of inherited well-rounded
pebbles together with the relatively unworn products of a
comparatively recent rejuvenation, and we are left to guess
the equivalent median roundness values of the original,
unadulterated deposition, obviously very high indeed.

These observations are perfectly consistent with the
supposed Tertiary situation described earlier and with the
theory from which it was inferred. Clearly the well-
rounded pebbles of size 7-30 mm are the mobile particles
of the long-established major Tertiary streams and the
large and less worn particles of irregular shape - or at
least many of them, for they are less distinctive - are
the corresponding lag and immovable particles. A critical
lag size (D_l) of about 30 mm suggests a competence (D_c)
of about 100 mm, which is consistent with our knowledge of
the granulometry and (as we shall see) the availability of
residual vein-quartz of the areas in question. The escape
size (D_e) of 7 mm indicates that the escape ratio (D_e/D_c)
was about 0.07, a figure to note in other assessment of
situations where t' is great and z' is of the order,
perhaps, of 50 kilometres.

Table 4. Size limits of commonly-occurring, well-rounded Tertiary quartz gravel particles formed in graded streams flowing across soft tropical regoliths.

The sizes are the intermediate diameters. Whilst the minimum sizes quoted are accurate estimates, representing measurements made after specific search for the smallest well-rounded pebbles, the maximum sizes are approximations, based on records and scaled photographs.
The limits relate to Wadell roundnesses of 0.70 and over.

(1) Gravels drawn from 'granitic areas', *not* providing abundant vein-quartz

Location	Minimum size (mm) (exact)	Maximum size (mm) (approx.)	Immediate origin
Sierra Leone			
- Bafi R.	7	25	Mainly terraces
- Meya R., nr. Koidu	8	>30	Floodplain and terraces
- Yengema neighbourhood	7	>22	Small streams
Guinea			
- 50 km north of Macenta	8		Small stream
Liberia			
- Lofa River	7		Terrace
Ivory Coast			
- Bandama R., west of Bouaké	8	25	Terrace
- Bagoé R., north of Boundiali	8		Channel and terraces
- Kohoué R., near Séguéla	9		Floodplain
Niger			
- Niger R., at Niamey	7	<30	Terrace
Nigeria			
- Gongola R., east of Bauchi	9		Terrace
Australia, New South Wales			
- Copeton, nr. Inverell	6 (granite quartz)		Tertiary headwater
- Backwater, nr. Glen Innes	8		deposit, certainly
- Airly Mt., N.E. of Bathurst	8		with inherited gravel

(2) Gravels drawn from 'schist areas', providing abundant vein-quartz

Location	Minimum size (mm)	Maximum size (mm)	Immediate origin
Sierra Leone			
- Tongo diamondfield	15	100	Floodplains and terrace
Ivory Coast			
- Kohoué R., near Séguéla		80	Terrace
Ghana			
- Birim River, near Oda	20	100	Terraces

Stream evolution

We will now turn our attention to the *short tributary streams* on the old landsurface. Here we have no need to go back into the distant past and in any case could not do so in the granitic areas, where the short streams would have disappeared. Instead we look at the present-day floodplain deposits and the adjacent terraces, together belonging to such streams as have lightly dissected the restricted but already well-developed and quite deeply weathered Quaternary erosion surfaces. These circumstances accurately reproduce the early stages of the Tertiary erosion surface, especially in the important respect that as soon as the nickpoint of a rejuvenated stream has quickly run its course to the very head of every headwater, there is henceforward virtually no possibility of further supply of sand or gravel to the stream. In the history of such a stream, even in the comparatively short term, this cut-off in supply is a well-defined *event* and it serves as the datum from which we can begin assessing the duration of travel (t') of the alluvium carried, and thus we can now have values of both t' and z' closely specified. Moreover, in West Africa generally the value of t' for the *lowest terrace* deposit (Vogt's 'gravier sous berge', or 'underbank gravel') was, at the time of its desertion by the rejuvenating stream, evidently much greater than the present value of t' for to-day's *meander-belt deposit*. This means that we can observe at will almost anywhere in the region, *provided the stream is poised throughout its length within the soft regolith*, the *four representative situations of the theory* as defined by long and short distances (z'_1 and z'_2) and long and short durations (t'_1 and t'_2), all linked by a fairly constant competence (D_c) of 100 mm and under.

This framework in space and time could provide the basis for some interesting quantitative research, but even without it certain tendencies are obvious from mere inspection of examples of the four situations, which moreover accord with the separate evidence of the Tertiary gravels, for which we have a third, equally distinctive value of t'.

For the first time in this study we are now assessing the important influence on stream processes of variation in the *duration of time* rated in absolute units. Normally this value cannot be identified with any one duration of time common to all aspects of a situation, but in the special circumstances now being examined single values of t' apply to almost every particle of gravel or sand within the drainage, with the exception of the inherited pebbles, usually easily distinguishable. We thus have in t' an index of the *maturity* of a deposit, whose single value must be reflected in every aspect of its make-up.

We will now compare the two deposits, terrace and present-day meander-belt, at a point lying roughly *one kilometre downstream* from the common (or almost common) source of the two unequally mature streams which produced them. The descriptions, summarised in Table 5, derive from my observations of a very large number of excavations in many streams of quite small competence (100 mm and less), where Quaternary regoliths, comparatively free of vein-quartz, were well-developed, mainly in Sierra Leone and

Table 5. West African quartz gravel streams: correlations of time, distance and the properties of the alluvium, as discussed in Section 16.3. The observations relate to graded streams of small competence (100 mm and less), poised throughout their lengths upon soft granitic regoliths, comparatively free of vein-quartz.

Duration of time since rejuvenation of stream (t')	Examples in West Africa	Distance along stream valley from source (z')	Typical alluvium profile *	Quartz gravel roundness	Heavy mineral properties
Very long (t'_3) ('very mature')	Streams which once flowed upon Tertiary erosion surfaces	'Short tributary' (say less than 10 km long)	The tributaries would have become 'extinct' and been buried by colluvium and lateritised long before qualifying as 'very mature'. However, whilst they were still active, their properties would have been the same as their recent counterparts', described below.		
			Properties inferred from the evidence of the dispersed gravels:		
		50 km	Very thin floodplain layer, open-work mobile layer of well-rounded gravel, and a lag-cum-immovable layer.	Mobile particles well-rounded (7-30 mm); lag particles sub-rounded and smooth (>30 mm)	Nothing but rare >2 mm durable minerals, well worn.
Long (t'_2) ('mature')	Low terrace (Vogt's 'gravier sous berge')	Very near source	Channel extinct. Lateritised colluvium and silt, over lag-cum-immovable layer	Angular to subangular.	Both durable and soft minerals, angular, usually scanty.
		1 km	Thin (or absent) mobile layer of gravel, over lag-cum-immovable layer.	Subrounded.	<0.5 mm: mainly durable minerals, scanty. >0.5 mm: mainly durable minerals, worn, often predominantly >2 mm.
		20 km	Thick mobile layer of fine gravel or gravelly sand, over lag-cum-immovable layer.		
Short (t'_1) ('immature')	Present-day meander-belt	Very near source	Clay and silt, over lag-cum-immovable layer.	Angular to subangular.	Same as below, but usually scanty.
		1 km	Thin mobile layer of sand, over lag-cum-immovable layer.		<0.5 mm: 'black sand' (i.e. mainly soft minerals), abundant. >0.5 mm: durable and soft minerals, all sizes, relatively little worn, abundant.
		20 km	Thick mobile layer of sand, over lag-cum-immovable layer.		

Examples of both terrace and present-day deposits were often observed in the same stream.

* usually omitting reference to the floodplain layer.

southern Guinea. The fact that one broad description suffices may be regarded as evidence of the force of the tendencies, although their manifestations were of course often recognisably subject to modification by special local circumstances. It is emphasised that the descriptions do not closely fit the different circumstances of *abundant* availability of quartz or other gravel, which are considered later (page 185).

(1) *Alluvium profile.* Erosion releases from the soft regolith much more sand than gravel and the immature present-day streams in granitic areas are sand streams, possessing well-defined mobile layers in which the mobile gravel pebbles are nonetheless closely scattered amongst the sand particles. By contrast the more mature terrace deposits commonly show no mobile layers at all or at best a few centimetres of fine gravel, indicating that at the time of their formation the bulk of the limited stock of the smaller particles had already escaped downstream. Both deposits, meander-belt and terrace, show lag-cum-immovable layers, which usually differ conspicuously in their matrices; that of the meander-belt is of coarse sand and fine gravel particles, but the matrix of the terrace gravel is commonly of clay and silt, with fine sand, testifying to the departure of the coarser particles and their replacement by products of infiltration, unrelated to direct fluvial action.

(2) *Quartz gravel rounding.* We will here consider *kind* as well as *degree* of roundness. There seem to be three different kinds of wear, in gravel streams, as undergone respectively by mobile, lag and fixed particles. Periodically picked up by the current and flung around in an unconstrained environment, *mobile particles* tend to lose quickly any idiosyncrancies of shape. The corners are knocked off and rudely rounded before any wear of re-entrant surfaces is apparent. The knocks and the abrasion are selectively applied to the sharper convexities and ultimately, as the little Tertiary pebbles show, the process produces a uniform oblong shape (the 'marbles' would not be allowed in any serious game), registering a high Wadell roundness. By contrast the *lag particles* are rarely tossed by the current, although as Schumm and Steven's observations have shown (see page 168) they may undergo sustained vibration within the constrained environment of a fairly rigid gravel framework. In any case lag particles are frequently abraded by impact from the smaller particles. In neither process are the forces great enough to remove protruberances and so the large particle, although it soon becomes perfectly smooth, yet retains its original general shape and only by chance registers a high Wadell roundness measure. As for the *immovable particles*, absolutely immobile, their properties are generally the same as of lag particles, but they must possess an unexposed *sole* resting on the floor and this will not be smoothed. Thus, as shown by the examples in Plate 9, we can often recognise the history of quartz pebbles by the kind of wear they have undergone - *mobile wear* or *lag wear* - which, related to the particle's size, informs of the approximate competence of the stream which produced it. Similarly we can

refer to *mobile roundness* and *lag roundness*. Often of
course the kind of roundness shown is not uniquely distinctive, as when the particle's competence ratio changed
appreciably as it travelled, although even then we may
often see how it had begun its journey as a mobile particle,
when the principal corners were all rudely rounded off,
but had ended as a lag particle in a finishing process
which reduced and smoothed every small-scale irregularity.
   Relating these conclusions to our study of quartz
gravels in small West African streams, we first observe
that the rounding of the mobile particles of the immature
meander-belt sand stream is too slight to show any wear
tendencies, due principally to the low rigour experienced
in a sand stream. We also note the fresh state of the
angular to subangular lag particles, which in their shel-
tered existence had not seen much attritive action of any
kind. However, the expected tendencies have already begun
to show in the more mature terrace gravels, in which both
mobile and lag particles are already subrounded, each displaying its particular kind of wear. The irregular cobble
shown in Plate 9 illustrates this. We have already considered the end-products of the processes in the very
mature Tertiary gravels and observed the distinction
between the well-rounded mobile particles and the irregularly shaped lag particles, which are nonetheless so
thoroughly smoothed that the surfaces are quite featureless.
   It may need to be emphasised that 'kind of roundness'
is quite different from the well-known property of
sphericity, which expresses the 'whole shape' of a particle
and not the detail. Sphericity is governed primarily by
the original shape of the particle, but can be systematically modified by wear, again under the control of the
competence ratio (D/D_c), as we shall see presently in
relation to Sneed and Folk's records from the Colorado
River of Texas.
   (3) *Heavy mineral occurrence*. The processes of wear
and escape may also be observed in any associated heavy
minerals, whose properties, especially for sizes larger
than 1 mm, I have observed over and over again during the
procedure of diamond recovery. There are two classes of
heavy mineral, one being that of the 'soft minerals',
such as ilmenite, hematite and 'laterite', and the other
that of the 'durable minerals', such as corundum, staurolite and garnet, all of which, in both classes, possess
specific gravities in the range 3.5 to 5.5. As ore-
dressing processes demonstrate, the behaviour of heavy
minerals is very strongly influenced by the superiority of
their specific gravities over that of quartz, which is
2.65, so that once entered into the sanctuary of a continuous lag gravel of quartz particles, they do not readily
leave it, even if of very small particle size. However,
within the lag layer they should also be very vulnerable
to both crushing and wear as a result of the frequent movement of the gravel particles *in situ*, as already discussed,
and indeed there is much evidence for this in consideration
of the comparative heavy mineral contents of the two deposits under study.

Stream evolution

In the immature present-day stream, both classes of
heavy mineral are found in the lag layer in comparative
abundance in all sizes available and the product of panning
the <0.5 mm range is commonly a copious 'black sand' composed mostly of the soft iron minerals. The contrast with
the adjacent terrace deposit may be striking, where all
the soft minerals are absent or nearly so, and the product
of panning is merely a very small quantity of light-
coloured material composed mostly of tiny, hard zircon
crystals. The >1 mm particles recovered from the terrace
normally consist mostly of the durable minerals, in much
smaller quantity and often notably restricted to the >2 mm
range, and showing appreciable wear. It is evident that
the heavy minerals have taken a severe pounding, which only
the larger and sounder representatives of the durable
class have survived. It is also interesting to note that
despite an abundance of laterite particles, of specific
gravity about 4.0, in the pediment gravels flanking the
stream, scarcely any laterite may be found in the lag
gravels of either of the stream deposits (the present-day
deposit having acquired most of its fresh material from
the floor). As for the Tertiary deposits, I can only
testify that wherever Tertiary well-rounded pebbles were
seen in a sample we could usually expect to recover a few
associated subrounded or even rounded particles of durable
mineral, such as corundum, or staurolite, almost exclusively of >2 mm size. In this case the size limitation may
equally well represent an escape size, because it also
applies to diamonds (of specific gravity 3.5), for there
is much independent evidence to show that diamonds smaller
than this size would not have been destroyed.

If we now follow the two deposits, meander-belt and
terrace, *along* the short stream, we discover similarly
consistent variations. *20 kilometres downstream from the
source*, the present-day immature stream shows an even
thicker sand layer, less pebbly than upstream, representing
the main surge of the quickly escaping sand, whilst the
mature terrace deposit is also possessed of a substantial
mobile layer but consisting either or fine gravel alone
(providing a relatively immature model of the Tertiary
mobile layer producing the well-rounded pebbles in a major
stream) or perhaps a pebbly sand, representing the rear of
the sand surge. Degree of roundness is governed principally by the maturity, which is the same all along the
active stream, and therefore the same roundness values are
seen as upstream.

In the opposite direction, *very near the source*, the
changes are very marked. Escape sizes rapidly increase
towards the source until, for both deposits, only the lag
particles are still retained. In consequence, as already
discussed, the competence for grade will have fallen towards and even below the critical value of about 30 mm,
where the stream no longer has the strength to scour its
bed. This situation heralds the 'extinction' of the
channelled stream. The first stage, often beginning in
the present-day stream, is the formation of a swamp underlain by silty alluvium stretching right down to the probably discontinuous lag-cum-immovable layer. The terrace

situation is essentially the same, but here the extinction
would have been completed, as indicated by an exceptionally
thick and often sloping covering to the alluvium on the
floor, representing the purely colluvial valley fill. This
phenomenon of progressive headwater extinction in swamps
is widespread on African erosion surfaces (as is readily
apparent from fairly low altitude air travel), and *anywhere*, as shown in Figure 30, it must be the principal
mechanism of progressive reduction in *drainage density* in
regions of low relief and light or zero gravel supply, un-
troubled by independent disturbance.

The enquiry so far has only related to streams of
small competence of 100 mm and below. This value of the
regional competence is restricted to the 'granitic areas'
where an otherwise fine-grained regolith contains only a
small quantity of residual vein-quartz. We will now consider possible *variations in the regional competence*. The
landmass may be locally crossed by belts of schists associated with very considerable quantities of vein-quartz, with
the result that streams flowing on or away from such areas
are much more heavily loaded with gravel and require com-
mensurately larger competences. The particle size distributions of these gravels may be no different from those we
have been considering, but the absolute *amount* of the
loading of the larger sizes alone is so much greater that
when the surge of the quickly travelling smaller gravel
sizes is spent and the total amount of loading of gravel
of all sizes is reduced to a value equivalent to the
initial loading in the granitic areas, this residual
gravel consists almost entirely of the larger sizes and
accordingly *continues* to require a large competence for
grade.

The situation is seen very clearly in terraces of the
Birim River in the humid forest region of southern Ghana,
where at Wenchi (near Oda), about 150 km from the stream's
source, thick mobile layers of quartz gravels show maximum
particle sizes (equal to the critical lag size $D_1 = 0.3D_c$)
a little larger than 100 mm, indicating a competence of
over 300 mm. The lag layers in this area are thin and discontinuous, witness to the limited range of particle size
of the loading, and the relatively large competence is
entirely the consequence of the great *amount* of the
loading. Much of the quartz in these still fairly immature
deposits is unsound and liable to breakage (facilitated by
the greater rigour imposed by the large competence, as will
be considered shortly) and we can see how the situation
would have developed here by looking 20 km downstream to
the same terraces at Edubia, where the local gravel supply
happens to be much reduced and the loading of the main
stream was evidently so much lighter that the 100 mm
cobbles are now all in the substantial lag layer appropriate to a competence for grade of only about 200 mm.
Soon any degradation permitting the competence to become
even smaller must stop because the ample inert lag layer,
consisting of the toughest residue of the largest particles
that travel, is now virtually both stationary and indestructible, and is becoming thick enough *alone* to maintain indefinitely a competence for grade of approximately

this same high value. So a large regional competence of
about 150-200 mm is established throughout the drainage.
Indeed these coarse, sub-rounded to rounded, mostly lag-
rounded, inherited lag particles continue to form thick lag
layers in all the streams in the quartz-ridden schist areas
in West Africa (as in Plate 5), always maintaining the
larger competence values and of course discouraging any
channel extinction in the headwaters.

The effect of all this on the roundness values of
mobile quartz particles is pronounced. In the Birim
valley, continuing my hunt for the smallest well-rounded
pebbles, I could find none smaller than about 20 mm (see
Table 4), as compared with the almost invariable 7-8 mm
in the granitic areas. The maximum sizes for high rounding
were correspondingly larger, about 100 mm as against 30 mm
in the granitic areas.

The same relationships are to be seen in Sierra Leone
in the Tongo diamondfield, near Panguma 50 kilometres
south of the Yengema field already referred to, but here
only in respect to Tertiary (or perhaps early Quaternary)
gravel relics inherited by the present-day small streams.
An example of a large mobile-rounded cobble from here is
shown in Plate 9, quite small, however, in comparison with
the largest specimens of these 'cannon balls' which measure
100 mm. The smallest well-rounded pebbles appropriately
measure about 15 mm. In a sense, however, these high
values are out of place, because this is a granitic area,
but there can be little doubt that the well-rounded
gravels have come from the nearby schistose Nimini Hills,
to the north-west, in a once heavily-loaded precursor of
the present-day streams which drain from that direction.
A variant of this situation is to be seen in the Ivory
Coast just north of Séguéla, where Tertiary relics of *both*
large and small ranges of well-rounded quartz particles
occur, as they must do in some places.

Another factor influencing mobile rounding must be the
rigour of the wearing process as governed by D_{max}, the
largest mobile particle size travelling. In the case of
quartz gravels, narrowly restricted in range of sizes as
supplied to the stream, this value is governed, as we have
just seen, immediately by the competence (D_c) but ultimately by the amount only - and not the size - of the
quartz gravel supply. In the case of rock gravels, particle size may, if large, alone be the principal control
regardless of the amount, but in any case, whatever the
cause, we can recognise that the larger the absolute sizes
of the mobile particles, the greater their rate of wear
with *time* (I_t). Thus for a given maturity (or value of
t'), the Wadell roundness values for the larger sized
middle-ranges (of roundness) for quartz particles may be
significantly higher. Of course this conclusion only
renders more impressive the very high roundness values
achieved by the tiny Tertiary quartz pebbles of the granitic
areas, emphasising the very high maturity of the deposits
of which they formed part.

Table 4 (page 179) shows that, with the exception of
the 6 mm value for Copeton, N.S.W., the *usual absolute
minimum size* of these well-rounded Tertiary quartz pebbles

is 7 mm, and we need to have an explanation for such a
limit. We have seen that the value of this escape size
(D_e) is linked to the competence (D_c) of the stream, which
is itself governed by the initial loading of the vein-
quartz particles. If we now consider the situation in
which the loading had been very light indeed, we can understand that eventually, after the escape of the abundant
sand particles which early on would have imposed a sand
regime, the remaining quartz gravel loading would be too
light to maintain other than a lightly-loaded gravel stream
possessing a very small competence (of say 70 mm or under),
whose inert condition would not allow the channel to keep
shifting briskly back and forth across the meander-belt.
As a result, the floodplain would remain undisturbed
sufficiently long to become indurated by incipient lateritisation (the first stages are often noticeable in present-
day floodplains in West Africa), perhaps beginning while
the sand regime was still in force, and the weak stream
would be trapped in a rigid channel. Thus there would
never be an active gravel stream or any opportunity for
prolonged pebble wear. This explanation is of course
speculation, but we can be fairly sure that both the amount
and the size distribution of the initial vein-quartz gravel
supply are the principal controls of the limiting competence. In this respect it is interesting to note that
the exceptional 6 mm well-rounded pebbles from Copeton,
New South Wales, are mostly not vein-quartz at all, but
whole quartz crystals derived from the granite itself,
which is extremely coarse-grained in this area. We can
accept that a moderate loading of such an exclusively very
fine-particled gravel would require a relatively very
small competence for grade, appropriate for a 6 mm escape
size. But this case is exceptional.

We may therefore be justified in supposing that in
normal circumstances 7 mm is the smallest size (intermediate diameter) of a quartz particle which may become
well-rounded by fluvial action alone, and conversely that
where smaller sizes of well-rounded quartz particles are
found another cause should be sought. For pebble sizes,
this cause could only be *marine action*. The significant
difference between the two kinds of action is that fluvial
transport is in one direction only and therefore, as we
have already observed, all processes involving such transport have to stop sooner or later as permanent base-level
is approached; whilst marine action can often continue
indefinitely for all particle sizes. Also of course marine
action can be sustained continuously, or at least very frequently, over long periods, giving the gravel no respite.
The distinction may be useful. My habit of measuring
small quartz pebbles did not stop when I was in England
and I soon discovered that there was no limiting (minimum)
escape size for the well-rounded quartz pebbles to be found
within the flint gravels of the River Thames. But of
course these pebbles would have been derived from any of
a variety of marine sedimentary sources known inside the
Thames drainage.

16.4   Quartz gravel rounding in a temperate environment

This enquiry into quartz rounding will be concluded by
return to the less settled environment of Quaternary
gravel streams in temperate climates, whose characters are
complicated not only by systematic changes in gravel composition, particle size and competence along the stream
(in the manner of Plumley's Black Hills streams discussed
on pages 147-150), but often also by irregular contamination from terraces by much coarser gravel, usually of
rock, transported at an earlier date in flows of larger
competence. In such cases, the variation of the competence
along the stream, which is the principal control of the
quartz rounding, may be both wide and erratic. Alternatively, if the floor is the source of fresh vein-quartz
(corresponding with the tropical situations discussed),
then almost certainly there will also be local supply of
rock gravel and then, even if the stream is continuously
at grade, the complex situation is quite beyond systematic
research. The only situations of interest are where
silica gravels alone, preferably of quartz, emerge from a
source area into a plain of easily eroded ground yielding
no gravel of any kind and stretching away a considerable
distance before approach to base-level or other inter-
ruption terminates the zone of interest.
        There seems to be record of only one such investigation
into quartz gravel rounding, which is that of Sneed and
Folk (1958), already mentioned, supported by Bradley's
later work (1970) on the same stream (mostly directed to
examination of the small quantities of rock gravel travelling). Sneed and Folk observed changes in the roundness
and certain other properties of 32-64 mm quartz pebbles
taken from channel bars and low terraces of the Colorado
River of Texas, along a distance of 267 miles (430 kilometres) from the point of last supply of quartz gravel.
The first 91 miles of this stretch cross an area providing
fresh chert, beyond which, near Austin, there is no further
supply of any fresh gravel constituents, although some
coarse inherited gravel comes in irregularly from terraces.
In this downstream stretch, where the Colorado now meanders
at grade, the only gravel particles sufficiently large,
abundant and durable to continue governing the stream's
competence are the silica gravels of chert and quartz,
which seem to show little change along the stream in their
common maximum sizes, registering about 120 mm for the
chert and 80 mm for the quartz. This interpretation of
Bradley's data is given tentatively and indeed there are
several aspects of the complex situation here about which
it is only possible to speculate. Nonetheless it is clear
that the gravel loadings are, or, more significantly, were
(in the stream precursors represented by the coarse-gravel
terraces) heavy enough to maintain, through their control
of the competence for grade, a fairly rapid travel velocity
for the quartz pebbles of the observed 32-64 mm range along
at least most of the distance studied (the possible exception being the last 6 miles only, where a regime change
now seems to be close or already begun). We also recognise
that the distance of travel (z) from the common source

upstream is effectively the same for all sizes in the range.

Sneed and Folk showed that the mean Wadell roundness of the quartz pebbles increased from 0.54 at the start (at the edge of the source area) to 0.61 within a defined stretch below the town of Austin, an understandably rapid increase reflecting the quick elimination of the sharper initial irregularities of shape. Thereafter to the end of the whole stretch studied, across a minimum distance of about 100 miles, the mean roundness increased only to 0.63, the small improvement, if statistically significant, presumably representing wear now spread more evenly over the individual particle surfaces. The authors speculated that the quartz roundness was approaching 'an asymptotic limiting roundness of 0.65', a conclusion which is per-fectly consistent with our recognition of relatively low competence ratios (D/D_c) and rapid travel velocities (U) prevailing throughout a brief duration of travel (t'). Plainly, the limiting roundness of 0.65 is significantly low in comparison with the 0.70 of the much smaller quartz pebbles from the invariably locally adulterated Tertiary gravels of West Africa (see page 178), for which we recog-nised that the original competence ratios were high enough to permit a much lower travel velocity and consequently a much longer duration of travel for an equivalent distance of travel. The marked difference in value is perfectly understandable in the light of the rounding theory. It also clearly demonstrates the interesting paradox, which may already have been recognised, that only a 'weak' stream can produce highly rounded quartz pebbles, given enough time of course.

The authors provided other significant information:

(1) For 'pebbles above and below this size range (32-62 mm), the usual increase of roundness with increasing size is clearly evident'. We have concluded that the rate of wear with distance (I_z) increases with increasing size and since at any point of observation the distance travelled (z) by these pebbles is effectively the same for all sizes, the roundness must increase with size.

(2) Within the 32-64 mm size range, the authors demon-strated that with increasing distance of travel the largest particles (>54 mm) became more rodlike without change in sphericity, indicating most wear on the intermediate axis; whilst the smallest particles (<38 mm) became more dis-coidal with increase in sphericity, indicating most wear on the long axis. These distinctions clearly result from the difference in behaviour between particles having higher and lower competence ratios (D/D_c), assuming no very great change in the competence (D_c). It is consistent with our conclusions about the processes operating in scour holes that larger mobile particles spend most of their time being passively moved by undercutting or being rolled along the surface of stationary alluvium, whilst the smaller ones are more frequently actually tossed *in situ*, and these two distinct types of movement must favour respectively wear on the intermediate axis and wear on the long axis. The effects accord with the theory and indeed it should be possible (in other circumstances) to correlate each of them with specific ranges in the value of the competence ratio.

CONCLUSION

In the Introduction I emphasised that any understanding of
natural streams which we might acquire through a deliberately reasoned, 'synthetic' and consequently truly theoretical approach could only be acceptable if consistently
confirmed by observation of actual streams. Despite the
persistent hazard of an unconscious misrepresentation of
evidence to suit the argument, I believe the quest to have
been successful in this respect, although of course would
not pretend that we have the right answer in every detail.
Nonetheless I am convinced that where error has crept in,
the right answer requires only minor adjustment to the
general statement. During my preliminary enquiries, con-
ducted over many years, I repeatedly found myself following
a wrong route, the fact of which, in due course, was always
amply demonstrated by contrary evidence observed, and
eventually reluctantly accepted, in actual streams. Now,
at last, the long road of the argument seems to be clear
all the way, and to remain clear. Undoubtedly it is a
long road, but truly no-one could expect it otherwise,
having regard to the complexity of the objective.

Two general conclusions encourage me in this confidence.
First, there is a *unity* to the theory, seemingly relevant
to every kind of natural stream and probably also, as
indicated on pages 158-160, to all hillslope processes
dependent on running water. Second, the theory seems to
explain adequately every process significantly contributing
to the steady state of first order equilibrium along any
kind of stream, graded or not. Of course, in making this
claim I acknowledge that the basic physical processes involved in stream action have throughout been recognised
only in their immediate physical effects, for we have not
explored their mechanics, except sometimes superficially.
But such enquiry is not needed in the context of first
order equilibrium, concerned only with *mean* physical
effects, constant as much for statistical as for physical
reasons. Our understanding is comparable to that of a
student of man's social and historical behaviour, who has
no need to know any more of human physiology than the
limits to what a man can do physically. But it is well
to have reflected in this way if only to be properly aware
that this study relates to only one facet of physical
fluvial science. Assuredly I do not make light of the
efforts of hydraulic investigators, whose different problems are so very much less tractable than the ones examined
here.

Although an extensive range of first order processes
has been considered in this study, certain omissions may
be noted. One relates to the assumption, stated on page 9
and maintained throughout the work, that 'the stream is
not constrained laterally by steep valley sides - in other

words it is not flowing in the notch of a *gorge*'. In this situation certain controls have to be considered which are independent of the main line of argument but which nonetheless are perfectly understandable. This book should have a chapter on this interesting topic, which possibly I may be able to add one day. The theory may also be usefully applied to the behaviour of *heavy minerals* in streams, particularly in regard to the critical competence ranges within which certain minerals of certain particle sizes are likely to be concentrated in graded streams of varying 'maturity'. This economically pertinent field of enquiry, briefly considered on pages 155 and 183, calls for a fuller discussion, with examples.

A recognised defect of this work, although, as often reiterated, not a crippling one, is the lack of accurate assessment of the few universal critical values which occupy important places in the theory. These are (1) the two *critical competence ratios* (D/D_c), nominally and frequently quoted as 0.3 and 0.001 (see page 37), and (2) the three *critical competences* (D_c), nominally quoted as 30 mm (the critical minimum competence, see page 114), 60 mm and 120 mm (distinguishing lightly, moderately and heavily-loaded sand streams, see page 102 and Figure 11). Although a primary aim of this work has been to establish the existence of critical values and not to demand their accurate assessment, a quantitative follow-up is desirable to add further conviction to the theory and maybe to render it more serviceable. Measurements should be made on a representative variety of graded streams of different sizes and classes. There is also need for detailed descriptive work illustrating the various *relationships* considered, such as those belonging to the concept of the complete, four-layered alluvium profile or that of the regime break.

POSTSCRIPT

As anticipated in the Conclusion on page 190, minor but
significant 'adjustments' to the general argument continue
to be required. The three points considered below emerged
too late for incorporation in the main text.

1. *The loading-competence relationship in a graded stream.*
The determination of the competence (D_c) of a graded stream
by the value of its loading (Q_R) is the 'cardinal relationship' first introduced on page 47 and afterwards used as the
key to understanding the channel properties of all kinds of
streams at or near to grade. However, it may not have been
sufficiently emphasised that the relationship is strictly
limited to first-order and second-order time, *with the loading
regarded as invariable.* In third-order time, with the loading
variable, the roles are reversed in that the competence is
then broadly prescribed by the 'attitude of the landscape'
and itself, both in determining the 'alluvium mobility' of
potential alluvium of varying particle sizes and in regulat-
ing the tempo of the competence-loading interaction (together
demonstrated in Figure 9 on page 85), governs both the size
and the amount of the loading. Happily all this can be ignored
in consideration of any one cross-section of a graded stream,
when the loading is the one and only significant arbitrary
component of the 'data' and the competence is a dependent
property of predictable value.

2. *The width-depth ratio* (see pages 106 and 121).
Another important, though secondary, control of the width-
depth ratio (W/H) of the channel is the first order value
of the *discharge* (Q), by virtue of its influence on the
depth (H), as discussed on page 117. We have seen that
the primary control is the *erodibility* (E_b) of the channel
bank, and it is obvious that a high bank is less stable
and therefore more readily erodible than a low one.
Consequently, other things being equal, we would expect
the W/H ratio of a large stream to be greater than that
of a small one. Common observation confirms this; a ratio
of 1:1 is often seen in streamlets, but it is unthinkable
in a stream like the Lower Mississippi, which, although a
moderately-loaded sand stream, understandably displays a
W/H ratio of more than 100:1, despite the maximum of 100:1
quoted for this class of stream in Table 3 on page 121.

3. *The channel sinuosity of a lightly-loaded sand stream*
(see page 118).
Although 'point bank erosion' (see Figure 15) must be
dominant in lightly-loaded streams (sand or gravel), the
process can operate only very slowly within the rigid,
almost inerodible channels characteristic of light loadings.
Consequently the sinuosity (P) actually achieved in these
circumstances is also very dependent on the duration of
time that has elapsed since the process began to operate.
It has not been possible to represent this factor in the
diagram of Figure 15 except very generally.

REFERENCES

Allen, J.R.L. 1970. *Physical processes of sedimentation.*
George Allen and Unwin, London.

Barrell, J. 1925. Marine and terrestrial conglomerates.
Bulletin of the Geological Society of America,
36, 279-342.

Blake, D.H. and Ollier, C.D. 1971. Alluvial plains of
the Fly River, Papua. *Zeitschrift für Geomorpho-
logie,* supplementband 12, 1-17.

Bradley, William C. 1970. Effect of weathering on
abrasion of granitic gravel, Colorado River (Texas).
Bulletin of the Geological Society of America,
81, 61-80.

Brush, L.M. and Wolman, M.G. 1960. Knickpoint behaviour
in noncohesive material: a laboratory study.
Bulletin of the Geological Society of America,
71, 59-74.

Burkham, D.E. 1972. Channel changes in the Gila River in
Safford Valley, Arizona, 1846-1970. *U.S. Geological Survey Professional Paper 655-G.*

Cailleux, A. and Tricart, J. 1964. *Initiation a l'étude
des sables et des galets.* Centre de Documentation
Universitaire, Paris.

Carey, Walter C. 1969. Formation of floodplain lands.
*Journal of the Hydraulics Division of the American
Society of Civil Engineers,* 95 (May), HY3, Paper
6574, 981-994.

Crickmay, C.H. 1960. Lateral activity in a river of
north western Canada. *Journal of Geology,* 68,
377-391.

Daniels, R.B. 1960. Entrenchment of the Willow Drainage
Ditch, Harrison County, Iowa. *American Journal of
Science,* 258, 161-176.

Doeglas, D.J. 1962. The structure of sedimentary deposits
of braided rivers. *Sedimentology* 1, 167-190.

Dury, G.H. 1966. The concept of grade. In Dury, G.H.
(ed) *Essays in geomorphology.* Heinemann, London.

Fahnestock, R.K. 1963. Morphology and hydrology of a
glacial stream - White River, Mount Rainier,

References

Washington. *U.S. Geological Survey Professional Paper* 422-A.

Fisk, H.N. 1944. *Geological investigation of the alluvial valley of the Lower Mississippi River.* Mississippi River Commission, Vicksburg, Miss.

Folk, R.L. and Ward, W.C. 1957. Brazos River Bar: a study in the significance of grain size parameters. *Journal of Sedimentary Petrology*, 27, 3-26.

Gilbert, G.K. 1914. The transportation of debris by running water. *U.S. Geological Survey Professional Paper* 86.

Green, J.F.N. 1949. The history of the River Dart, Devon. *Proceedings of the Geologists' Association*, 60, 105-124.

Hack, J.T. 1957. Studies of longitudinal stream profiles in Virginia and Maryland. *U.S. Geological Survey Professional Paper* 294-B.

Hickin, E.J. 1974. The development of meanders in natural river-channels. *American Journal of Science*, 274, 414-442.

Hjulström, F. 1935. Studies of the morphological activity of rivers as illustrated by the River Fyris. *Bulletin of the Geological Institution, University of Upsala*, 25, 221-527.

Kalinske, A.A. 1943. The role of turbulence in river hydraulics. *Second Hydraulics Conference, Iowa University Studies in Engineering, Bulletin* 27, 266-279.

Krumbein, W.C. 1941a. The effects of abrasion on the size, shape and roundness of rock fragments. *Journal of Geology*, 49, 482-520.

Krumbein, W.C. 1941b. Measurement and geological significance of shape and roundness of sedimentary particles. *Journal of Sedimentary Petrology*, 11, 64-72.

Kuenen, Ph.H. 1956. Experimental abrasion of pebbles. 2. Rolling by current. *Journal of Geology*, 64, 336-368.

Kuenen, Ph.H. 1959. Experimental abrasion. 3. Fluviatile action in sand. *American Journal of Science*, 257, 172-190.

Lane, E.W. 1938. Notes on the formation of sand. *Transactions of the American Geophysical Union, 19th Annual Meeting*, 505-508.

Lane, E.W. 1940. Notes on limit of sediment concentration. *Journal of Sedimentary Petrology*, 10, 95-96.

Lane, E.W. and Borland, W.M. 1954. River-bed scour during floods. *Transactions of the American Society of Civil Engineers*, 119, 1069-1080.

Lane, E.W. and Carlson, E.J. 1954. Some observations on the effect of particle shape on the movement of coarse sediments. *Transactions of the American Geophysical Union*, 35, 453-462.

Leliavsky, S. 1955. *An introduction to fluvial hydraulics*. Constable, London.

Leopold, L.B. 1973. River channel change with time: an example. *Bulletin of the Geological Society of America*, 84, 1845-1860.

Leopold, L.B., Bagnold, R.A., Wolman, M.G. and Brush, L.M. 1960. Flow resistance in sinuous or irregular channels. *U.S. Geological Survey Professional Paper*, 282-D.

Leopold, L.B. and Miller, J.P. 1956. Ephemeral streams - hydraulic factors and their relation to the drainage net. *U.S. Geological Survey Professional Paper* 282-A.

Leopold, L.B., Wolman, M.G. and Miller, J.P. 1964. *Fluvial processes in geomorphology*. Freeman, San Francisco.

Lewis, W.V. 1944. Stream trough experiments and terrace formation. *Geological Magazine*, 81, 241-253.

Mackin, J.H. 1948. Concept of the graded river. *Bulletin of the Geological Society of America*, 59, 463-512.

Mackin, J.H. 1963. Rational and empirical methods of investigation in geology. In Albritton, C.R. (ed) *The fabric of geology*. Addison-Wesley Pub. Co., Reading, Mass.

Matthes, G.H. 1947. Macroturbulence in natural stream flow. *Transactions of the American Geophysical Union*, 28, 255-266.

Morisawa, Marie 1968. *Streams: their dynamics and morphology*. McGraw-Hill, New York.

Moss, A.J. 1963. The physical nature of common sandy and pebbly deposits. Part 2. *American Journal of Science*, 261, 297-343.

Nordin, C.F. and Beverage, J.P. 1965. Sediment transport in the Rio Grande, New Mexico. *U.S. Geological Survey Professional Paper* 462-F.

References

Nordin, C.F. and Culbertson, J.K.   1961.   Particle-size
    distribution of stream bed material in the Middle
    Rio Grande Basin, New Mexico.   *U.S. Geological
    Survey Professional Paper* 424-C, 323-326.

Pettijohn, F.J.   1956.   *Sedimentary rocks*.   Harper, New
    York.

Plumley, W.J.   1948.   Black Hill terrace gravels: a study
    in sediment transport.   *Journal of Geology*, 56,
    526-577.

Powers, M.C.   1953.   A new roundness scale for sedimentary
    particles.   *Journal of Sedimentary Petrology*, 23,
    117-119.

Rubey, W.W.   1952.   Geology and mineral resources of the
    Hardin and Brussells quadrangles (Illinois).
    U.S. Geological Survey Professional Paper 218.

Ruxton, B.P. and Berry, L.   1961.   Weathering profiles
    and geomorphic position on granite in two tropical
    regions.   *Revue de Géomorphologie Dynamique*, 12,
    16-31.

Scheidegger, A.E.   1961.   *Theoretical geomorphology*.
    Springer-Verlag, Berlin.

Scheidegger, A.E. and Langbein, W.B.   1966.   Probability
    concepts in geomorphology.   *U.S. Geological Survey
    Professional Paper* 500-C.

Schumm, S.A.   1960.   The shape of alluvial channels in
    relation to sediment type.   *U.S. Geological Survey
    Professional Paper* 352-B.

Schumm, S.A.   1963.   Sinuosity of alluvial rivers on the
    Great Plains.   *Bulletin of the Geological Society
    of America*, 74, 1089-1100.

Schumm, S.A.   1968.   River adjustment to altered hydrologic
    regimen - Murrumbidgee River and paleochannels,
    Australia.   *U.S. Geological Survey Professional
    Paper* 598, 1-65.

Schumm, S.A.   1969.   River metamorphosis.   *Journal of the
    Hydraulics Division of the American Society of
    Civil Engineers*, 95 (January), HY1, Paper 6352,
    255-273.

Schumm, S.A. and Khan, H.R.   1972.   Experimental study of
    channel patterns.   *Bulletin of the Geological
    Society of America*, 83, 1755-1770.

Schumm, S.A. and Lichty, R.W.   1963.   Channel-widening and
    flood-plain construction along Cimarron River in
    south western Kansas.   *U.S. Geological Survey
    Professional Paper* 352, 71-88.

Schumm, S.A. and Lichty, R.W. 1965. Time, space and causality in geomorphology. *American Journal of Science*, 263, 110-119.

Schumm, S.A. and Parker, R.S. 1973. Implication of complex response of drainage systems for Quaternary alluvial stratigraphy. *Nature Physical Sciences* 243 (128), 99-100.

Schumm, S.A. and Stevens, M.A. 1973. Abrasion in place: a mechanism for rounding and size reduction of coarse sediments in rivers. *Geology* 1, 37-40.

Scott, C.H. and Stephens, H.D. 1966. Special sediment investigations, Mississippi River at St. Louis, Missouri, 1961-1963. *U.S. Geological Survey Professional Paper* 1819-J.

Sneed, E.D. and Folk, R.L. 1958. Pebbles in the Lower Colorado River, Texas: a study in particle morpho-genesis. *Journal of Geology*, 66, 114-150.

Speight, J.G. 1965. Flow and channel characteristics of the Angabunga River, Papua. *Journal of Hydrology*, 3, 16-36.

Thomas, M.F. 1974. *Tropical geomorphology*. Macmillan, London.

Tricart, J. and Schaeffer, R. 1950. L'indice d'émoussé des galets, moyen d'étude des systèmes d'érosion. *Revue de Géomorphologie Dynamique*, 1, 151-179.

Vogt, J. 1956. *Rapport provisoire de mission en moyenne Côte d'Ivoire*. Service de Géologie et de Prospection Minière (S.G.P.M.), Dakar.

Vogt, J. 1959. Aspects de l'évolution morphologique récente de l'Ouest Africain. *Annales de Géographie*, 367, 193-206.

Vogt, J. 1962. Les facteurs de la dynamique de l'Adour moyen. *Revue de Géomorphologie Dynamique*, 13, 49-72.

Walker, E.H. 1957. The deep channel and alluvial deposits of the Ohio Valley in Kentucky. *U.S. Geological Survey Water Supply Paper* 1411.

Wentworth, C.K. 1922. A field study of the shapes of river pebbles. *Bulletin of the U.S. Geological Survey*, 730-C, 103-114.

Wolman, M.G. 1955. The natural channel of Brandywine Creek, Pennsylvania. *U.S. Geological Survey Professional Paper* 273.

References

Wolman, M.G. and Leopold, L.B. 1957. River flood plains:
    some observations on their formation. *U.S. Geo-
    logical Survey Professional Paper* 282-C, 87-107.

Wooldridge, S.W. and Linton, D.L. 1955. *Structure,
    surface and drainage in south-east England.*
    George Philip, London.

Yatsu, E. 1955. On the longitudinal profile of the graded
    river. *Transactions of the American Geophysical
    Union*, 36, 655-663.

Yatsu, E. 1959. On the discontinuity of grain size
    frequency distribution of fluvial deposits and its
    geomorphological significance. *Proceedings of the
    International Geographical Union Regional
    Conference in Japan*, 1957, 224-237.

AUTHOR INDEX

PLACE INDEX

SUBJECT INDEX